I0842019

# STARTUP FROM SCRATCH

*A beginner's guide to starting up in India.*

## Aryan Pratap Singh Tomar

To the fearless visionary dreamers and relentless innovators behind the unstoppable force of Entrepreneurship in India

# Table of Content


| Ch. No | Topic | Page |
|:---:|:---|:---:|
|  | Before You Start | 1 – 2 |
| 1. | Why Start a Startup? | 3 – 6 |
| 2. | Identifying Your Passion and Interests | 7 – 11 |
| 3. | Finding and Evaluating Your Startup Idea | 12 – 16 |
| 4. | Conducting Market Research | 17 – 23 |
| 5. | Identifying Your Target Customer | 24 – 26 |
| 6. | Crafting Your Value Proposition | 27 – 30 |
| 7. | Co-founders and Advisors | 31 – 37 |
| 8. | Building Your Startup Team | 38 – 42 |

| 9. | Understanding Your Competitors | 43 – 46 |
|---|---|---|
| 10. | Creating Your Minimum Viable Product | 47 – 52 |
| 11. | Iterating & Refining Your Product/Service | 53 – 60 |
| 12. | Developing Your Brand | 61 – 71 |
| 13. | Building Your Online Presence | 72 – 92 |
| 14. | Basics of Marketing | 93 – 138 |
| 15. | Marketing Jargons | 139 – 191 |
| 16. | Customer Relationship Management | 192 – 196 |
| 17. | Managing Your Finances | 197 – 207 |
| 18. | Raising Capital for Your Finances | 208 – 212 |
| 19. | Business Plan | 213 – 234 |

| 20. | Creating a Pitch Deck | 235 – 238 |
|---|---|---|
| 21. | Scaling & Growing your Startup | 239 – 243 |
| 22. | Overcoming Challenges & Staying Motivated | 244 – 247 |
| 23. | Legal & Regulatory Compliance | 248 – 260 |
| 24. | Few Jargons in Startup | 261 – 264 |
| | Conclusion | 265 – 266 |

# Before You Start

Are you someone who has ever dreamt of starting a startup, achieving financial independence, or making a mark in the business world? Perhaps you've had countless ideas swirling in your mind but lacked the knowledge and guidance on how to bring them to life. Starting a startup can seem like a daunting task, especially when you have no clue where to begin. That's where this book, "Startup from Scratch," comes in. It is designed to provide you with the basic knowledge and insights you need to embark on your entrepreneurial journey.

This book is for anyone who has ever felt the burning desire to start their own venture but felt overwhelmed by the vastness of the startup landscape. Whether you're a first-time entrepreneur or have dabbled in small business ventures before, this guide will equip you with the essential understanding and tools to get your startup off the ground.

In "Startup from Scratch," we'll cover a wide range of topics, exploring the crucial aspects that lay the foundation for a successful startup. From identifying your passion and interests to evaluating startup ideas, conducting market research, and defining your target customer, we'll guide you through the process of finding your unique niche in the market.

Co-founders and advisors play a vital role in a startup's success. We'll delve into the dynamics of building your startup team and understanding the importance of collaboration and shared vision. Additionally, we'll help you navigate the competitive landscape by providing insights on analysing your competitors and crafting a compelling value proposition.

One of the fundamental principles of startup development is the concept of the Minimum Viable Product (MVP). We'll explore how to develop your MVP, iterate and refine your product or service, and ultimately create a brand that resonates with your target audience. Building a strong online presence and understanding the basics of marketing jargons will be essential in promoting your startup and attracting customers.

As you progress in your entrepreneurial journey, managing your finances and raising capital will become crucial. We'll delve into the world of financial management, providing insights on budgeting, financial planning, and different methods of raising capital for your startup. Developing a solid business plan and crafting a persuasive pitch deck will also be covered, giving you the tools to communicate your vision effectively to potential investors.

Scaling and growing your startup is the ultimate goal. We'll explore strategies and best practices for expanding your operations, overcoming challenges, and staying motivated along the way. Additionally, we'll touch upon a few key jargons commonly used in the startup world, ensuring you're well-versed in the language of entrepreneurship.

"Startup from Scratch" aims to be your comprehensive guide, offering practical advice, valuable insights, and actionable steps to help you navigate the intricacies of starting a startup. Whether you're looking to disrupt an industry or solve a specific problem, this book will provide you with the foundational knowledge and inspiration to turn your dreams into reality.

Remember, starting a startup requires perseverance, dedication, and a willingness to embrace both successes and failures. By immersing yourself in the knowledge and wisdom shared in this book, you'll be better prepared to face the challenges and seize the opportunities that lie ahead.

Now, let us embark on this transformative journey together and unlock the potential of your startup from scratch!

# Chapter 1: Why Start a Startup?

## Introduction:

The concept of entrepreneurship has always been fascinating to many individuals, who aspire to build something of their own from scratch. Starting a startup is an exciting journey that requires a lot of hard work, dedication, and passion. In this chapter, we will discuss why starting a startup can be a great idea, the challenges that come along with it, and how to prepare yourself for the journey ahead.

## Why Start a Startup?

There are numerous reasons why an individual might want to start a startup. For instance, you might have a unique idea that you are passionate about, or you desire to be your own boss and have control over your work. Perhaps you see a gap in the market that you believe you can fill, or you want to create a product or service that can help people in some way. Whatever your reason might be, starting a startup can be an exciting and rewarding experience.

One of the benefits of starting a startup is the potential to create wealth for yourself and others. Successful startups can generate significant profits and provide a platform for growth and expansion. For instance, Flipkart, an Indian e-commerce company, started in 2007, with the aim of providing online shopping to the Indian population. Over time, they expanded their services to include a range of products, including electronics, fashion, and groceries. In 2018, Walmart acquired a majority stake in Flipkart for $16 billion, which is an example of how a startup can generate significant wealth for its founders and investors.

Another reason to start a startup is to pursue your passion and create something that you believe in. For instance, Paytm, an Indian mobile payment and financial services company, started in 2010 with the aim of providing digital payment solutions to the Indian population. The founder, Vijay Shekhar Sharma, was passionate about creating a convenient and secure way for people to transact digitally. Today, Paytm has grown into a leading player in the Indian digital payments market.

## Challenges of Starting a Startup:

Starting a startup is not easy, and there are many challenges that you will face along the way. One of the biggest challenges is uncertainty. When you start a startup, you are entering into uncharted territory. You don't know how successful your product or service will be, or how the market will respond. You will need to be comfortable with ambiguity and have the ability to adapt to changing circumstances.

Another challenge is the need for funding. Starting a startup requires capital, and you will need to find investors or other sources of funding to get your business off the ground. In India, there are many government initiatives and private investors that support startups. For instance, the Government of India's 'Startup India' initiative provides funding, mentoring, and other resources to startups. Additionally, private investors such as Sequoia Capital and Accel Partners have invested in many successful Indian startups, including Flipkart and Paytm.

Building a strong team is also a challenge. You will need to find people who share your vision and are willing to work hard to make it a reality. Additionally, you will need to be able to manage and motivate your team to achieve your goals. For instance, Byju's, an Indian edtech startup, started in 2011 with the aim of providing online education to students across India. Today, they have a team of over 11,000 employees who work towards their mission of transforming education in India.

## Preparing Yourself for the Journey Ahead:

Before you start a startup, it is important to prepare yourself for the journey ahead. This includes developing your skills, building your network, and understanding the market and industry that you want to enter.

Developing your skills is essential for success in entrepreneurship. You will need to have a deep understanding of your product or service, as well as the industry and market that you are entering. This means you should spend time researching and studying the industry, trends, and consumer behaviours to understand what is driving demand, what challenges the industry is facing, and what opportunities may be present. Understanding your product or service is equally important. You should be knowledgeable about every aspect of your offering, from its features and benefits to its pricing strategy and unique selling proposition.

To develop the necessary skills, you may need to take courses, attend seminars or workshops, read books or articles, or seek advice and mentorship from experts in the field. Networking with other entrepreneurs, investors, and industry professionals can also be a valuable way to gain insights and knowledge.

## Building Your Network

In addition to developing your skills and knowledge, building a strong network is also crucial for success in entrepreneurship. Your network can provide support, advice, mentorship, and connections to potential investors or partners.

There are several ways to build your network, including attending networking events, participating in startup incubator programs, and joining online communities or forums. In India, there are numerous startup incubator programs and networking events that can help entrepreneurs connect with other like-minded individuals and industry professionals.

## Understanding the Market and Industry

Understanding the market and industry is crucial for success in entrepreneurship. You need to have a deep understanding of your target audience, their needs and preferences, and the competitive landscape. This will help you identify gaps in the market and create a product or service that meets the needs of your customers.

To understand the market and industry, you should conduct market research, analyse trends and data, and keep a pulse on consumer behaviours and preferences. This will help you make informed decisions about your product or service, pricing strategy, and marketing campaigns.

## Developing a Clear Vision and Plan

Finally, to start a successful startup, you need to have a clear vision for your business and a well-defined plan for how you will achieve your goals. This includes developing a business plan, setting realistic targets, and creating a roadmap for how you will achieve them.

A business plan is a document that outlines your company's goals, strategies, and financial projections. It should also include an analysis of the market and competition, as well as a description of your products or services and pricing strategy. The business plan serves as a roadmap for your startup and helps you stay focused on your goals.

Setting realistic targets is also important. You should break down your goals into smaller, achievable targets that can be measured and tracked. This will help you stay motivated and on track towards achieving your larger goals.

Creating a roadmap for how you will achieve your goals is the final step in developing a clear vision and plan for your startup. Your roadmap should outline the steps you will take to achieve your targets, including product development, marketing campaigns, and funding rounds.

# Conclusion

Starting a startup can be an exciting and rewarding journey, but it requires preparation, hard work, and dedication. To be successful, you need to develop your skills and knowledge, build a strong network, understand the market and industry, and have a clear vision and plan for your business. With the right mindset and support, you can overcome the challenges and create a successful startup that makes a difference in the world.

# Chapter 2: Identifying Your Passion and Interests

Starting a successful startup requires passion and a deep commitment to your work. If you are not passionate about your business, it can be challenging to stay motivated and overcome the inevitable obstacles that come with entrepreneurship. Therefore, identifying your passions and interests is a crucial step towards starting a successful startup. This chapter will provide you with the guidance you need to identify your passion and interests and use them to create a successful startup.

## Self-reflection

The first step towards identifying your passion and interests is self-reflection. Self-reflection involves examining your values, interests, and personal qualities. It is essential to take some time out and think deeply about what motivates you and what you enjoy doing.

One effective way to start self-reflection is to make a list of your interests, hobbies, and activities you enjoy. Ask yourself why you enjoy them and what they offer you. You can also consider the challenges you have faced and the things that you have learned from them.

During self-reflection, it is essential to be honest with yourself. Your business should reflect your genuine interests and passions, and not what you think others want you to do. Additionally, consider seeking feedback from people you trust, such as family and friends, to help you gain a different perspective on your interests and strengths.

## Explore New Things

It's possible that you may not know what you're passionate about yet. In that case, it's important to explore new things. Attending workshops, trying new activities, and engaging with people who are doing things that interest you can be a great way to explore new interests.

Exploration is critical, especially in the early stages of your startup. As you explore new interests, you will discover what you are passionate about and what you are not. It is essential to keep an open mind and try new things, even if they seem intimidating or challenging.

## Identify the Intersection

Once you have identified your passions and interests, the next step is to identify how they can be applied to a business idea. This requires finding the intersection between your passions and the needs of the market. For example, let's say that you are passionate about cooking and healthy eating. You could start a business that offers healthy meal delivery services.

In the Indian context, many successful startups have been founded by identifying the intersection between their passions and market needs. For instance, Byju's, a popular edtech startup, was founded by Byju Raveendran, who was passionate about teaching and making learning fun. Similarly, Paytm was founded by Vijay Shekhar Sharma, who was passionate about mobile technology and digital payments.

## Consider the Market

It is important to research the market and see if there is a demand for your product or service. Conducting market research, talking to potential customers, and analysing the competition will help you identify gaps in the market and create a product or service that meets the needs of your customers.

In India, there are several market research firms that can help you understand your target market better. Additionally, many successful startups use social media and other digital platforms to conduct market research and gather feedback from potential customers.

## Start Small

Starting a business can be overwhelming, but it's important to start small. You don't have to quit your job and invest all your savings into a business. Starting small will help you test your idea on a small scale and see if there is a demand for your product or service. You can start by offering your product or service to friends and family or at a local market.

Starting small also allows you to refine your product or service and get feedback from potential customers. This feedback can be used to make necessary adjustments and improvements to your offering. It also helps to build credibility and gain traction for your business.

## Embrace Failure

Starting a business comes with its fair share of failures and setbacks. It's important to embrace failure as a learning opportunity and not let it discourage you. Failure is a natural part of the process, and it's how you respond to failure that ultimately determines your success. Learn from your mistakes, make adjustments, and keep moving forward.

Example: The Story of Paper Boat

Paper Boat is a popular Indian beverage company that offers traditional Indian drinks with a modern twist. The founders, Neeraj Kakkar and James Nuttall, were passionate about preserving traditional Indian recipes that were at risk of being lost to modernisation. They launched Paper Boat in 2013 with a small team and limited resources.

They started by testing their idea at local markets and small stores. The initial response was positive, and they used this feedback to refine their product and build a following. They slowly expanded their product range and distribution network, and Paper Boat became a household name in India.

**Find Inspiration from Role Models:** Another way to identify your passions and interests is to look to your role models. Think about the people you admire and the work they do. What qualities do they possess that you admire? What skills or interests do they have that align with your own? By identifying these qualities, you can start to uncover your own passions and interests.

For example, if you admire Elon Musk for his innovation and ability to disrupt multiple industries, you may be interested in starting a tech company that revolutionizes an industry. Alternatively, if you admire the philanthropic work of Bill Gates, you may be interested in starting a social enterprise that solves a specific societal issue.

**Consider Your Values:** Your values can also be a guide in identifying your passions and interests. Consider what is most important to you in life, whether it's family, health, community, or social justice. These values can inspire ideas for a startup that aligns with your personal beliefs.

For instance, if you value community and social justice, you may want to start a non-profit that addresses issues of food insecurity in your local community. If you value health and wellness, you may consider starting a wellness center or a health and fitness app.

**Use Your Personal Experiences:** Your personal experiences can also be a source of inspiration for your startup idea. Think about any problems or challenges you have faced in your life and how you overcame them. This could spark an idea for a product or service that solves a similar problem for others.

For example, if you have struggled with mental health issues in the past, you may be interested in starting a mental health app that connects users with therapists and provides resources for self-care. If you have experience in the hospitality industry and have noticed inefficiencies in hotel operations, you may consider starting a hotel management software company.

**Look for Opportunities in Emerging Industries:** Another way to identify your passions and interests is to look for opportunities in emerging industries. As technology continues to advance, new industries are emerging, and there may be opportunities to create a business that aligns with your interests.

For instance, with the rise of the gig economy and remote work, there is a growing need for co-working spaces and tools that facilitate remote collaboration. If you are interested in creating a more sustainable future, you may consider starting a green energy company that develops new technologies for renewable energy.

**Use Mind Mapping Techniques:** Mind mapping is a technique that can help you visually organize your thoughts and ideas. Start by writing down your core interests and passions in the center of a piece of paper. Then, branch out from those core interests with related sub-topics. For example, if one of your core interests is cooking, you may branch out to sub-topics such as healthy eating, meal planning, and recipe development. This technique can help you uncover connections between your interests and identify potential business ideas.

## Conclusion:

Identifying your passions and interests is a critical step in starting a successful startup. By engaging in self-reflection, exploring new things, finding the intersection between your passions and market needs, considering your values and personal experiences, looking for opportunities in emerging industries, and using mind mapping techniques, you can uncover ideas that align with your interests and skills. By starting small and embracing failure as a learning opportunity, you can turn your passion into a successful business venture.

# Chapter 3: Finding and Evaluating Your Startup Idea

One of the most important steps in starting a successful startup is finding and evaluating your startup idea. Your idea is the foundation on which you will build your business, so it's essential that you choose a good one. In this chapter, we will discuss some methods for generating and evaluating startup ideas.

## Generating Startup Ideas

1. **Identify problems and pain points:** One of the best ways to come up with a startup idea is to identify problems and pain points in your own life or the lives of others. Look for areas where there is a need for a better solution or a more efficient way of doing things.

For example, if you are someone who often struggles to find healthy food options on-the-go, you may consider developing a food delivery service that specializes in healthy and nutritious meals. Or, if you are a parent who has a hard time finding affordable and reliable childcare services, you may consider developing an app that connects parents with trusted childcare providers in their area.

2. **Leverage your expertise:** Consider your own areas of expertise and experience. You may have unique insights or skills that can be turned into a profitable business. For example, if you have experience in web development, you may consider starting a web design agency. Or, if you have a passion for fashion and experience in retail, you may consider starting an online clothing boutique.

3. **Look for emerging trends:** Keep an eye out for emerging trends in your industry or in the wider world. These trends can indicate potential areas of growth and innovation. For example, the rise of the gig economy has led to the development of new businesses that connect freelance workers with clients. Similarly, the growing interest in

sustainable living has led to the development of businesses that focus on eco-friendly products and services.

## Evaluating Startup Ideas

Once you have generated a list of potential startup ideas, you need to evaluate them to determine which ones are most viable. Here are some factors to consider:

- **Market Demand**

The first and most important factor to consider when evaluating startup ideas is market demand. Is there a market for your product or service? Are people actually interested in what you are offering? Conducting market research can help you determine the potential demand for your idea. You can use tools such as surveys, focus groups, and online research to gather data on your target market.

Market research can help you identify your potential customers, their needs, and preferences. You can also use it to determine the size of your target market and estimate the potential revenue for your business. This information can help you decide whether your idea is worth pursuing or not.

- **Competition**

Another important factor to consider when evaluating startup ideas is competition. Who are your competitors? How many are there? How does your product or service differ from theirs? You need to identify your competitors and analyse their strengths and weaknesses.

Understanding your competition can help you differentiate your business and offer something unique to your customers. You can also learn from your competitors' mistakes and avoid making the same ones. It is important to note that having competitors is not necessarily a bad thing. It can indicate that there is a market for your product or service.

- **Scalability**

Scalability is another important factor to consider when evaluating startup ideas. Can your business scale as it grows? Will you be able to handle an increase in demand for your product or service? It is important to have a plan for growth and expansion.

You need to consider the resources, infrastructure, and personnel required to scale your business. This can include hiring more staff, investing in technology, and expanding your operations. You also need to consider the potential risks and challenges of scaling your business.

- **Cost**

Cost is another critical factor to consider when evaluating startup ideas. How much will it cost to start and run your business? What are the potential revenue streams? Consider the costs of manufacturing, marketing, staffing, and other expenses.

You need to have a clear understanding of the financial requirements of your business. You can create a budget to estimate the costs of starting and running your business. You should also consider the potential revenue streams and how long it will take to break even.

- **Passion**

Finally, it is important to consider your passion for your idea when evaluating startup ideas. Are you truly passionate about your idea? Starting a business is hard work, and you will face challenges and setbacks along the way. You need to have a strong passion for your idea to stay motivated and committed to your vision.

Passion is also important because it can inspire others to believe in your idea. If you are passionate about your business, it can be contagious and attract employees, investors, and customers who share your vision.

## Example:

Let's say you have identified a problem with finding affordable and reliable pet care services in your area. You decide to start a pet care business that offers affordable and trustworthy pet care services to pet owners in your community.

To evaluate the viability of your idea, you would need to conduct market research to determine if there is demand for your services. You could survey pet owners in your community to determine if they are interested in your services and how much they are willing to pay for them.

You would also need to research your competitors to determine how you can differentiate your business. Are there other pet care businesses in your area? What services do they offer? How can you offer something unique and valuable to your customers?

You would also need to consider the scalability of your business. Can you handle an increase in demand as your business grows? Will your idea be able to adapt to changes in the market and industry trends? These are important questions to ask yourself when evaluating your startup idea.

Another factor to consider is the potential market for your product or service. Is there a demand for what you're offering? Are there already established competitors in the market? If so, what makes your idea unique and how will it stand out from the competition? These are all important questions to ask when evaluating your startup idea.

One way to test the potential market for your idea is through market research. This can involve conducting surveys or focus groups to gather feedback on your product or service from potential customers. It can also involve analysing industry trends and the behaviour of your target market.

It's important to also consider the feasibility of your startup idea. Do you have the resources, skills, and knowledge to turn your idea into a viable business? Can you secure funding to support your startup in its early stages?

Another important factor to consider is the legal and regulatory requirements for starting a business in India. This can include registering your business, obtaining necessary licenses and permits, and complying with tax laws.

When evaluating your startup idea, it's important to be honest with yourself and willing to make changes or pivot if necessary. Remember, the most successful startups are often the ones that are willing to adapt and evolve over time.

For example, let's say you have an idea for a mobile app that helps people track their daily exercise and nutrition. Before launching the app, you conduct market research and discover that there are already several established fitness tracking apps in the market. However, you also discover that there is a demand for a more personalized approach to fitness tracking, with features such as personalized meal plans and coaching services. Based on this feedback, you decide to pivot your idea and incorporate these features into your app, making it stand out from the competition and better meet the needs of your target market.

Overall, finding and evaluating your startup idea is a crucial step in starting a successful business. By considering factors such as market demand, feasibility, scalability, and legal requirements, you can ensure that your idea has the potential to succeed and thrive in the competitive world of startups.

# Chapter 4: Conducting Market Research

Market research is a crucial step in starting and growing any business. It involves gathering and analysing data about the target market, competition, and industry trends to make informed business decisions. Without proper market research, a startup risks launching a product or service that fails to meet the needs of the market, resulting in wasted time, resources, and money.

In this chapter, we'll discuss the different types of market research, the steps involved in conducting market research, and the tools and techniques you can use to gather and analyse data.

## Types of Market Research

There are two main types of market research: primary research and secondary research.

Primary research involves gathering data directly from the source through surveys, focus groups, and other methods. This type of research allows you to gather specific information about your target market, such as their preferences, needs, and behaviours.

Secondary research involves gathering data from existing sources, such as industry reports, government data, and competitor analysis. This type of research allows you to gather information about industry trends, market size, and competitor activity.

## Steps in Conducting Market Research

1. **Define Your Objectives:**

Before conducting market research, it's essential to have a clear understanding of your objectives. These objectives could include determining the potential demand for your product, identifying your target market, understanding your competition, and more. The clearer you are about your objectives, the more focused and targeted your research will be.

To define your objectives, you should first ask yourself what questions you need to answer to inform your business decisions. These could include questions about your target market, your competition, your product's unique selling proposition (USP), or your pricing strategy. Once you have a list of questions, you can prioritize them and determine which ones are most critical to answer.

It's also important to consider what information you already have and what information you still need. This can help you determine which research methods are best suited to your objectives.

## 2. Identify Your Target Market:

Identifying your target market is an essential step in market research. You need to know who your ideal customer is so that you can tailor your product, marketing, and sales strategies to their needs and preferences.

To identify your target market, you should consider demographic factors such as age, gender, income, and geographic location. You can also look at psychographic factors such as interests, values, and lifestyle. It's essential to be as specific as possible when defining your target market. This will help you create more effective marketing messages and reach your ideal customers more efficiently.

In addition to identifying your target market, you may also want to consider conducting market segmentation. This involves dividing your target market into smaller, more specific groups based on factors such as behaviour, needs, or preferences. Market segmentation can help you tailor your marketing strategies to each group and improve the effectiveness of your campaigns.

## 3. Choose Your Research Methods:

Once you have defined your objectives and identified your target market, you need to choose the best research methods to gather the data you need. The research methods you choose will depend on the nature of your objectives and the type of information you need to collect.

Some common research methods include surveys, focus groups, interviews, observation, and online research. Surveys are an excellent way to gather quantitative data and get a broad understanding of your target market. Focus groups and interviews are better suited for qualitative data and can help you gain deeper insights into your customers' needs and preferences. Observational research can be useful for understanding customer behaviour and identifying patterns and trends.

When choosing your research methods, it's essential to consider factors such as cost, time, and accessibility. You should also consider the potential biases that may be present in each method and how you can mitigate these biases to ensure the accuracy and reliability of your data.

## 4. Collect Data:

Once you have chosen your research methods, you need to collect data from your target market. To ensure the accuracy and reliability of your data, it's essential to collect data from a large enough sample size.

When collecting data, it's important to consider the data collection method. For example, if you are conducting a survey, you may want to use a mix of online and offline methods to reach a broader audience. You may also want to consider incentivizing participants to increase response rates.

It's important to be organized when collecting data. This means having a clear plan for how you will collect and store the data. You should also ensure that your data collection methods comply with relevant data privacy regulations.

## 5. Analyse Data:

Once you have collected your data, the next step is to analyse it. This involves identifying patterns, trends, and insights that will help you make informed business decisions.

Data analysis can be a complex process, and there are many different techniques and tools available. Some common methods include descriptive statistics, regression analysis, and data visualization.

When analysing your data, it's important to look for patterns, trends, and insights that will help you make informed business decisions. Look for recurring themes and issues that your target market is facing, as well as any gaps or unmet needs that your product or service could potentially fill.

It's also important to consider the validity and reliability of your data. Ensure that your sample size is large enough to provide accurate and reliable results. If necessary, consider conducting additional research or consulting with experts in your field to verify your findings.

Once you have analysed your data, use it to make informed business decisions. Use the insights gained from your market research to inform your product development, marketing strategy, pricing, and distribution.

Market research is an ongoing process, and it's important to continue gathering data and analysing trends over time. Stay up to date with changes in your industry, and regularly check in with your target market to ensure that your business is meeting their needs and expectations.

## Tools and Techniques for Market Research

- **Surveys:** Surveys are a way of asking a lot of people what they think about a particular topic. Imagine you have a big group of friends, and you want to know what they like to eat. You could ask them one by one, but that would take a long time. Instead, you could make a survey and ask everyone at the same time. Surveys can be done online or in-person, and they can ask both simple questions like "What is your favourite colour?" or more detailed questions like "What do you think about this product?".

For example, a company in India that sells clothes might want to know what types of clothes people like to wear. They could make a survey and ask people questions like "What is your favourite colour for clothes?" or "Do you prefer traditional or modern clothes?".

- **Focus Groups:** Focus groups are a way of gathering a small group of people together to talk about a particular product or service. It's like having a big brainstorming session with a small group of people. The company can ask questions and get feedback from the group. Focus groups are great for getting detailed feedback and opinions on a product or service.

For example, a company in India that sells phones might want to know what features people look for in a phone. They could gather a group of people together and ask them questions like "What is the most important feature you look for in a phone?" or "What would make you choose one phone over another?".

- **Interviews:** Interviews are a way of getting detailed information from individuals. It's like having a one-on-one conversation with someone, but with a purpose. The company can ask questions and get detailed answers from the person being interviewed. Interviews are great for getting personal insights and opinions.

For example, a company in India that sells food might want to know what types of food people like to eat. They could interview people one-on-one and ask them questions like "What is your favourite type of food?" or "What type of food do you like to eat when you're feeling happy?".

- **Observational Research:** Observational research is a way of watching people and recording their behaviour. It's like being a detective and observing people without them knowing it. The company can watch people in a natural setting, like a store or a park, and see how they behave. Observational research is great for getting insights into customer behaviour.

For example, a company in India that sells toys might want to know what toys children like to play with. They could go to a park and watch children play with different toys, and see which toys they play with the most.

- **Online Research:** Online research is a way of gathering data from online sources like social media, customer reviews, and online forums.

It's like looking at what people are saying about a particular topic online. The company can see what people are saying about their product or service, and get real-time insights into customer opinions and preferences.

For example, a company in India that sells cars might want to know what people think about their new car model. They could look at online forums where people are talking about cars, and see what they are saying about their new model.

## Example of Market Research in Action

Let's say you're planning to launch a new line of organic food products in India. You could conduct market research to gather information about the market size, demand for organic food, and competitor activity.

To conduct primary research, you could survey a sample of individuals to gather information about their dietary preferences and buying habits. You could also conduct focus groups to gather more detailed feedback on specific product offerings.

To conduct secondary research, you could analyse existing industry reports and government data to gather information about the size of the organic food market in India, growth projections, and regulatory requirements.

By conducting this research, you could gain valuable insights into the organic food market in India, and make informed decisions about your product offerings, pricing strategy, and marketing efforts.

Once you have a better understanding of your target audience and competitors, you can begin to identify gaps in the market and areas where you can differentiate your product or service.

One example of a company that successfully identified a gap in the market is Airbnb. The founders of Airbnb noticed a lack of affordable accommodation options during a design conference in San Francisco, and realized that there was an opportunity to create a platform that would connect travellers with locals who could offer spare rooms or apartments for rent. By conducting market research and identifying this gap in the market, Airbnb was able to create a successful business model that disrupted the traditional hotel industry.

In addition to identifying gaps in the market, market research can also help you evaluate the potential demand for your product or service. For example, if you are considering starting a business that sells organic pet food, you may want to conduct research to determine the size of the pet food market, the demand for organic products, and the purchasing behaviour of pet owners.

Finally, market research can also help you determine the pricing strategy for your product or service. By understanding what your competitors are charging and how much your target audience is willing to pay, you can set a price that is both competitive and profitable.

## Conclusion

In conclusion, market research is a vital step in the process of starting a successful startup. By taking the time to understand your target audience, competitors, and market demand, you can make informed decisions that will help you differentiate your product or service and create a competitive advantage. While it may be tempting to skip this step and dive straight into launching your business, investing time and resources into market research can ultimately save you from costly mistakes and increase your chances of success.

Remember, starting a business is a journey that requires patience, dedication, and hard work. Conducting thorough market research can help you lay a solid foundation for your startup and increase your chances of success in the long run. So, take the time to gather data, analyse your findings, and use your insights to inform your business strategy. By doing so, you will be well on your way to turning your passion and ideas into a thriving startup that makes a meaningful impact on the world.

# Chapter 5: Identifying Your Target Customer

Identifying your target customer is a crucial step in starting a successful startup. Your target customer is the group of people who are most likely to buy your product or service. By understanding who your target customer is, you can create products and services that cater to their needs, which in turn can increase your chances of success.

## 1. Conduct Market Research

The first step in identifying your target customer is to conduct market research. This will help you understand who your potential customers are, what their needs and preferences are, and how you can meet those needs. You can use a variety of methods to conduct market research, including surveys, focus groups, and online research.

## 2. Develop Customer Personas

Once you have gathered data through market research, the next step is to develop customer personas. Customer personas are fictional representations of your ideal customer. They should include demographic information, such as age, gender, income, and education level, as well as psychographic information, such as values, interests, and behaviour.

For example, if you are developing a mobile app for budget travellers, your customer personas might include:

- Young adults between the ages of 18 and 30
- Students or recent graduates with limited income
- Adventurous individuals who enjoy exploring new places
- Tech-savvy individuals who rely heavily on their mobile devices

By developing customer personas, you can get a better understanding of who your target customer is, what they want, and how you can reach them.

### 3.  Analyse Your Competition

Another important step in identifying your target customer is to analyse your competition. Look at what your competitors are doing and who they are targeting. Identify any gaps in the market that your startup can fill.

For example, if you are developing a new line of natural skincare products, you might look at what other companies are offering and identify a gap in the market for affordable, all-natural products. By filling this gap, you can attract customers who are looking for an affordable, all-natural option.

### 4.  Consider Customer Behaviour

When identifying your target customer, it's important to consider customer behaviour. What motivates your customers to make a purchase? What factors influence their buying decisions?

For example, if you are developing a new line of luxury watches, you might consider what factors influence a customer's decision to purchase a high-end watch. Is it the brand name? The quality of materials? The design?

By understanding customer behaviour, you can create products and marketing strategies that appeal to your target customer.

### 5.  Use Data Analytics

Data analytics is a powerful tool for identifying your target customer. By analysing data from your website, social media accounts, and other sources, you can gain insights into who your customers are, what they want, and how they behave.

For example, if you run an e-commerce website, you might use data analytics to track which products are most popular among your customers. By understanding what products are popular, you can create similar products that are likely to appeal to your target customer.

Let's take the example of a street food vendor in India who is trying to identify their target customer. After conducting market research, the vendor discovers that their potential customers are primarily office workers who are looking for a quick and affordable lunch option. The vendor then develops customer personas, which include office workers between the ages of 25-45, who have limited time and are looking for healthy and delicious food. Based on this information, the vendor analyses their competition and identifies a gap in the market for healthy street food options that are both affordable and quick to serve.

To cater to this target customer, the street food vendor might consider offering a variety of healthy options such as salads, sandwiches, and wraps that can be prepared quickly and easily. The vendor might also consider offering special discounts or loyalty programs to attract regular office customers.

When it comes to customer behaviour, the street food vendor might consider what factors influence a customer's decision to purchase street food. For example, the vendor might offer samples or free tastings to entice customers to try their food, or create an attractive and inviting display to draw customers in.

By using data analytics, the street food vendor can track the popularity of different menu items and adjust their offerings accordingly. For instance, if a particular dish is particularly popular, the vendor might consider offering more variations of it or introducing new dishes that are similar.

## Conclusion

Identifying your target customer is essential for the success of your startup. By conducting market research, developing customer personas, analysing your competition, considering customer behaviour, and using data analytics, you can gain a better understanding of who your target customer is and how to reach them. Remember, the more you know about your target customer, the better you can create products and services that meet their needs and increase your chances of success.

# Chapter 6: Crafting Your Value Proposition

One of the key aspects of a successful startup is creating a value proposition that resonates with your target audience. Your value proposition is the promise of value that you will deliver to your customers and sets you apart from your competitors. In this chapter, we will explore the steps involved in crafting a compelling value proposition.

## 1. Understand Your Customer's Needs

The first step in creating a value proposition is to understand your customer's needs. This involves identifying the pain points that your target audience is experiencing and the problems they are looking to solve. Once you have identified these needs, you can tailor your value proposition to address them directly.

For example, Swiggy, an Indian food delivery startup, identified the need for quick and reliable food delivery services. They created a value proposition that emphasized their ability to deliver food from a variety of restaurants quickly and efficiently, addressing a major pain point for customers.

## 2. Differentiate Yourself from Competitors

Your value proposition should also differentiate you from your competitors. This means identifying what sets your startup apart and highlighting those unique features in your messaging.

For instance, Oyo Rooms, an Indian hotel aggregator startup, differentiates itself from traditional hotel booking platforms by offering affordable and standardized accommodations across a wide range of price points. They crafted a value proposition that emphasized their unique selling point (USP) of providing a comfortable and affordable stay at any budget.

## 3. Focus on Benefits, Not Just Features

When crafting your value proposition, it's essential to focus on the benefits your startup provides, rather than just the features. Benefits are what your customers gain from using your product or service, while features are the technical aspects of what you offer.

For example, Cure.fit, an Indian health and fitness startup, focuses on the benefits of their offering – a one-stop-shop for all your fitness and wellness needs. They provide access to fitness classes, healthy meal plans, and mental wellness services, emphasizing the overall health and wellbeing benefits of using their platform.

## 4. Use Clear and Simple Language

Your value proposition should be easy for your customers to understand. Using clear and simple language will help your message resonate with your target audience.

For instance, Paytm, an Indian mobile wallet and e-commerce platform, crafted a value proposition that is easy to understand for their customers. Their value proposition is "One App, One Tap, One Payment," emphasizing the simplicity and ease of use of their platform.

## 5. Create a Customer Persona

To craft a compelling value proposition, it's important to have a clear understanding of who your target customer is. Creating a customer persona can help you to identify your customer's goals, challenges, pain points, and motivations.

For example, if you are launching a health and wellness startup, your customer persona may be a busy working professional who is looking for a convenient way to stay healthy and fit. Understanding their needs and priorities can help you to tailor your value proposition to address their specific pain points.

## 6. Test and Refine Your Value Proposition

Once you have crafted your value proposition, it's important to test it with your target audience. This will help you to identify any areas that may need refining and ensure that your messaging resonates with your customers.

For example, Ola, an Indian ride-hailing startup, tested their value proposition of providing affordable and reliable transportation services in the Indian market. They refined their messaging to emphasize the affordability and convenience of their platform, which helped to differentiate them from their competitors.

Let's say you are starting a meal kit delivery service that specializes in healthy and organic meal options. By creating a customer persona for your target audience, you can tailor your value proposition to meet their specific needs and preferences.

Your customer persona might be a busy professional in their mid-thirties who values health and convenience. They are concerned about the quality of their food, but don't have the time to shop for and prepare healthy meals every day.

With this customer persona in mind, you can create a value proposition that speaks directly to their pain points and desires. For example, your value proposition might emphasize the convenience of having healthy and delicious meals delivered right to their door, saving them time and stress. You might also emphasize the high-quality, organic ingredients used in your meals, which will give your customers peace of mind knowing that they are eating healthy food.

By creating a customer persona and tailoring your value proposition to meet their needs and preferences, you can create a compelling message that resonates with your target audience and sets you apart from your competitors.

## Conclusion

In conclusion, crafting a compelling value proposition is an essential step in building a successful startup. By understanding your customer's needs, differentiating yourself from your competitors, focusing on benefits rather than features, using clear and simple language, creating a customer persona, and testing and refining your messaging, you can create a value proposition that resonates with your target market and sets your startup up for success.

To make sure that your value proposition is effective, you need to keep refining it and making it better over time. This means being open to feedback from your customers and making changes based on what you learn.

Additionally, your value proposition should be integrated into all aspects of your business, from your website and marketing materials to your customer service and product development. It should be clear and consistent across all channels so that your customers know exactly what they can expect from your startup.

Finally, it's important to remember that your value proposition is not set in stone. As your business grows and evolves, you may need to update it to reflect changes in your market or target audience. By staying flexible and adaptable, you can continue to create value for your customers and drive growth for your startup.

In summary, creating a compelling value proposition is a critical component of building a successful startup. By following the steps outlined in this chapter, you can craft a value proposition that resonates with your target audience, differentiates you from your competitors, and communicates the benefits of using your product or service. Keep refining and testing your value proposition over time, and be willing to make changes as needed to ensure that it continues to drive growth and success for your startup.

# Chapter 7: Co-founders and Advisors

When starting a business, one of the most important decisions you will make is whether to go solo or with a co-founder. While going solo may seem like the easier option, having a co-founder can bring many benefits, such as shared responsibilities, complementary skill sets, and emotional support. This chapter will discuss the advantages of having a co-founder, the ideal co-founder mix, how to check co-founder fitment, optimum equity split between co-founders, finding and compensating co-founders, and the role of advisors.

## Going Solo or with a Co-founder:

Going solo or having a co-founder is one of the most critical decisions an entrepreneur needs to make when starting a business. While it may be tempting to go solo, having a co-founder can provide a number of benefits, such as a division of labour, sharing of risk and financial burden, and access to additional skills and expertise.

However, there are also drawbacks to having a co-founder. Differences in vision, leadership style, and decision-making can create conflicts that may be difficult to resolve. In addition, sharing equity and decision-making power with a co-founder may result in less control over the business.

Before making the decision to go solo or have a co-founder, it's important to consider your strengths and weaknesses as an entrepreneur. If you have a specific skill set or expertise, it may make sense to bring on a co-founder with complementary skills to fill any gaps. On the other hand, if you are confident in your abilities and have a clear vision for your business, going solo may be the best option.

Another important factor to consider is your personal relationships. Bringing on a friend or family member as a co-founder may seem like a good idea, but it can also put strain on the relationship if the business encounters challenges. It's important to have open and honest communication with any potential co-founders and to make sure everyone is aligned on the vision and goals for the business.

Ultimately, the decision to go solo or have a co-founder is a personal one that should be based on a number of factors. It's important to weigh the potential benefits and drawbacks, consider your own strengths and weaknesses, and have open communication with any potential co-founders before making a decision.

## The Ideal Co-founder Mix:

Choosing the right co-founder(s) can be one of the most crucial decisions you make when starting a business. You need to find someone who not only shares your passion and vision for the company but also brings different skills, experiences, and perspectives to the table.

The ideal co-founder mix depends on the nature of your business, your strengths and weaknesses, and the industry you are in. Generally, co-founders with complementary skills and experiences tend to work well together. For example, if you are a technical person, you may need a co-founder with business or marketing experience. If you are a businessperson, you may need a co-founder with technical skills.

It's important to look for someone who shares your values, work ethic, and level of commitment. You should also consider whether you can work well together and communicate effectively. Building a startup can be stressful and challenging, so it's important to have a co-founder you can rely on and trust.

In some cases, having multiple co-founders can be beneficial, as it can bring a diversity of skills and perspectives to the team. However, having too many co-founders can also lead to conflicts and decision-making challenges. Ideally, you should aim to have a small team of co-founders who can work together effectively.

Ultimately, the ideal co-founder mix will depend on your specific business and the skills and experiences you need to bring your vision to life. Take the time to find the right co-founder(s) who can complement your skills and help you build a successful startup.

# How to Check Co-founder Fitment?

Choosing the right co-founder is critical to the success of your startup. To ensure that you find the right co-founder, it is important to evaluate their skills, experience, and personality fit with you and your business. Here are some steps you can take to check co-founder fitment:

1. **Determine your strengths and weaknesses:** Before you start looking for a co-founder, take the time to identify your own strengths and weaknesses. This will help you find someone who complements your skillset and can fill the gaps in your expertise.

2. **Evaluate potential co-founders' skills and experience:** Look for a co-founder who has skills and experience that complement yours. For example, if you are a tech expert, you might want to find a co-founder who has a background in sales or marketing.

3. **Assess their commitment:** Starting a startup requires a lot of hard work and dedication. It is important to ensure that your co-founder is committed to the vision of the company and is willing to put in the necessary time and effort.

4. **Check their personality fit:** A co-founder is someone with whom you will be working very closely. It is important to ensure that your personalities and working styles are compatible. You should look for someone who shares your values, communication style, and work ethic.

5. **Consider their network:** A co-founder with a strong network can be a valuable asset to your startup. Look for someone who has connections in your industry and can help you make valuable business contacts.

6. **Conduct a trial period:** Consider starting with a trial period to see how well you and your potential co-founder work together. This can be a short-term project or a temporary employment period to evaluate how well you both complement each other.

## Optimum Equity Split between Co-founders

When starting a business with a co-founder, one of the most important and often challenging decisions is determining the equity split between the co-founders. Equity is essentially ownership in the company, and it's crucial to get the split right to ensure a fair and sustainable partnership.

There is no hard and fast rule for how to split equity between co-founders, as each situation is unique. However, there are some general guidelines and factors to consider when determining the equity split.

One factor to consider is the contributions each co-founder will make to the business. This includes not only financial contributions but also skills, experience, and connections. If one co-founder is investing significantly more money into the business than the other, it may make sense for them to receive a larger equity stake. Similarly, if one co-founder has specific expertise or connections that are vital to the success of the business, they may also deserve a larger stake.

Another factor to consider is the roles and responsibilities of each co-founder. It's essential to define clear roles and responsibilities early on in the partnership to avoid conflicts down the road. If one co-founder is taking on more of the day-to-day operations and management of the business, they may deserve a larger stake.

It's also important to consider the long-term vision and goals of the business. If one co-founder has a stronger vision for the company's direction and growth, they may deserve a larger stake.

When it comes to determining the actual percentage split, there are a few different methods that co-founders can use. One common method is the "equal split" approach, where each co-founder receives an equal percentage of the company's equity. However, this may not always be the most appropriate or fair approach, especially if one co-founder is making a larger investment or has more significant responsibilities.

Another method is the "dynamic equity" approach, where the equity split is adjusted over time based on each co-founder's contributions and performance. For example, if one co-founder's contributions to the business decrease over time, their equity stake may be reduced accordingly.

It's also essential to consider vesting when determining the equity split. Vesting is essentially a schedule that determines when co-founders receive their equity stake. For example, a common vesting schedule is four years, with co-founders receiving 25% of their equity stake each year. This helps ensure that co-founders are committed to the business for the long term and incentivizes them to stay with the company.

## How to Find Right Co-founders?

Finding the right co-founder(s) for your startup is crucial as they will be your partners, support system, and will help you build your business. Here are some tips for finding the right co-founders:

1. **Networking:** Attend events, conferences, and meetups related to your industry to meet like-minded people who are interested in startups. You can also join online forums and groups to connect with people who share the same passion as you.
2. **Industry-specific platforms:** There are several industry-specific platforms such as AngelList, FoundersNation, and Startup Weekend that can help you find potential co-founders. These platforms have a large database of entrepreneurs, investors, and advisors.
3. **Personal network:** Reach out to your personal network such as friends, family, colleagues, and alumni networks to see if anyone is interested in starting a business with you. This can be a great option as you already have a good understanding of their strengths, weaknesses, and work style.
4. **Co-founder dating sites:** There are several co-founder dating sites such as CoFoundersLab and FounderDating that help connect entrepreneurs with potential co-founders. These platforms allow you to create a profile, browse through potential co-founders, and connect with them.
5. **Compatibility:** Finding the right co-founder is not just about their skillset and experience, but also about their personality, work ethic, and values. It's important to find someone who shares your vision and is passionate about the same things as you. You should also look for

someone who complements your skill set and can bring a different perspective to the table.

6. **Assessing skills and experience:** When looking for a co-founder, it's important to assess their skills and experience. You want someone who can bring expertise and experience to areas where you lack. It's important to have a mix of technical and business skills among your co-founders.

7. **Communicating your vision:** When looking for a co-founder, it's important to clearly communicate your vision, mission, and goals. This will help you attract the right people who are aligned with your vision and are willing to work towards achieving your goals.

Once you have found potential co-founders, it's important to assess their fitment. Here are some factors to consider:

1. **Work style:** It's important to assess their work style and see if it complements yours. You want someone who can work well under pressure, is proactive, and can handle ambiguity.

2. **Communication:** Communication is key in any partnership. You want someone who is a good communicator and is willing to have honest and open conversations.

3. **Conflict resolution:** Conflicts are bound to happen in any partnership. It's important to assess how they handle conflicts and whether they are open to compromise.

4. **Commitment:** Starting a business requires a lot of commitment and hard work. It's important to assess their commitment and see if they are willing to put in the effort and time required to build a successful business.

## Role of Advisors

Having advisors can be immensely beneficial for a startup, especially for first-time entrepreneurs. Advisors can provide valuable guidance and expertise, as well as connections and access to resources. They can also help entrepreneurs avoid common mistakes and pitfalls.

The role of advisors can vary depending on the needs and goals of the startup. Some advisors may be more involved in day-to-day operations, while others may provide more high-level strategic guidance. It's important for entrepreneurs to identify what they need from an advisor and seek out individuals who have the relevant experience and expertise.

Advisors can come from a variety of backgrounds, including industry experts, investors, and successful entrepreneurs. When considering potential advisors, it's important to evaluate their track record and reputation, as well as their compatibility with the startup's mission and values.

Once advisors have been identified, it's important to establish clear expectations and communication channels. This includes setting regular check-ins and providing updates on the startup's progress. It's also important to be open to feedback and criticism from advisors, as they can provide valuable insights that can help improve the business.

In terms of compensation, advisors may receive equity in the startup, a monthly or yearly retainer fee, or a combination of both. It's important for entrepreneurs to establish clear terms and expectations for compensation upfront to avoid any confusion or misunderstandings down the line.

## Conclusion

In conclusion, building a startup team is a crucial step in the success of your business. Whether you decide to go solo, find a co-founder or bring on advisors, it's important to carefully consider your options and choose the right people to work with. A good mix of skills, values, and personalities is key to a successful partnership, and checking for fitment is crucial to ensure you are all aligned towards the same goals. Additionally, it's important to consider equity splits, compensation, and legal agreements to avoid potential conflicts down the road. By finding the right co-founders or advisors, you can benefit from their expertise, experience, and network to help grow your business. Remember to communicate openly, be transparent about your expectations, and establish a strong foundation of trust and respect to ensure a successful working relationship.

# Chapter 8: Building Your Startup Team

Building a successful startup requires more than just a great idea. It requires a team of dedicated and passionate individuals who are committed to turning that idea into a reality. As an entrepreneur, building the right team can be the difference between success and failure. In this chapter, we will discuss the steps you can take to build the perfect team for your startup.

## Step 1: Define your team's roles and responsibilities

The first step to building a great team is to define the roles and responsibilities that need to be filled. Start by identifying the key areas of your business that require attention. This could include marketing, sales, operations, and product development. Once you have identified these areas, create job descriptions for each role that outline the responsibilities, required skills, and qualifications needed.

For example, if you are building a software startup, you may need a software engineer, a product manager, a marketing specialist, and a salesperson. Each role has different responsibilities and requires specific skills and qualifications. Be clear about what you are looking for in each role, and communicate these requirements clearly in your job descriptions.

## Step 2: Hire for cultural fit

Cultural fit is crucial when building a team for your startup. You want to hire individuals who share your values and are passionate about your vision. When interviewing candidates, focus on their values and work ethic, as well as their skills and experience. Look for individuals who are willing to take on challenges, work collaboratively, and are passionate about your product or service.

For example, if your startup is focused on sustainability, look for candidates who share a passion for environmentalism and sustainability. If you prioritize innovation, look for candidates who are willing to take risks and think outside the box.

### Step 3: Leverage your network

Your personal and professional network can be a valuable resource when building a team for your startup. Reach out to your network and let them know that you are looking for talented individuals to join your team. Ask for referrals and recommendations, and be sure to follow up on any leads.

You can also attend networking events, startup meetups, and industry conferences to connect with potential team members. These events are great opportunities to meet like-minded individuals who are passionate about entrepreneurship and may be interested in joining your team.

### Step 4: Use online resources

There are several online resources you can use to find potential team members for your startup. LinkedIn, AngelList, and Indeed are all great platforms for posting job openings and finding candidates. You can also join online communities and forums related to your industry or niche to connect with potential team members.

Additionally, you can use freelance platforms like Upwork and Fiverr to hire contractors or freelancers for short-term projects or to fill specific roles in your startup.

### Step 5: Offer competitive compensation and benefits

Offering competitive compensation and benefits is crucial when building a team for your startup. You want to attract and retain top talent, so you need to offer compensation and benefits packages that are competitive with other companies in your industry.

Be sure to research the average salaries and benefits packages for the roles you are hiring for, and aim to offer packages that are at or above this average. This will help you attract top talent and ensure that your team members feel valued and appreciated.

### Step 6: Foster a positive and supportive work environment

Creating a positive and supportive work environment is essential for building a great team. You want your team members to feel valued, respected, and supported. Encourage open communication, collaboration, and teamwork. Provide opportunities for professional development and growth, and offer regular feedback and recognition.

Additionally, create a work environment that fosters creativity and innovation. Allow your team members to take risks and experiment with new ideas. Encourage them to challenge the status quo and think outside the box.

## Step 7: Conduct skills and personality assessments

Skills assessments can help you evaluate potential team members' skills and qualifications in a more objective and consistent manner. Personality assessments can also be useful for determining whether a candidate will be a good fit for your team's culture and values. These assessments can help you make more informed hiring decisions and ensure that you are hiring the right people for the right roles.

## Step 8: Develop a comprehensive onboarding program

Developing a comprehensive onboarding program can help new team members get up to speed quickly and start contributing to your startup as soon as possible. Your onboarding program should include an introduction to your company culture, values, and mission, as well as training on your products, services, and processes. This will help new team members feel more comfortable and confident in their roles and increase their chances of success.

## Step 9: Establish clear communication channels

Establishing clear communication channels is essential for ensuring that your team members can communicate effectively with each other and with you. Make sure that everyone knows how to reach each other, whether through email, phone, chat, or in-person meetings. Encourage regular check-ins and provide opportunities for team members to share feedback, concerns, and ideas.

## Step 10: Foster a culture of continuous learning and improvement

Finally, it's important to foster a culture of continuous learning and improvement within your startup team. Encourage your team members to pursue professional development opportunities, such as attending conferences, taking courses, or joining industry associations. Provide opportunities for cross-functional collaboration and encourage team members to share knowledge and expertise with each other. By fostering a culture of continuous learning and improvement, you can help your team members stay engaged, motivated, and inspired.

## Conclusion

In conclusion, building a great startup team is an essential part of turning an idea into a successful business. It requires a lot of effort, time, and resources to find the right people with the right skills, experience, and mindset to complement your own strengths and weaknesses. However, once you have built a cohesive and effective team, it can be the most valuable asset in scaling your startup and achieving your vision.

Remember, building a startup team is not just about hiring people with impressive resumes or offering high salaries. It is about finding people who share your passion, commitment, and values, and who are willing to work hard, learn, and grow with you. It is also about creating a positive and supportive culture where everyone feels valued, heard, and motivated to contribute their best work.

So, take your time to define your startup's vision, mission, and values, and then identify the specific roles and skills needed to achieve your goals. Use various channels, such as job boards, social media, referrals, and events, to attract potential candidates, and then screen them carefully to ensure they fit your team's culture and expectations.

When evaluating candidates, look beyond their technical skills and experience and also consider their personality, communication style, and work ethic. It can also be helpful to conduct team interviews or work simulations to see how candidates interact with your existing team and how they handle different scenarios and challenges.

Once you have found the right people, invest in their development and growth through training, coaching, and mentorship. Provide them with clear goals and expectations, regular feedback and recognition, and opportunities for ownership and decision-making.

Finally, ensure that your team's compensation and benefits packages are competitive and aligned with their performance and contributions. Consider offering equity, profit sharing, or other non-monetary incentives that align with your team's long-term goals and aspirations.

# Chapter 9: Understanding Your Competitors

In the world of startups, competition is a fact of life. No matter what industry or niche you are in, chances are there are already established players in the market. This can be intimidating for new entrepreneurs, but it doesn't have to be. By understanding your competitors, you can gain valuable insights that can help you differentiate your offering and carve out a unique place in the market. In this chapter, we will explore the importance of understanding your competitors and provide practical tips for conducting a competitive analysis.

## Why Understanding Your Competitors is Important?

There are several reasons why understanding your competitors is important for the success of your startup:

1. **Identify gaps in the market:** By analysing your competitors, you can gain insights into the gaps in the market that have not been addressed by your competitors. Understanding these gaps can help you develop a unique value proposition that sets your offering apart from your competitors. For example, if your competitors are offering a certain product or service that lacks a certain feature, you can introduce that feature in your product or service and gain a competitive advantage. By identifying and capitalising on the gaps in the market, you can better serve your customers and grow your business.

2. **Benchmark your performance:** By comparing your performance to that of your competitors, you can gain valuable insights into how your business is performing relative to others in the same industry. This can help you identify areas where you are falling behind and work to improve them. For example, if your competitor's customer retention rate is higher than yours, you can analyse their strategy and implement changes to improve your own retention rate. By benchmarking your

performance against your competitors, you can stay competitive and ensure your business is meeting the needs of your customers.

3. **Identify potential partnerships:** By analysing your competitors, you may identify potential partners or suppliers who can help you grow your business. For example, if your competitor has a supplier who provides high-quality raw materials, you may consider approaching that supplier to see if they can provide the same materials to your business. Similarly, if your competitor has a partnership with a complementary business, you may consider forming a similar partnership with that business to expand your reach. By identifying potential partners through your competitors, you can build relationships that can help your business grow.

4. **Identify potential threats:** By analysing your competitors, you can identify potential threats to your business, such as new entrants or changes in consumer preferences. For example, if a new competitor enters the market offering a similar product or service, you can adjust your strategy to stay competitive. Similarly, if your competitor's customers are shifting their preferences towards a new feature or benefit, you can adapt your offering to meet those changing preferences. By identifying potential threats through your competitors, you can proactively address them and stay ahead of the competition.

5. **Learn from their mistakes:** By analysing your competitors' successes and failures, you can learn from their mistakes and avoid making the same ones yourself. For example, if your competitor made a mistake in their marketing strategy that resulted in a loss of customers, you can avoid making the same mistake by implementing a different strategy. Similarly, if your competitor had a successful product launch, you can analyse their strategy to learn what worked well and apply those learnings to your own product launches. By learning from your competitors' successes and failures, you can improve your own strategy and increase your chances of success.

## How to Conduct a Competitive Analysis

1. **Identify Your Competitors:** The first step in conducting a competitive analysis is to identify your competitors. This includes both direct and indirect competitors. Direct competitors are businesses that offer similar products or services to yours, while indirect competitors are businesses that offer different products or services that could potentially satisfy the same customer need. For example, a restaurant may have direct competitors in other restaurants that offer similar cuisine, but also indirect competitors in fast food chains or delivery services.

2. **Analyse Your Competitors' Offerings:** Once you have identified your competitors, the next step is to analyse their offerings. This includes their products or services, pricing, marketing, distribution channels, and customer service. This will give you a sense of how your competitors are positioning themselves in the market and where you may be able to differentiate your offering.

3. **Analyse Their Marketing:** In addition to analysing your competitors' offerings, it is important to analyse your competitors' marketing and branding strategies. How are they positioning themselves in the market? What messaging and visuals are they using to appeal to their target audience? By analysing their marketing efforts, you can gain insights into what messaging and visuals resonate with your target audience and how you can position your own startup to stand out in the market.

4. **Understand Their Customers:** To truly understand your competitors, you need to understand their customers. This includes their target audience, demographics, and psychographics. You can gather this information through online research, surveys, or by talking to their customers directly. This will give you a sense of what drives customer loyalty and what areas your competitors may be neglecting.

5. **Analyse Their Strengths and Weaknesses:** Once you have gathered all of this information, you can analyse your competitors' strengths and weaknesses. This will give you a sense of where you may be able to outcompete them and where you may need to improve your own offering.

6. **Identify Opportunities and Threats:** Based on your analysis, you can identify potential opportunities and threats to your business. This

includes emerging trends, changes in consumer preferences, or shifts in the competitive landscape. By anticipating these changes, you can proactively adapt your strategy and stay ahead of the curve.

7. **Pricing:** Another important aspect of understanding your competitors is analysing their pricing strategies. Are they pricing their products or services higher or lower than you? What factors are they considering when setting their prices? Are they offering any discounts or promotions? By analysing these pricing strategies, you can determine whether you need to adjust your own pricing strategy or if you can offer additional value to justify a higher price point.

8. **Distribution:** Another key aspect of understanding your competitors is analysing their distribution channels. How are they reaching their target audience? Are they using online channels, physical retail stores, or a combination of both? By understanding their distribution channels, you can determine whether there are any gaps in the market that your own startup can fill or if there are opportunities to collaborate with complementary businesses.

9. **Innovation:** Lastly, it is important to stay up to date on your competitors' product and service offerings. Are they introducing any new products or services that could impact your own startup? How are they evolving their offerings to stay relevant in the market? By keeping an eye on their product and service offerings, you can ensure that your own startup is constantly innovating and staying ahead of the competition.

In conclusion, understanding your competitors is essential to building a successful startup. By analysing their strengths and weaknesses, pricing strategies, marketing and branding efforts, distribution channels, and product and service offerings, you can gain insights into what you need to do to differentiate yourself from the competition and position your startup for success in the market. So, take the time to research and analyse your competitors, and use the insights you gain to inform your own business strategy and decision-making.

# Chapter 10: Creating Your Minimum Viable Product

In the world of startups, creating a Minimum Viable Product (MVP) is a crucial step in bringing your idea to life. An MVP is a basic version of your product or service that you can test with early users to gather feedback and determine if there is a market for your idea. By creating an MVP, you can quickly and cost-effectively test your assumptions and refine your product before investing too much time and money into development.

## What is an MVP?

An MVP (Minimum Viable Product) is a version of a product with just enough features to satisfy early customers and provide feedback for future product development. It is a strategy used by startups and companies to quickly launch a product into the market with minimal resources, time, and investment. The purpose of an MVP is to test the viability of a product idea, validate assumptions, and gather customer feedback to refine and improve the product.

An MVP is not a scaled-down version of the final product, but rather a product with only the core features that address the primary problem that the product is designed to solve. The focus is on delivering value to the customer with minimal development efforts and investment. The goal is to launch the product as soon as possible and then iterate and improve the product based on customer feedback.

An MVP is not just about building a product with minimum features but about building a product that solves a real problem for a specific group of customers. The key is to identify the core problem that the product solves, create a solution that is simple and easy to use, and test it in the market to validate the assumptions and gather feedback.

The MVP approach is popular in the startup world as it allows entrepreneurs to validate their idea with minimal resources and investment before building a full-fledged product. This reduces the risk of failure and saves time and resources.

## Why Create an MVP?

Creating an MVP is an essential step for any startup or business to validate its product idea before investing a significant amount of time, money, and resources in its development. An MVP allows entrepreneurs to test their product hypothesis, gather feedback from potential customers, and make informed decisions on future product development.

An MVP is a simple and functional version of a product or service that is developed with minimum resources and features to solve a specific problem faced by the target customers. It is the initial version of a product that is created with the bare minimum features required to test the product's potential in the market. By creating an MVP, businesses can test the waters and get early feedback from their customers, which can help them refine and improve the product over time.

One of the primary reasons to create an MVP is to minimize the risk of failure. By creating an MVP, entrepreneurs can avoid the costly mistake of investing a significant amount of time and resources in developing a product that may not have a market fit. An MVP allows them to test the product hypothesis and gather feedback from their customers before investing a significant amount of time, money, and resources in product development.

Creating an MVP also helps businesses to validate their assumptions about the product and its market fit. An MVP allows entrepreneurs to test their product idea in the real world and gather feedback from potential customers, which can help them validate their assumptions about the product and its market fit. By validating their assumptions, entrepreneurs can make informed decisions about product development and pivot their product strategy if necessary.

## Steps to Create an MVP

1. **Identify the core features:** The first step in creating an MVP is to identify the core features that will solve the customer's problem. This requires a deep understanding of the target market and their needs. Start by brainstorming a list of features, then narrow it down to the essentials that will create value for the customer.

For example, if you are creating a food delivery app, the core features might include the ability to order food, track delivery, and pay for the order. The app might also have additional features such as a rewards program, but these can be added later in the development process.

2. **Develop a prototype:** Once you have identified the core features, it's time to create a prototype. This can be done using wireframes or a simple mockup. The prototype should provide a visual representation of the product, including the user interface and basic functionality.

For example, a food delivery app prototype might include a home screen with options to order food and track delivery. The prototype should be user-friendly and provide a seamless experience for the user.

3. **Test the prototype:** After creating the prototype, it's time to test it with potential customers. This can be done using a small focus group or by sending it out to a larger sample of users. The goal is to gather feedback on the prototype's functionality and identify any areas for improvement.

For example, the food delivery app prototype might be tested by a small group of potential users who order food and provide feedback on the ordering process, delivery time, and overall experience.

4. **Build the MVP:** Once the prototype has been tested and refined, it's time to build the MVP. This involves building a functional product with the core features identified in step one. The MVP should provide value to the customer and be scalable for future development.

For example, the food delivery app MVP might include the ability to order food from multiple restaurants, track delivery in real-time, and pay for the order. The

MVP should be designed with the end user in mind and provide a seamless experience.

5. **Launch and iterate:** After building the MVP, it's time to launch it to the market. This involves marketing the product and collecting feedback from early customers. The goal is to use this feedback to iterate on the product and make improvements based on customer needs.

For example, the food delivery app might launch in a small market and gather feedback from early customers on the ordering process, delivery time, and user experience. This feedback can be used to make improvements to the MVP and prepare for future growth.

6. **Scale and expand:** Once the MVP has been validated and improved based on customer feedback, it's time to scale and expand. This involves adding additional features and expanding the product to new markets.

For example, the food delivery app might add additional features such as a rewards program or expand to new markets to attract new customers and grow the business.

## Tips for Creating an Effective MVP

1. **Identify your target market:** Before creating an MVP, it is essential to identify your target market and understand their needs and pain points. Conduct thorough market research and gather data about your potential customers to build an MVP that resonates with them. Consider factors such as demographics, psychographics, and behaviour patterns. By doing so, you can tailor your MVP to meet the specific needs of your target market and increase your chances of success.

2. **Focus on the core features:** An MVP should only include the core features that are essential to solving the customer's problem. Avoid adding unnecessary features that can increase the development time and cost. Prioritize the features that are critical to delivering value to your customers. By focusing on the core features, you can launch your MVP faster, gather feedback, and iterate based on that feedback.

3. **Keep it simple:** An MVP should be simple and easy to use. The goal is to create something that users can understand and use without needing any training. Avoid adding too much complexity that can confuse your users. Keep the interface clean and intuitive, with a focus on delivering the core value proposition of your product. By keeping your MVP simple, you can reduce development time, lower costs, and increase user adoption.

4. **Test and iterate:** An MVP is not a one-time effort. It is an ongoing process of testing and iterating based on the feedback you receive from your customers. Be open to feedback and willing to make changes to your product based on that feedback. Gather feedback through user testing, surveys, and analytics. Use this feedback to iterate on your MVP and improve its value proposition.

5. **Create a user-friendly interface:** The user interface (UI) of your MVP plays a crucial role in the success of your product. Make sure your MVP has a clean and intuitive UI that makes it easy for users to navigate and use your product. Use design principles that align with your target market's preferences and behaviour patterns. By creating a user-friendly interface, you can increase user adoption, engagement, and retention.

6. **Use existing tools and technologies:** Don't reinvent the wheel. Instead of creating everything from scratch, use existing tools and technologies to speed up the development process. There are many tools available that can help you create an MVP quickly and easily. This can help you save time, reduce costs, and focus on delivering value to your customers.

7. **Measure and track user engagement:** It's important to track user engagement metrics such as user retention, time spent on the app, and user behaviour to understand how users are interacting with your product. Use analytics tools to track these metrics and make data-driven decisions. By measuring and tracking user engagement, you can identify areas of your MVP that need improvement and iterate based on that feedback.

8. **Be agile:** Creating an MVP requires an agile mindset. You need to be flexible and open to change. Be willing to pivot your product strategy

based on the feedback you receive from your customers. Use an agile development methodology that prioritizes frequent feedback loops and rapid iteration. This can help you launch your MVP faster and more efficiently.

9. **Keep your team small:** An MVP should be created with a small team. Avoid adding too many people to the development process as it can slow down the process and increase communication overhead. Keep your team small and focused on delivering the core value proposition of your product. This can help you reduce costs, improve communication, and increase speed.

10. **Be clear about your goals:** Finally, be clear about your goals and what you want to achieve with your MVP. Set realistic expectations and be prepared to adjust them based on the feedback you receive from your customers. Communicate your goals clearly to your team, stakeholders, and customers. By being clear about your goals, you can focus your efforts on what matters most and avoid wasting time and resources on features or activities that do not align with your objectives.

# Chapter 11: Iterating and Refining Your Product or Service

Iterating and refining your product or service is a crucial step in the growth of any business. It involves evaluating and improving your offerings based on customer feedback, market trends, and changing consumer needs. In this chapter, we will discuss the importance of iterating and refining your product or service and how it can lead to success in the Indian market.

Iterating and refining your product or service means making continuous improvements and adjustments to make it better over time.

For example, imagine you are baking cookies for your friends. You bake the cookies and your friends try them and give you feedback that they're a little too sweet. You take their feedback and make adjustments to the recipe, like using less sugar, and bake another batch. Your friends try the new batch and love it! You just iterated and refined your cookie recipe based on feedback to make it better.

In the world of startups, iterating and refining means taking feedback from customers and making changes to the product or service to better meet their needs. This could involve adding new features, improving the user interface, or making the product or service more affordable. By continuously iterating and refining, startups can improve their product or service and stay competitive in the market.

## Why Iteration is Important?

The Indian market is highly competitive, with new products and services being launched every day. To stand out in such a crowded marketplace, you need to continuously improve your offerings to meet the ever-changing needs and expectations of your customers. Iteration allows you to do just that. It enables you to test new ideas, make improvements, and adapt to changes in the market. Here are some key benefits of iteration:

1.  **Improved Customer Satisfaction**

Customer satisfaction is crucial to the success of any business. Iterating your product or service based on customer feedback can help you identify and address issues that may be impacting their satisfaction. This can lead to better customer experiences and increased loyalty.

For example, a popular food delivery service in India received customer feedback that their delivery times were too long. In response, they iterated their delivery process by introducing more delivery partners and optimizing their routes. This led to shorter delivery times and increased customer satisfaction.

## 2. Increased Market Share

Iterating your product or service can also help you gain a competitive advantage in the Indian market. By continuously improving your offerings, you can stay ahead of your competitors and attract new customers. This can lead to increased market share and revenue.

For example, a popular e-commerce platform in India iterated their mobile app to improve the user experience. They added new features such as one-click ordering and personalized recommendations, which led to an increase in app downloads and usage. This helped them gain a larger market share and stay ahead of their competitors.

## 3. Cost Savings

Iterating your product or service can also lead to cost savings in the long run. By identifying and addressing issues early on, you can avoid costly mistakes and reduce the risk of failure. This can save you time and money in the long run.

For example, a fintech startup in India iterated their product based on customer feedback and market trends. They discovered that their pricing model was not competitive compared to their competitors. By iterating their pricing model, they were able to reduce their costs and increase their profit margins.

# How to Iterate and Refine Your Product or Service?

Iterating and refining your product or service requires a systematic approach. Here are some key steps you can take to ensure that you are iterating effectively:

### 1.  Gather Customer Feedback

The first step in iterating your product or service is to gather feedback from your customers. This can be done through surveys, focus groups, or one-on-one interviews. Ask your customers what they like about your product or service, what they don't like, and what improvements they would like to see.

For example, a health and wellness startup in India gathered customer feedback through surveys and discovered that their users were having trouble navigating their app. Based on this feedback, they iterated their app by simplifying the navigation and adding more intuitive features.

### 2.  Analyse Market Trends

In addition to customer feedback, it is important to analyse market trends when iterating your product or service. Keep an eye on your competitors and see what they are doing. Look for new technologies, emerging trends, and changes in consumer behaviour.

For example, a ride-hailing service in India analysed market trends and discovered that there was a growing demand for eco-friendly transportation. In response, they iterated their service by introducing electric vehicles, which helped them attract environmentally conscious customers.

### 3.  Test and Iterate

Once you have gathered customer feedback and analysed market trends, it's time to use this information to improve your product or service. This is where iteration and refinement come into play.

Iteration involves making small changes or adjustments to your product or service based on the feedback you've received. This can include tweaking features, changing the user interface, or adjusting pricing. The goal is to make incremental improvements that enhance the user experience and better align with customer needs and preferences.

Refinement, on the other hand, involves making more significant changes to your product or service based on the insights you've gained. This could involve pivoting to a new market segment, repositioning your brand, or even overhauling your entire product or service offering. The goal is to make substantive changes that address fundamental issues and position your product or service for long-term success.

In India, many startups have successfully leveraged iteration and refinement to improve their offerings and achieve sustainable growth. One such example is Flipkart, India's largest e-commerce marketplace. When the company first launched in 2007, it focused primarily on selling books online. However, the founders quickly realized that to succeed in India's diverse and complex market, they needed to expand their offerings and cater to a wider range of customer needs.

Over the years, Flipkart iterated and refined its platform, adding new categories such as electronics, fashion, and home goods. The company also introduced innovative features such as cash on delivery, which helped address the challenges of India's largely unbanked population. By continually listening to customer feedback and adapting to market trends, Flipkart grew into a multibillion-dollar company and was eventually acquired by Walmart in 2018.

So, how can you iterate and refine your product or service in India's unique business landscape? Here are some key steps to consider:

## 1. Prioritize Feedback

To effectively iterate and refine your product or service, you need to prioritize customer feedback. This means actively seeking out feedback from your target audience, whether through surveys, focus groups, or user testing. You should also monitor social media and online reviews to see what customers are saying about your product or service.

Once you've gathered feedback, analyse it carefully to identify patterns and trends. Look for areas where customers are consistently expressing dissatisfaction or areas where they are asking for new features or capabilities. Use this information to prioritize your iteration and refinement efforts.

## 2. Experiment

Iteration and refinement require experimentation. This means trying out new ideas and features and seeing how they resonate with your target audience. Start small by making small changes and testing them with a select group of customers. This could involve A/B testing different versions of your website, or offering a new feature to a small subset of users.

As you gain insights from these experiments, you can make more informed decisions about which changes to make and how to refine your product or service.

## 3. Be Agile

To effectively iterate and refine your product or service, you need to be agile. This means being able to quickly adapt to changing market conditions and customer needs. This requires a flexible mindset and a willingness to pivot your strategy if needed.

For example, if you find that a particular feature is not resonating with your target audience, you may need to pivot to a new feature or even a new product or service offering altogether. Being agile also means being able to move quickly to address critical issues or capitalize on emerging trends.

## 4. Stay Focused

While iteration and refinement are important, it's also important to stay focused on your overall vision and goals. Don't get distracted by shiny new features or market trends that don't align with your core value proposition.

Instead, use iteration and refinement to enhance your product or service in ways that support your overall vision and goals. This means staying true to your brand, your mission, and your unique value proposition.

## 5. Use Data to Drive Decision Making

Data should be at the heart of your iteration and refinement efforts. Use analytics tools to track key metrics such as user engagement, conversion rates, and customer satisfaction. This data can help you make more informed decisions about which features to add, which to remove, and how to improve the overall user experience.

For example, if you notice that customers are consistently abandoning your checkout process at a certain step, you may need to redesign that step to make it more user-friendly and intuitive. By using data to inform your decision making, you can avoid making assumptions and instead make changes based on concrete evidence.

## 6. Collaborate with Your Team

Iterating and refining your product or service should be a collaborative effort that involves your entire team. This means fostering an environment where everyone feels comfortable sharing their ideas and opinions, and where feedback is welcomed and valued.

Encourage team members from different departments to work together on iteration and refinement projects. For example, your marketing team may have valuable insights into how to improve the user experience on your website, while your product development team may have ideas for new features or functionality.

## 7. Celebrate Successes and Learn from Failures

Finally, it's important to celebrate successes and learn from failures as you iterate and refine your product or service. When you make a successful change, take the time to acknowledge the team members who contributed to that success and recognize the impact it has had on your customers.

At the same time, don't be afraid to acknowledge when things don't go as planned. Use these experiences as opportunities to learn and grow, and to refine your approach moving forward.

Here are some specific strategies you can use to iterate and refine your product or service:

1. **Conduct regular user testing:** In addition to collecting feedback from your customers, conducting regular user testing can help you identify specific pain points and usability issues with your product or service. This can involve observing how customers interact with your product or service and using that feedback to make data-driven decisions about improvements. For example, if you're running a mobile app, you might conduct user testing to see how people are using your app and where they're running into issues.

2. **Implement A/B testing:** A/B testing can help you optimize your product or service by testing two different versions and seeing which one performs better. This can involve testing different features, pricing structures, or marketing campaigns to see which one generates better results. For example, you might test two different versions of your website's landing page to see which one generates more conversions.

3. **Collect and analyse customer feedback:** Gathering feedback from your customers is critical to identifying areas for improvement and refining your product or service. This can involve collecting feedback through surveys, customer reviews, social media, or other channels, and using that feedback to inform your iteration and refinement process. For example, if you're running an e-commerce business, you might collect feedback from customers about their experience with your website, shipping process, or customer service, and use that feedback to improve those areas.

4. **Stay up to date with market trends:** Keeping up with market trends can help you identify new opportunities and stay ahead of the competition. This can involve using tools like Google Trends or social media monitoring to track trends in your industry, and using that information to inform your iteration and refinement process. For example, if you're running a fashion e-commerce business, you might use social media monitoring to track the latest fashion trends and use that information to inform your product design and marketing strategy.

5. **Build a culture of experimentation:** Fostering a culture of experimentation can help you encourage innovation and drive continuous improvement. This can involve creating a safe space for

failure and learning, and encouraging your team to experiment with new ideas and approaches. For example, you might host regular hackathons or innovation sprints to encourage your team to generate new ideas and experiment with new approaches to product development or marketing. By integrating these specific strategies with the key steps outlined earlier, you can create a robust iteration and refinement process that helps you deliver more value to your customers and stay ahead of the competition.

## Conclusion

In conclusion, iterating and refining your product or service is a crucial step in the success of any business, especially for startups. By actively seeking out customer feedback, experimenting with new ideas, being agile, and staying focused on your goals, you can continuously improve your product or service and stay ahead of the competition.

For entrepreneurs just starting out, iteration and refinement can help you identify what works and what doesn't, and make the necessary changes to improve your product or service. For established businesses, iteration and refinement can help you stay relevant in a constantly evolving market and ensure that your product or service continues to meet the needs of your customers.

Regardless of your stage in the business journey, the key to effective iteration and refinement is to stay connected to your customers and remain open to feedback and new ideas. By embracing a culture of experimentation and continuous improvement, you can drive innovation and ultimately achieve long-term success.

# Chapter 12: Developing Your Brand

## What is a Brand?

A brand is more than just a name or a logo. It's the image that comes to mind when we think about a particular product or company. It's what makes one product different from another and helps us to choose what to buy. It's the identity of a company that sets it apart from the others.

For example, when you think of a burger, what comes to your mind? McDonald's? KFC? Burger King? These are all brands, and each of them has a unique identity that makes them different from one another. They have their own logo, colours, slogans, and marketing strategies that make them easily recognizable to people.

A brand represents a company's values, personality, and promise to its customers. It's like a personality for the business. Just like how you have a personality that makes you unique and different from your friends, a brand has its own personality too. For example, some brands may be seen as adventurous, while others may be seen as luxurious or eco-friendly.

A brand also represents a company's reputation. If a company consistently provides high-quality products or services, then it builds a positive reputation and becomes known for its reliability. This reputation is a part of the brand that sets it apart from other businesses.

A brand is not just for big companies; even small businesses can have their own brands. In fact, building a strong brand can help small businesses compete with larger ones. A strong brand can create trust, loyalty, and credibility, which are important for businesses to succeed.

In India, we see many examples of strong brands. For example, when we think of toothpaste, we may think of Colgate, which is a well-known brand in India. Similarly, when we think of cars, we may think of Maruti Suzuki or Tata Motors.

These are all examples of brands that have a strong identity and reputation in India.

# Why is Branding Important?

## 1. Differentiation

In today's highly competitive market, it's essential to stand out from the crowd. A strong brand can help businesses differentiate themselves from their competitors. A well-defined brand with a unique personality, values, and message can help businesses create a distinct identity in the market. A good example of differentiation through branding is the Indian brand Amul. Amul has established a unique identity by creating memorable ads with catchy slogans like "Utterly Butterly Delicious" and "The Taste of India."

## 2. Recognition

Recognition is one of the critical benefits of branding. When a brand is established, it becomes easier for customers to identify and remember it. A strong brand makes it easier for customers to distinguish a particular product or service from its competitors. An excellent example of recognition through branding is Coca-Cola. The Coca-Cola brand has been around for over a century, and the company has created an iconic logo and advertising campaigns that make it easy for customers to recognize the brand.

## 3. Trust

Trust is essential in building a long-term relationship with customers. A strong brand builds trust with customers, making it more likely that they will choose a particular business over its competitors. Customers are more likely to trust a brand that has a strong reputation and consistently delivers high-quality products or services. An example of trust through branding is the Indian airline IndiGo. IndiGo has established itself as a reliable and trustworthy airline by consistently delivering excellent customer service, on-time flights, and affordable fares.

### 4. Loyalty

Loyalty is another benefit of branding. A strong brand creates customer loyalty, leading to repeat business and positive word-of-mouth marketing. Customers who are loyal to a brand are more likely to continue to use its products or services and recommend them to others. An excellent example of loyalty through branding is the Indian brand Tata. Tata has created a strong brand by delivering high-quality products and services, and as a result, has built a loyal customer base.

### 5. Premium Pricing

Branding can also help businesses charge premium prices for their products or services. A strong brand with a reputation for quality and reliability can command a higher price point than its competitors. An example of premium pricing through branding is Apple. Apple has established itself as a premium brand by delivering high-quality products with sleek designs and innovative features. As a result, Apple can charge premium prices for its products.

### 6. Helps to create a strong company culture:

A strong brand creates a sense of purpose and direction for employees, helping to foster a positive company culture. When employees understand the brand values and mission, they are more likely to feel engaged and motivated in their work. Example: Tata Group is a brand that is known for its strong company culture. Its brand values of integrity, excellence, and responsibility are reflected in the company's operations and policies. This has helped the company to build a strong reputation and loyal customer base.

### 7. Helps to attract top talent:

A strong brand can help to attract top talent to a company. Employees want to work for companies that have a positive reputation and are aligned with their values. Example: Google is a brand that is known for its strong employer brand. The company's brand values of innovation, collaboration, and diversity have helped it to attract top talent from around the world.

### 8. Facilitates brand extensions:

A strong brand can facilitate the extension of the brand into new product categories or markets. When a brand has a positive reputation and emotional connection with customers, it is easier to introduce new products or expand into new markets. Example: Nestle is a brand that has successfully extended its brand into new product categories and markets. The company's strong brand reputation and loyal customer base have helped it to introduce new products and expand into new markets with ease.

## 9.  Builds Emotional Connections:

A strong brand can build emotional connections with customers, leading to stronger brand loyalty and advocacy. When customers feel connected to your brand, they are more likely to become repeat customers and recommend your products or services to others. Example: The Indian brand Fevicol has built a strong emotional connection with customers through their humorous and relatable advertising campaigns. As a result, Fevicol has become a household name for adhesives, and customers feel a sense of loyalty towards the brand.

## 10.Supports Business Growth:

A strong brand can support business growth by providing a solid foundation for future marketing and expansion efforts. When customers recognize and trust your brand, it becomes easier to introduce new products or expand into new markets. Example: The Indian brand Godrej has built a strong brand identity based on their commitment to sustainability and innovation. This has allowed them to expand their product offerings into a variety of industries, including home appliances, furniture, and personal care products.

## 11.Increases Perceived Value:

A strong brand can increase the perceived value of your products or services, allowing you to charge higher prices and increase profit margins. When customers associate your brand with quality and value, they are willing to pay more for your products or services. Example: The Indian brand Royal Enfield has built a strong brand identity around their classic motorcycles and adventurous lifestyle. As a result, customers are willing to pay a premium for Royal Enfield motorcycles, increasing their perceived value in the market.

## 12. Builds credibility:

A strong brand can establish credibility and authority in the market. It can make your business appear more professional and trustworthy, which can be especially important for new or unknown businesses. Example: An Indian customer might prefer to buy a smartphone from a well-known brand like Samsung or Apple because they have established a reputation for quality and reliability, even if the price is higher than a lesser-known brand.

## 13. Supports marketing efforts:

Finally, a strong brand can support your marketing efforts and make them more effective. When customers already recognize and trust your brand, it can be easier to attract their attention and persuade them to make a purchase. Example: A well-known Indian brand like Maggi has been able to use its strong brand identity and reputation for quick and easy meals to support its marketing efforts and attract new customers through advertisements and social media campaigns.

## 14. Creates a Sense of Community:

Branding can create a sense of community among customers, employees, and stakeholders. When people identify with a brand, they feel like they belong to a larger group that shares their values and interests. For example, the brand Royal Enfield has a passionate community of customers who share a love for classic motorcycles. By fostering this sense of community, Royal Enfield has created a loyal customer base that continues to support the brand through repeat purchases and positive word-of-mouth marketing.

## 15. Builds Trust with Stakeholders:

Branding can build trust with stakeholders, including customers, employees, investors, and partners. A strong brand communicates the values and mission of the business, and demonstrates a commitment to delivering quality products or services. For example, Tata Group, one of India's largest conglomerates, has built a strong brand based on its commitment to social responsibility and ethical business practices. This has helped build trust with customers, employees, and investors, who believe in the company's values and mission. As a result, Tata Group has been able to attract and retain top talent, form successful partnerships, and expand its business operations both domestically and internationally.

## Key Elements of Developing a Brand

Developing a brand involves a variety of elements that work together to create a unique identity that customers can recognize and connect with. In this section, we will discuss the key elements of developing a brand that resonates with your target audience.

1. **Define Your Brand Identity** The first step in developing a brand is to define your brand identity. Your brand identity includes the visual elements of your brand, such as your logo, colour palette, typography, and imagery. It also includes the tone of voice and personality of your brand, which sets it apart from competitors.

Your brand identity should be consistent across all marketing channels, from your website to social media pages to physical stores. A consistent brand identity creates a recognizable and trustworthy brand.

2. **Understand Your Target Audience** To develop a brand that resonates with your audience, you must understand your target audience. Identify your target demographic, including age, gender, location, interests, and values. Research their pain points, needs, and wants. Develop a brand that meets their expectations and solves their problems.

For example, if your target audience is working professionals, they may value reliability and efficiency. Your brand identity should reflect these values, such as through a streamlined website and fast customer service.

3. **Develop Your Brand Messaging** Your brand messaging is the language and tone you use to communicate with your audience. It should convey your brand's unique value proposition and resonate with

your target audience. Develop messaging that speaks to their needs, interests, and values.

For example, if your brand offers eco-friendly products, your messaging should focus on the environmental benefits and how your products help consumers reduce their carbon footprint.

4.  **Establish Your Brand Voice** Your brand voice is the personality of your brand, and it should be consistent across all marketing channels. Establish a brand voice that resonates with your target audience and sets your brand apart from competitors.

For example, if your brand is aimed at young adults, your brand voice might be informal, friendly, and humorous. If your brand is more professional, your brand voice may be formal, authoritative, and informative.

5.  **Design Your Logo and Visual Identity** Your logo and visual identity are critical elements of your brand. Your logo should be simple, memorable, and representative of your brand values. Your visual identity, including your colour palette and typography, should be consistent across all marketing channels.

For example, the Indian clothing brand Fabindia uses earthy colours and traditional motifs in their logo and visual identity to reflect their focus on traditional Indian handicrafts.

6.  **Develop Your Brand Guidelines** Brand guidelines are rules and guidelines for using your brand identity. They ensure consistency across all marketing channels and customer touchpoints, and help protect your brand from being used improperly. Your brand guidelines should include information on logo usage, colour palette, typography, tone of voice, and other key elements of your brand identity.

For example, the Indian beverage brand Paper Boat has a strong visual identity, using bold colours and playful illustrations. Their brand guidelines ensure that their marketing materials are consistent in their use of colour, typography, and imagery.

7. **Build Your Online Presence** In today's digital age, building an online presence is critical for developing your brand. Your online presence includes your website, social media profiles, online content, and search engine optimization. Your online presence should be consistent with your brand identity and tailored to your target audience.

For example, the Indian e-commerce brand Myntra has a strong online presence, using social media to connect with their audience and create a personalized shopping experience. Their website is visually appealing and easy to navigate, with a consistent brand identity across all pages.

8. **Create Quality Content** Quality content is a crucial element of developing a strong brand. Your content should reflect your brand values and be tailored to your target audience. It can include blog posts, videos, social media posts, and other types of content.

For example, the Indian skincare brand Plum Goodness creates blog posts and social media content that educates their audience about skincare, using ingredients that are safe and environmentally friendly. Their content helps establish them as an authority in the skincare space and reinforces their brand values.

9. **Focus on Customer Experience** Customer experience plays a significant role in developing a strong brand. Providing excellent customer service and creating a positive experience for your customers can help build brand loyalty and word-of-mouth marketing.

For example, the Indian hospitality brand OYO Rooms focuses on providing a seamless and personalized experience for their guests. They use customer feedback to improve their services and ensure that their customers have a memorable stay, which helps establish them as a trusted brand in the hospitality industry.

10. **Consistently Evaluate and Adapt Your Brand** It's essential to regularly evaluate and adapt your brand to meet the changing needs and expectations of your target audience. Regularly monitor your

brand's performance and make changes as needed to ensure that it continues to resonate with your audience.

For example, the Indian retail brand Titan has evolved its brand identity over the years to remain relevant and appeal to younger audiences. They have adapted their messaging and visual identity to reflect changing consumer trends while still staying true to their core values.

11. **Define Your Unique Selling Proposition** Your unique selling proposition (USP) is what sets your brand apart from competitors. It is the specific benefit that your brand offers that cannot be found anywhere else. Identify your USP and use it as a key element of your brand messaging.

For example, the Indian dairy brand Amul has a strong USP of offering high-quality, affordable dairy products. Their messaging focuses on the benefits of consuming dairy and the superior taste and quality of their products.

12. **Create a Memorable Tagline** A tagline is a brief statement that encapsulates your brand's message and value proposition. It should be memorable, catchy, and communicate the essence of your brand in a few words.

For example, the Indian telecommunications company Airtel uses the tagline "Jo Tera Hai Woh Mera Hai" which translates to "What's yours is mine". This tagline communicates their focus on customer satisfaction and personalized service.

13. **Build a Brand Story** A brand story is a narrative that communicates the history, values, and mission of your brand. It creates an emotional connection with your audience and helps them understand why your brand exists and what it stands for.

For example, the Indian snack brand Haldiram's has a brand story that emphasizes the importance of traditional Indian recipes and ingredients. This narrative has helped them connect with their audience and build a loyal following.

14. **Foster Brand Advocacy** Brand advocacy is the process of turning satisfied customers into brand ambassadors who promote your brand to others. Foster brand advocacy by providing excellent customer service, creating a positive brand experience, and encouraging customers to share their experiences with others.

For example, the Indian hotel chain Taj Hotels offers a loyalty program that rewards customers for their loyalty and encourages them to share their experiences with others. This has helped them build a strong network of brand advocates who promote their brand to others.

15. **Monitor Your Brand Reputation** Your brand reputation is the perception that customers have of your brand. It is essential to monitor your brand reputation to identify potential issues and respond to customer feedback. Use social media monitoring tools and customer feedback surveys to stay informed about your brand's reputation.

For example, the Indian ride-hailing company Ola uses social media monitoring tools to track customer feedback and respond to customer complaints in real-time. This has helped them maintain a positive brand reputation and build trust with their customers.

## Conclusion

In conclusion, branding is a crucial aspect of building a successful business. A brand represents the identity of your business, its values, and its offerings, and it allows you to connect with your target audience. By defining your brand identity, understanding your target audience, developing your brand messaging, establishing your brand voice, designing your logo and visual identity, developing your brand guidelines, building your online presence, and creating quality content, you can create a brand that resonates with your audience and sets your business apart from competitors.

In India, where there is a diverse and growing market, branding is particularly important. With a strong brand, businesses can establish trust and loyalty with their customers, differentiate themselves from competitors, and succeed in the marketplace. From traditional Indian handicrafts to modern e-commerce brands, businesses in India have the opportunity to create unique and memorable brands that connect with a wide range of consumers.

# Chapter 13: Building Your Online Presence

In today's digital age, building an online presence is essential for businesses and individuals alike. Your online presence includes your website, social media profiles, online content, and search engine optimization. In this chapter, we will discuss the key elements of building an online presence that resonates with your audience.

**Know Your Audience:** Knowing your audience is a crucial element of building an online presence. It involves understanding the people you want to reach with your content and tailoring your messaging to their needs and interests. By knowing your audience, you can create content that resonates with them, build trust and loyalty, and ultimately grow your brand.

The first step in knowing your audience is to identify your target demographic. This includes factors such as age, gender, location, income, education, and occupation. Understanding these demographic characteristics can help you create content that appeals to their interests and needs.

For example, if your target audience is young adults interested in fitness, you may want to create content around topics such as healthy eating habits, workout routines, and stress management techniques. Understanding your audience's age group can also help you determine which social media platforms they are likely to use, as different age groups tend to have different preferences when it comes to social media.

Once you have identified your target demographic, you need to research their pain points, needs, and wants. This involves understanding their challenges, problems, and desires, and creating content that helps them address these issues. You can conduct research through surveys, focus groups, or social media listening tools to gain insights into your audience's needs and preferences.

For example, if your target audience is working parents, you may want to create content around topics such as time management, meal planning, and affordable family activities. By understanding their pain points, you can create content that provides solutions and adds value to their lives.

Another important aspect of knowing your audience is understanding their values and beliefs. This includes understanding their attitudes towards social issues, political views, and cultural values. By understanding their values and beliefs, you can create content that aligns with their worldview and strengthens your relationship with them.

For example, if your target audience is environmentally conscious, you may want to create content around topics such as sustainable living, eco-friendly products, and reducing waste. Understanding their values and beliefs can also help you determine which causes and charities to support, as aligning with causes that are important to your audience can help build trust and loyalty.

**Develop Your Brand Identity:** Developing a strong brand identity is essential for building an online presence that resonates with your target audience. Your brand identity includes a range of visual and non-visual elements that come together to create a cohesive and recognizable image of your brand. A strong brand identity helps to differentiate your brand from competitors and creates a lasting impression in the minds of your target audience.

The visual elements of your brand identity include your logo, colour palette, typography, and imagery. Your logo is the centerpiece of your brand identity and should be simple, memorable, and representative of your brand's values and personality. It should be easily recognizable and scalable to different sizes and formats.

Your colour palette should be consistent across all your marketing materials, including your website, social media profiles, and advertising campaigns. The colours you choose should reflect your brand's values and personality and resonate with your target audience. For example, a financial services brand might use blue and green to convey stability and growth, while a fashion brand might use bright, bold colours to reflect their creativity and energy.

Typography is another important visual element of your brand identity. Your choice of fonts should be consistent across all your marketing materials and reflect your brand's personality and values. For example, a luxury brand might use a classic serif font to convey sophistication and elegance, while a tech startup might use a modern sans-serif font to reflect their innovation and forward-thinking approach.

Imagery is also an important component of your brand identity. Your choice of images should reflect your brand's personality and values and resonate with your target audience. For example, a fitness brand might use images of athletes and active lifestyles to convey their focus on health and wellness, while a food brand might use images of delicious, visually appealing dishes to entice their audience.

Non-visual elements of your brand identity include your tone of voice and personality. Your tone of voice should be consistent across all your marketing materials and reflect your brand's personality and values. For example, a brand focused on sustainability might use a serious, educational tone to convey the importance of environmental responsibility, while a brand focused on fun and entertainment might use a playful, humorous tone to engage their audience.

Your brand personality should also be consistent across all your marketing materials and reflect your brand's values and purpose. For example, a brand focused on health and wellness might adopt a nurturing, caring personality to convey their focus on wellbeing and self-care, while a brand focused on adventure and travel might adopt a bold, adventurous personality to reflect their spirit of exploration and discovery.

Developing a strong brand identity takes time and effort, but it is essential for building an online presence that resonates with your target audience. By creating a cohesive and recognizable image of your brand, you can differentiate yourself from competitors, create a lasting impression in the minds of your audience, and build a loyal customer base.

**Develop your Website:** In today's digital age, having a website is essential for building an online presence. A website serves as the digital storefront for your brand and is often the first point of contact for potential customers. It is crucial to develop a website that is visually appealing, easy to navigate, and optimized for search engines.

The first step in developing a website is to determine its purpose. What do you want your website to achieve? Is it a platform for selling products or services, providing information, or building brand awareness? Your website's purpose will inform its design and content.

Next, it's essential to choose a domain name that reflects your brand identity and is easy to remember. Your domain name should be relevant to your brand, easy to spell, and avoid using hyphens or numbers.

Once you have your domain name, it's time to select a hosting provider. A hosting provider is a company that stores your website's files and makes them accessible on the internet. It's important to choose a hosting provider that provides reliable service and offers features that meet your website's needs.

When designing your website, it's crucial to consider the user experience (UX). The UX refers to how users interact with your website, including how easy it is to navigate, load time, and overall usability. A website with a poor UX can lead to high bounce rates and low engagement.

One key element of UX is responsive design. Responsive design ensures that your website is optimized for different screen sizes, from desktops to mobile devices. With more people accessing the internet on their mobile devices, having a mobile-friendly website is critical for reaching a wider audience.

In terms of design, it's important to consider your brand identity and create a website that reflects it. This includes using your brand colours, typography, and imagery to create a cohesive look and feel. Your website's design should be visually appealing while also being easy to read and navigate.

When creating content for your website, it's important to keep your target audience in mind. Your content should be relevant, informative, and engaging, providing value to your audience. It's also essential to optimize your content for search engines by using relevant keywords and meta descriptions.

In addition to creating quality content, it's important to include calls to action (CTAs) on your website. CTAs encourage visitors to take a specific action, such as making a purchase, subscribing to a newsletter, or contacting you for more information. A well-placed CTA can lead to increased engagement and conversions.

Finally, it's essential to test your website before launching it. This includes checking for broken links, ensuring that all forms and CTAs are working correctly, and testing its responsiveness on different devices. By testing your website, you can identify and fix any issues before it goes live.

**Utilize Social Media:** Social media platforms such as Facebook, Twitter, Instagram, LinkedIn, and many others have revolutionized the way we communicate and interact with each other. They have also provided businesses and individuals with a powerful tool for building an online presence. Social media platforms allow you to connect with your audience, share content, and promote your brand. In this section, we will discuss how to utilize social media to build a strong online presence.

The first step to utilizing social media is to identify which platforms your target audience uses the most. This will help you to focus your efforts on the most effective platforms. For example, if your target audience is primarily young adults, you may want to focus on platforms like Instagram and Snapchat. On the other hand, if your target audience is primarily professionals, LinkedIn may be the most effective platform.

Once you have identified the most effective social media platforms for your target audience, it is important to create a strong social media strategy. Your strategy should include the type of content you will share, the frequency of your posts, and the tone of your messaging. It is also important to engage with your audience by responding to comments and messages, asking for feedback, and providing customer support.

One of the most effective ways to utilize social media is to share quality content that resonates with your audience. This can include blog posts, articles, images, videos, and other forms of media. Your content should be informative, engaging, and relevant to your audience. It should also reflect your brand identity and be consistent with your messaging.

A great example of a brand that utilizes social media effectively is Amul, an Indian dairy cooperative. Amul has a strong social media presence with engaging and humorous content that resonates with their audience. Their "utterly butterly delicious" advertising campaign is a classic example of how to create memorable content that connects with your audience.

In addition to sharing quality content, it is also important to engage with your audience on social media. This can include responding to comments and messages, asking for feedback, and providing customer support. By engaging with your audience, you can build strong relationships with your customers and improve your brand's reputation.

Another effective way to utilize social media is to collaborate with other brands and influencers in your industry. This can help you to reach a wider audience and build credibility. For example, Indian beauty brand, Lakme, collaborated with fashion bloggers and influencers to promote their products and increase their reach on social media.

It is also important to track and analyse your social media metrics to determine the effectiveness of your social media strategy. Metrics such as engagement rates, reach, and follower growth can provide valuable insights into what is working and what is not. This information can help you to adjust your strategy and improve your social media presence over time.

**Create Quality Content:** Creating quality content is an essential element of building an online presence. It is one of the most effective ways to engage your audience and establish your brand as a thought leader in your industry. High-quality content can help drive traffic to your website, increase your social media following, and improve your search engine rankings.

There are different types of content that businesses can make, such as blog posts, videos, infographics, podcasts, whitepapers, and e-books. A blog is a type of website where you can write about things that you are interested in or that you know a lot about. Videos can show people how to do things or give them a tour of your business. Infographics are pictures that make it easier to understand facts and numbers. Podcasts are like talk shows that people can listen to while they are doing other things. Whitepapers and e-books are like really long articles that teach people about a specific topic in-depth. The key is to create content that resonates with your audience and provides them with value. Your content should be informative, engaging, and relevant to your target audience.

One of the most popular forms of content is blog posts. Blogging is an excellent way to establish your brand as a thought leader and to provide your audience with valuable information. Your blog should focus on topics that are relevant to your industry and your audience. Use your blog to share your thoughts, insights, and opinions on industry trends, news, and best practices. Make sure your blog posts are well-written, informative, and engaging. Include high-quality images, infographics, or videos to make your content more visually appealing.

Another effective way to create quality content is through videos. Video content is one of the most engaging forms of content and is a great way to connect with your audience. You can create videos on a wide range of topics, such as product demonstrations, customer testimonials, how-to guides, or behind-the-scenes glimpses of your business. Use video content to showcase your products or services in action and to provide your audience with valuable insights.

Infographics are another great way to create quality content. Infographics are visually appealing and can help simplify complex information. Use infographics to share statistics, facts, or data relevant to your industry. Make sure your infographics are easy to read and visually appealing. Use a clear and concise design that makes it easy for your audience to understand the information you are presenting.

Podcasts are becoming increasingly popular as a way to create quality content. Podcasts are a great way to provide your audience with valuable information and to establish your brand as a thought leader in your industry. Use podcasts to share insights, discuss industry trends, or interview experts in your field. Make sure your podcasts are well-produced and engaging.

Finally, whitepapers and e-books are excellent ways to create quality content. These longer-form pieces of content allow you to dive deep into a particular topic and provide your audience with in-depth insights and information. Use whitepapers and e-books to provide your audience with valuable information that they can't find anywhere else. Make sure your whitepapers and e-books are well-designed, easy to read, and provide your audience with value.

**Use Search Engine Optimization (SEO):** Search Engine Optimization, or SEO, is a crucial component of building an online presence. It refers to the practice of improving the visibility of your website in search engine results pages (SERPs) by optimizing your content and website structure.

In simpler terms, think of SEO as a way to help people find your website more easily when they search for something related to your business or industry. When someone types a query into a search engine like Google, the search engine uses an algorithm to determine which websites to display in the results. SEO is all about understanding how this algorithm works and optimizing your website accordingly to improve your chances of appearing higher in the search results.

One important aspect of SEO is keyword research. Keywords are the phrases or words that people type into a search engine when they are looking for something. By identifying the keywords that your target audience is searching for, you can optimize your website content to include those keywords, making it more likely that your website will show up in the search results for those queries. For example, if you run a bakery, you might want to optimize your website for keywords like "best cupcakes" or "wedding cakes" to attract customers who are looking for those types of products.

Another aspect of SEO is website structure. Search engines prefer websites that are well-organized and easy to navigate. This means that you should make sure your website is mobile-friendly, has fast loading times, and is easy to navigate. You should also make sure that your website has a clear hierarchy and that your content is structured in a logical way.

Content is also an important factor in SEO. Search engines prefer websites that have high-quality, relevant content. This means that you should create content that is useful, informative, and engaging for your target audience. You should also make sure that your content is optimized for keywords and includes relevant meta descriptions and tags.

In addition to on-page optimization, off-page optimization is also important for SEO. This refers to the practices you can use to promote your website and build links to it from other websites. This can include tactics like guest blogging, social media marketing, and influencer outreach. By building links to your website from other high-quality, authoritative websites, you can improve your website's credibility and visibility in the search results.

One key thing to keep in mind with SEO is that it is an ongoing process. The search engines are constantly updating their algorithms, so you need to stay up-to-date with the latest best practices and adjust your strategy accordingly. This means that you need to be willing to invest time and resources into your SEO efforts to see results.

For example, let's say you run a pet store that sells high-quality dog food. You might start by doing some keyword research to identify the most popular search terms related to dog food. You could then optimize your website content to include those keywords, such as by creating blog posts about the benefits of high-quality dog food or including those keywords in your product descriptions. You could also work on building links to your website from other pet-related websites, such as through guest blogging or influencer outreach.

**Build Relationships with Customers:** Building relationships with customers is a vital aspect of building an online presence. It is essential to establish a connection with your customers so that they feel valued and connected to your brand. By building strong relationships with your customers, you can create a loyal customer base that will return to your business time and time again.

To build relationships with customers, it is important to understand who your customers are and what they want. You need to be able to put yourself in their shoes and understand their needs and wants. This will allow you to create content and marketing strategies that resonate with them and help build trust and credibility with your brand.

One of the best ways to build relationships with customers is to engage with them on social media. Social media platforms such as Facebook, Twitter, and Instagram provide an opportunity to connect with your customers and create a dialogue. Respond to comments and messages, ask for feedback, and share content that is relevant and interesting to your audience. By engaging with your customers, you can create a sense of community and establish a personal connection with them.

Another way to build relationships with customers is to provide exceptional customer service. Customers want to feel valued and heard, and providing them with excellent customer service can help achieve this. Respond promptly to customer inquiries and complaints, be helpful and empathetic, and go above and beyond to exceed their expectations. By providing exceptional customer service, you can build trust and create a positive reputation for your brand.

Email marketing is another effective way to build relationships with customers. By sending regular newsletters and promotional emails, you can keep your customers informed about your business and offer exclusive promotions and discounts. Personalize your emails and make them engaging and relevant to your audience.

Another effective way to build relationships with customers is through customer loyalty programs. Customer loyalty programs incentivize customers to continue doing business with you by offering rewards or other benefits. These programs can help you build long-term relationships with customers and increase customer retention.

It is also important to collect customer feedback and use it to improve your business. Ask for feedback after a purchase or experience, and use the feedback to improve your products or services. This will show your customers that you value their opinions and are committed to providing the best experience possible.

Finally, building relationships with customers involves being authentic and transparent. Customers appreciate honesty and transparency, so make sure you are open and upfront about your business practices, policies, and values. This will help you build trust with your customers and establish a reputation as a trustworthy business.

**Utilize Online Advertising:** Online advertising is a powerful tool for building an online presence and reaching potential customers. It involves placing ads on various online platforms such as search engines, social media, and websites to promote your products or services. The goal of online advertising is to attract new customers, increase brand awareness, and ultimately drive sales.

Imagine that you have a lemonade stand that you want to promote. You could create a poster and hang it up around the neighbourhood, but what if you want to reach more people? You could create an ad on a popular website or social media platform to attract more customers. This is similar to what businesses do when they utilize online advertising.

There are several types of online advertising that businesses can use, such as search engine advertising, social media advertising, display advertising, and email advertising. The key is to choose the right type of advertising for your business and target audience.

Search engine advertising involves placing ads on search engines like Google or Bing. These ads appear at the top of the search results when someone searches for a specific keyword. For example, if someone searches for "lemonade stands in my area," an ad for your lemonade stand could appear at the top of the search results. This is a great way to attract customers who are actively searching for your product or service.

Social media advertising involves placing ads on social media platforms like Facebook, Instagram, or Twitter. These ads can appear in the user's feed or as a sponsored post. Social media advertising allows businesses to target their ads to specific demographics based on factors like age, gender, location, and interests. For example, if you have a lemonade stand, you could target your ads to parents with young children who live in your area.

Display advertising involves placing ads on websites or apps. These ads can be in the form of banner ads, pop-ups, or video ads. Display advertising can be targeted to specific demographics or based on the user's browsing behaviour. For example, if someone has been searching for lemonade stands online, they might see an ad for your lemonade stand while browsing a website.

Email advertising involves sending promotional emails to a list of subscribers. This type of advertising is effective because it reaches people who have already expressed interest in your business by subscribing to your email list. You can use email advertising to promote special offers, new products or services, or to drive traffic to your website or social media pages.

In addition to choosing the right type of advertising, it's important to create effective ads. Your ads should be eye-catching, informative, and relevant to your target audience. Use high-quality images and engaging copy to grab the user's attention. Be sure to include a clear call to action, such as "Visit our website to learn more" or "Click here to get started."

Online advertising can be highly targeted, which means you can reach specific groups of people based on their interests, demographics, and behaviours. For example, if you sell toys for kids, you can target parents with young children who live in a certain area or have shown an interest in educational toys. This helps you to reach the right people and maximize your return on investment.

Online advertising can also be cost-effective. You can set a budget and bid for ad placements, which means you only pay when someone clicks on your ad or takes a specific action, such as making a purchase. This allows you to control your spending and optimize your campaigns for better results.

It's important to understand that online advertising requires continuous testing and optimization. It's not a set-it-and-forget-it solution, and requires constant monitoring and adjustment to achieve optimal results. You need to test different ad formats, messaging, targeting, and landing pages to see what works best for your business. It's also important to track your metrics such as click-through rates, conversion rates, and return on investment to measure your success and make data-driven decisions.

For example, if you are running a social media ad campaign, you can test different ad formats such as images, videos, or carousel ads. You can also test different messaging or calls-to-action to see what resonates best with your audience. Additionally, you can use A/B testing to compare two versions of an ad or landing page to see which one performs better.

**Track and Analyse Your Metrics:** Tracking and analysing your metrics is a crucial aspect of building and maintaining a successful online presence. It allows you to evaluate the performance of your website, social media accounts, and online marketing efforts, and make data-driven decisions to improve your online strategy.

Metrics are simply measurements of your online activity, such as the number of website visitors, the bounce rate, time spent on site, conversion rates, and more. These metrics provide valuable insights into the behaviour of your online audience and the effectiveness of your online presence. By analysing these metrics, you can identify areas for improvement, optimize your online strategy, and achieve your business goals.

One of the most important metrics to track is website traffic. Website traffic refers to the number of people who visit your website. You can track this metric using tools like Google Analytics. By analysing your website traffic, you can identify which pages are most popular, how long people are spending on your site, and where your traffic is coming from. This information can help you improve your website's user experience and better understand your audience.

Another important metric to track is engagement on your social media accounts. This includes likes, comments, shares, and followers. Social media engagement is a measure of how interested and invested your audience is in your brand. By tracking your social media metrics, you can identify which content resonates most with your audience and adjust your social media strategy accordingly.

Conversion rates are also critical to track. Conversion rates measure the percentage of visitors to your site who take a specific action, such as filling out a form or making a purchase. By analysing your conversion rates, you can identify which pages and content are driving the most conversions, and optimize your site to increase your conversion rates.

It's also important to track metrics related to your online advertising efforts. This includes metrics such as click-through rates, cost per click, and cost per acquisition. By tracking these metrics, you can optimize your online advertising campaigns to ensure you're getting the best return on investment.

To make the most of your metrics, it's important to regularly analyse and interpret them. Look for patterns, trends, and areas for improvement. For example, if you notice a high bounce rate on a particular page of your website, it may be an indication that the content isn't engaging enough or that the page isn't user-friendly. By identifying these issues and making changes, you can improve your website's performance and achieve better results.

**Stay up to date with Trends and Technology:** In today's fast-paced digital world, it is essential to stay up-to-date with the latest trends and technology in order to build and maintain an effective online presence. This is especially important for businesses operating in India, where the online market is rapidly expanding and becoming increasingly competitive.

Staying current with trends and technology allows you to stay ahead of the curve and maintain a competitive edge in your industry. This means keeping an eye on emerging technologies, social media platforms, and changes in consumer behaviour. By staying up-to-date, you can anticipate changes in the market and adapt your online strategy accordingly.

One of the most important things businesses can do to stay up-to-date with trends and technology is to regularly read and follow relevant blogs and publications. This will help businesses stay informed about the latest developments in their industry and the wider world of technology. For instance, following blogs and publications like YourStory, Inc42, Economic Times, etc., can help businesses stay informed about the latest news, trends, and updates in the Indian startup ecosystem.

Another way to stay updated with trends and technology is by attending industry events and conferences. These events offer businesses the opportunity to network with peers, learn from industry experts, and gain insights into the latest trends and technologies.

One trend that has become increasingly important in recent years is mobile optimization. With the widespread use of smartphones and tablets, it is essential to ensure that your website and online presence are mobile-friendly. This means optimizing your website for smaller screens, ensuring fast load times, and providing a seamless user experience across all devices.

Another trend to watch is the rise of video content. Video is quickly becoming one of the most popular forms of online content, with platforms like YouTube gaining millions of users every day. This presents a great opportunity for businesses to create engaging and shareable video content that can help build their brand and reach new audiences.

Artificial Intelligence (AI) and Machine Learning (ML) are also rapidly changing the online landscape, with businesses using these technologies to automate tasks, personalize experiences, and improve customer service. By staying current with these emerging technologies, businesses can streamline their operations and offer more personalized experiences to their customers.

Social media platforms are constantly evolving, with new features and algorithms being introduced all the time. It is essential to stay current with these changes in order to maintain an effective social media strategy. For example, Instagram's recent introduction of Reels, a short-form video feature, has presented a new opportunity for businesses to create engaging video content and reach new audiences.

Search Engine Optimization (SEO) is another area where staying up-to-date is crucial. The algorithms used by search engines like Google are constantly evolving, which means that SEO strategies that worked in the past may no longer be effective. By staying current with the latest SEO trends and best practices, businesses can ensure that their website ranks highly in search results and attracts more traffic.

**Leverage Influencer Marketing:** Leveraging influencer marketing is a great way to build your online presence and reach a wider audience. In India, influencer marketing has become one of the most popular ways for brands to connect with their target audience. Influencer marketing involves partnering with social media influencers who have a large following and influence over their followers' purchasing decisions. These influencers can help promote your brand or product and increase your reach and credibility.

One of the most significant advantages of influencer marketing is that it allows brands to connect with their audience in a more authentic way. People trust influencers, and when an influencer promotes a product, their followers are more likely to trust that product. In addition, influencers often have a deep understanding of their followers' interests and preferences, which means they can tailor their content to be more appealing to their followers. This, in turn, can lead to higher engagement rates and increased conversions.

To leverage influencer marketing effectively, brands must identify the right influencers to partner with. This involves identifying influencers whose values align with your brand and whose followers are likely to be interested in your product. For example, if you sell makeup products, you may want to partner with beauty influencers who have a large following in India. It's also essential to ensure that the influencer's followers are authentic and engaged. One way to do this is to look at their engagement rates and the quality of the comments on their posts.

Once you have identified the right influencers to partner with, it's important to develop a mutually beneficial relationship. Influencers will only promote brands that align with their values and that they genuinely believe in. Brands should, therefore, focus on building relationships with influencers and providing them with value. This could involve providing them with free products or services or offering them a commission for every sale that they generate.

It's also important to be transparent when working with influencers. The Advertising Standards Council of India (ASCI) has issued guidelines for influencer marketing that require influencers to disclose when they are being paid to promote a product. Brands should, therefore, ensure that influencers are transparent about their relationships and that they disclose any sponsored content.

Finally, it's important to measure the impact of your influencer marketing campaigns. This involves tracking metrics such as engagement rates, click-through rates, and sales. This data can help you identify which influencers are most effective at promoting your brand and which types of content generate the most engagement.

**Engage in Online Community Building:** Engaging in online community building is an important aspect of building an online presence. Online communities are groups of people who share common interests, goals, and passions, and they can be found on various platforms such as social media, forums, and blogs. Building relationships with these communities can help businesses increase their brand awareness, build credibility, and ultimately drive sales.

In India, online communities are thriving, with millions of people coming together online to discuss topics ranging from sports to food to fashion. By identifying and engaging with these communities, businesses can tap into a captive audience of potential customers.

Online community building refers to the process of creating and nurturing a community of people who share common interests, goals or beliefs through online platforms such as social media, forums, and blogs. This can be done by individuals or businesses to connect with their audience, build relationships, and foster brand loyalty.

For businesses, online community building can lead to increased brand awareness, customer engagement, and ultimately, sales. By creating a space where customers can share their experiences, ask questions, and give feedback, businesses can establish themselves as trustworthy and reliable sources of information. This, in turn, can help to attract new customers and retain existing ones.

It is important to note that online community building is not a one-way street. To build a strong online community, one must also actively listen to the community and respond to their needs. This means responding to comments and messages, addressing concerns and complaints, and being open to feedback and suggestions.

One example of successful online community building in India is the Facebook group "Humans of Bombay". This group was created by photographer and blogger Karishma Mehta, with the aim of sharing stories of everyday people in Mumbai. The group has grown to over 2.7 million members and has become a platform for people to share their own stories, connect with others, and build a community of like-minded individuals.

One way to engage in online community building is to participate in online forums and discussions related to your industry. By offering valuable insights and expertise, businesses can position themselves as thought leaders in their field, gaining the trust and respect of community members. For example, a company that sells gardening tools could participate in a forum for gardening enthusiasts, offering tips and advice on how to maintain a beautiful garden. Over time, members of the community may start to see this company as a reliable source of information, leading to increased brand awareness and potentially, sales.

Another way to engage in online community building is to create or join groups on social media platforms like Facebook or LinkedIn. These groups can be focused on specific topics or industries, and provide a platform for members to share ideas and connect with others in their field. By creating a group, businesses can position themselves as a hub for discussions and knowledge sharing, helping to build a loyal following. For example, a company that sells eco-friendly products could create a group focused on sustainability, encouraging members to share tips on how to reduce their carbon footprint. By doing so, they are not only providing value to their customers but also building a community of like-minded individuals who are more likely to support their business.

In addition to participating in existing online communities or creating groups, businesses can also host their own online events. These events can take various forms, including webinars, live streams, or virtual conferences, and provide a platform for businesses to connect with their customers in real-time. By hosting an event, businesses can build relationships with their customers and gain valuable insights into their needs and preferences. For example, a company that sells fitness equipment could host a virtual workout session, allowing customers to try out their products and connect with other fitness enthusiasts.

**Utilize Chatbots and AI:** In today's fast-paced world, businesses are constantly searching for ways to improve their online presence and customer service. One way to achieve this is by utilizing chatbots and artificial intelligence (AI) technology. Chatbots are computer programs that simulate human conversation, while AI refers to machines that can learn and perform tasks that typically require human intelligence.

Chatbots and AI can be used in a variety of ways to enhance a business's online presence. One way is by improving customer service. Chatbots can be programmed to respond to frequently asked questions and provide information about a business's products or services. This can free up human employees to focus on more complex customer issues, while still providing customers with quick and efficient support.

Another way chatbots and AI can be used is to personalize the customer experience. By analysing a customer's behaviour and preferences, AI algorithms can recommend products and services that the customer is more likely to be interested in. This can lead to increased sales and customer satisfaction.

Chatbots and AI can also be used to automate repetitive tasks. For example, a chatbot can be used to schedule appointments or process orders, freeing up human employees to focus on more strategic tasks. This can help a business save time and money, while improving overall efficiency.

In India, chatbots and AI technology are already being used by a number of businesses, both large and small. For example, HDFC Bank has implemented an AI-powered chatbot called EVA to help customers with their banking needs. The chatbot can answer questions about bank accounts, credit cards, loans, and more.

In addition to improving customer service and the customer experience, chatbots and AI can also provide valuable insights into customer behaviour and preferences. By analysing data from customer interactions, businesses can gain a better understanding of what customers want and need. This can help businesses improve their products and services, as well as their marketing strategies.

**Implement E-commerce Features:** In today's world, online shopping has become an integral part of our lives. With the advent of technology and the internet, e-commerce has grown significantly, and it has become easier for businesses to sell their products and services online. If you want to build an online presence, implementing e-commerce features is a must.

E-commerce, or electronic commerce, refers to the buying and selling of products or services online. With e-commerce, you can sell your products 24/7, reach a wider audience, and increase your revenue. There are several e-commerce features that you can implement to make your online business more successful.

One of the most important e-commerce features is an online store. An online store is a website where customers can browse and purchase products or services. It should be easy to navigate and visually appealing to attract and retain customers. Indian e-commerce giants like Flipkart, Amazon and Myntra have a user-friendly interface, which makes shopping online easier for their customers.

Another essential e-commerce feature is a secure payment gateway. Customers want to be sure that their personal and financial information is safe when shopping online. A secure payment gateway ensures that all transactions are encrypted and protected from hackers. Popular payment gateways in India include Paytm, Razorpay, and PayU.

In addition to online stores and payment gateways, another important e-commerce feature is a product catalog. A product catalog is a list of all the products or services that you offer on your online store. It should be detailed and provide all the necessary information that customers need to make informed decisions. For example, if you are selling clothes online, your product catalog should include the size chart, material, colour options, and care instructions.

One of the most significant advantages of e-commerce is the ability to reach a wider audience. To take advantage of this, you can implement social media integration on your website. Social media integration allows customers to share your products with their friends and followers on social media platforms like Facebook, Instagram, and Twitter. This can increase your visibility and bring in more customers.

Another way to increase your reach is by implementing mobile responsiveness. With the increasing use of smartphones, it is crucial to have a website that is optimized for mobile devices. A mobile-responsive website ensures that your customers have a seamless shopping experience regardless of the device they are using. Many Indian businesses have adopted this feature, and this has helped them to reach a wider audience.

Lastly, you can implement customer reviews and ratings. Customer reviews and ratings are essential in building trust and credibility with your customers. They provide social proof that your products or services are of good quality and can help potential customers make informed decisions. Many e-commerce platforms in India, like Amazon and Flipkart, have integrated this feature and it has proved to be beneficial for their businesses.

# Chapter 14: Basics of Marketing

## Market:

A market is a place or a concept where individuals or businesses come together to buy and sell goods or services. It can be a physical location, such as a marketplace or a store, or it can be a virtual space facilitated by technology, like an online marketplace or e-commerce platform.

Imagine you're setting up a food delivery startup, and you're eager to understand your potential customer base. Let's explore the concept of a market together.

A market is like a bustling bazaar, filled with people seeking goods or services. It's the space where buyers and sellers interact, where transactions take place. To truly understand your market, you need to dive deeper and explore its different dimensions.

First, we have the available market. Picture it as a vast landscape of customers who currently purchase similar products or services. These are the people who are already engaging with the existing players in the food delivery industry. To succeed, you'll need to study this market, understand their preferences, and find a unique way to stand out.

Within the vast expanse of the available market, there exists a unique segment that's eager to purchase goods or services without any additional marketing efforts from your end. These customers are drawn to your offering naturally, like moths to a flame. They already recognize the value and relevance of your product, making them your initial consumer base.

The market minimum represents the minimum size of this customer segment. It's the baseline, the starting point that your business can count on, even without actively promoting your product. These are the early adopters, the enthusiasts who genuinely resonate with what you offer. They might have heard about your product through word-of-mouth, stumbled upon it online, or perhaps encountered it mistakenly. Regardless of how they found you, they're ready and willing to become your customers.

Now, let's shift our attention to the exciting part—the market potential. Think of it as the vast expanse of untapped opportunities, waiting to be explored. It includes customers who are not currently using food delivery services but have the potential to become your future customers. To tap into this potential, you'll need to understand their needs, preferences, and barriers to adoption. This segment represents your growth opportunity, your chance to expand the market and make a significant impact.

## Marketing Mix

The marketing mix refers to the combination of elements that a company uses to promote its product or service, including product, price, place, and promotion, to meet customer needs and achieve its marketing objectives. It is a strategic approach to effectively reach target customers and drive business success.

### Product:

In the dynamic world of marketing, the first element of the marketing mix is the product. Let's embark on a journey to understand the significance of a product and how it caters to the needs of customers in the Indian market.

Imagine you are a passionate entrepreneur, determined to create a product that resonates with the aspirations of your target audience. You begin by asking yourself some essential questions: What does your client desire from your service or product? How will they use it? Where will they use it?

As you delve deeper into understanding your customers' needs, you start to envision the features that your product must possess to meet those needs. You carefully analyse the market and make sure that your product offers essential features that your competitors might have missed. You aim to create something that truly serves your customers, eliminating any unnecessary features that may not add value to their experience.

Now, it's time to give your product a name, a name that reflects its essence and captures the attention of your target audience. You understand the power of a catchy name that can leave a lasting impression in the minds of customers.

Differentiation is key in a competitive market. You analyse your competitors' offerings and identify what sets your product apart. You strive to create a unique selling proposition, highlighting the aspects that make your product stand out. It could be superior quality, innovative features, or a distinctive design.

Visual appeal plays a significant role in attracting customers. You carefully consider the appearance of your product, thinking about its shape, colour, and sizes available. You aim to create a product that not only meets functional needs but also appeals to your customers' aesthetic sensibilities.

As you shape your product, you keep in mind the diverse tastes and preferences of Indian consumers. You ensure that your product aligns with the cultural nuances and aspirations of the Indian market. Whether it's clothing, electronics, or home goods, you strive to create a product that resonates with the hearts of Indian consumers.

Through your journey in understanding the importance of a product in the marketing mix, you realize that it's not just about creating something to sell. It's about crafting an experience, meeting the needs of your customers, and delivering value that goes beyond their expectations.

As you bring your product to life, you infuse it with passion, creativity, and a deep understanding of your customers' desires. You envision a product that becomes a part of people's lives, solving their problems, and bringing joy and satisfaction. With a clear vision of your product, its features, differentiation, and visual appeal, you are ready to embark on the next steps of your marketing journey.

**Price:**

As we continue our journey through the marketing mix, we now arrive at the second element: price. The price of a product is not just a number, but a reflection of its value and a crucial factor that determines your firm's profit and survival in the Indian market.

Imagine you are a savvy entrepreneur, ready to introduce your product to the world. One of the most critical decisions you face is determining the price at which customers will be willing to pay to enjoy your offering. It's not a decision to be taken lightly, as the price you set has a profound impact on your entire marketing strategy, sales, and the demand for your product.

To understand the significance of pricing, you must first recognize that it shapes the perception of your product in the eyes of consumers. When setting the price, you need to carefully consider the perceived value that your product offers. Indian consumers, like people around the world, evaluate the worth of a product based on the price tag attached to it. A higher price may create an impression of exclusivity or superior quality, while a lower price might be associated with affordability and value for money.

Several factors influence the determination of price. One important consideration is the demand for your product. If the demand is high, you may choose to set a slightly higher price to capture the perceived value and generate higher profits. Conversely, if the demand is lower, you might adopt a more competitive pricing strategy to attract customers and gain market share.

The cost of the ingredients or materials used to create your product also plays a significant role in pricing. As an astute entrepreneur, you analyse the cost structure of your product, taking into account raw materials, manufacturing expenses, overhead costs, and other financial considerations. You strive to strike a balance between ensuring profitability and offering a price that is attractive to your target audience.

Competition is another factor that influences pricing decisions. In the vibrant Indian market, you need to be aware of your competitors and their pricing strategies. You assess the prices charged by similar products in the market and make strategic choices to position your product competitively. You might opt for a pricing strategy that is either higher or lower than your competitors, depending on your product's unique features, quality, and perceived value.

Understanding customer perception is vital in setting the right price. You put yourself in the shoes of your target customers, considering their willingness to pay and their perception of value. You conduct market research, gather feedback, and listen to the voices of Indian consumers. This allows you to align your pricing strategy with the expectations and purchasing power of your target audience.

As you navigate the complex landscape of pricing, you realize that it's a delicate balancing act. You aim to maximize profits while also ensuring that your product remains accessible to your intended market. You seek to create a price that not only covers costs but also provides a fair exchange of value for your customers.

With careful consideration of factors such as demand, cost, competition, and customer perception, you arrive at a price that reflects the value of your product in the Indian market. It becomes a price that captures the attention of customers, conveys the quality of your offering, and sets the stage for a successful marketing journey.

Remember, the price you set is more than just a number. It is a strategic decision that influences your brand perception, sales, and overall success in the Indian market. Let your pricing strategy be a reflection of the value you offer, the needs of your customers, and your aspirations as an entrepreneur seeking to make a positive impact.

## Place:

As we delve deeper into the marketing mix, we now arrive at the third element: place. Picture yourself as an entrepreneur, ready to position and distribute your product in a way that resonates with the Indian market and ensures accessibility to potential buyers.

To start, you ponder the question of where your clients are likely to search for and discover your product. Do they prefer the convenience of online shopping or do they enjoy visiting physical stores? Understanding your target audience's preferences is key to effectively placing your product.

In the vast landscape of Indian commerce, you contemplate the various distribution channels available to you. Will you opt for an online store, where customers can conveniently browse and purchase your product with just a few clicks? Or do your potential clients frequent traditional brick-and-mortar stores, bustling malls, or local supermarkets? By identifying the places where your target audience typically shops, you can strategically position your product for maximum visibility and accessibility.

As you consider your distribution strategy, you realize that intermediaries play a crucial role in connecting your product to the end consumer. These intermediaries could be distributors, wholesalers, or retailers who facilitate the flow of your product from production to consumption. You evaluate the different distribution channels and identify the main intermediaries who can effectively reach your target market. It could be a network of retailers or distributors spread across various regions in India.

You also contemplate the length of the distribution channel that is feasible for your product. Will you adopt a direct distribution approach, where you sell your product directly to the end consumer, or will you involve multiple intermediaries? Understanding the complexity of your product, its target market, and the resources at your disposal helps you determine the most efficient and effective distribution channel length.

Differentiating your distribution strategy from that of your competitors is crucial. You analyse the methods employed by your rivals and seek opportunities to stand out. Perhaps you offer additional services, such as faster delivery or personalized customer support. Maybe you forge strategic partnerships with renowned retailers or leverage emerging e-commerce platforms to reach a wider audience. Your aim is to create a unique distribution strategy that sets your product apart and enhances the overall customer experience.

In the dynamic marketplace, you also consider the importance of a strong sales force. Depending on your product and target market, you assess whether you need a dedicated team of sales representatives who can effectively communicate the value of your product, build relationships with retailers, and drive sales. The strength of your sales force can greatly impact the placement and distribution of your product, enabling you to capture market share and foster customer loyalty.

With a deep understanding of your target audience's shopping habits, the available distribution channels, and the role of intermediaries, you strategically position your product in a place that maximizes its visibility and accessibility to potential buyers. You craft a distribution strategy that aligns with your product's unique characteristics, outshines your competitors, and delivers an exceptional customer experience.

Remember, the placement of your product is not just about its physical location, but also about its presence in the minds and hearts of your target audience. Let your distribution strategy be a reflection of your commitment to meet customer needs, provide convenience, and create value at every touchpoint. By strategically placing your product in the right channels and ensuring its availability where your customers are, you set the stage for success in the vibrant and diverse Indian market.

## Promotion:

As we explore the final element of the marketing mix, let's dive into the exciting world of promotion. Imagine yourself as an entrepreneur, eager to spread the word about your product and capture the attention of the Indian market.

Promotion is the art of communicating the value and benefits of your product to your target audience. It's about crafting compelling messages that resonate with your customers and inspire them to take action. So, how do you effectively promote your product in the diverse and vibrant landscape of India?

First and foremost, you must understand your customers and their needs. What motivates them? What challenges do they face? By gaining deep insights into their desires and pain points, you can tailor your promotional efforts to strike a chord with their hearts and minds.

In the age of technology, digital marketing has become a powerful tool to reach and engage with your audience. You ponder the various online platforms where your target market spends their time - social media, search engines, e-commerce websites, and more. You craft engaging content, captivating visuals, and persuasive ads that showcase the unique value your product offers. Through targeted digital campaigns, you ensure that your promotional messages reach the right people at the right time.

But don't overlook the power of traditional marketing channels. In India, print media, television, and radio still play a significant role in capturing the attention of a wide audience. You consider running advertisements in popular newspapers, magazines, or television channels that your target audience frequently engages with. The key is to strike a balance between online and offline promotion, leveraging the strengths of each channel to amplify your brand's reach.

Word-of-mouth marketing is another powerful promotional tool in the Indian context. Indians value personal recommendations and opinions from trusted sources. You foster positive customer experiences and encourage satisfied customers to spread the word about your product. This could be through testimonials, online reviews, or referral programs that incentivize customers to share their positive experiences with their friends and family.

In the spirit of India's diverse cultural fabric, you explore the possibility of collaborating with influencers or celebrities who have a strong influence on your target audience. These influential personalities can help endorse your product and create a buzz that resonates with their followers. Whether it's a Bollywood actor, a renowned sports personality, or a popular social media influencer, their endorsement can significantly boost your product's visibility and credibility.

Special promotions, discounts, and loyalty programs are also effective ways to drive customer engagement and encourage repeat purchases. Indians appreciate value for their money, and offering attractive deals can capture their attention and entice them to choose your product over competitors. Whether it's festive discounts, exclusive offers, or rewards for loyal customers, you design promotional strategies that align with the Indian consumer's love for savings and benefits.

Lastly, you recognize the importance of measuring the effectiveness of your promotional efforts. You track key metrics, such as reach, engagement, conversion rates, and customer feedback, to evaluate the success of your marketing campaigns. This data-driven approach allows you to optimize your promotional strategies and make informed decisions to continually improve your reach and impact.

Remember, promotion is not just about shouting from the rooftops about your product. It's about crafting meaningful messages, leveraging digital and traditional channels, harnessing the power of word-of-mouth, and creating compelling experiences that resonate with the diverse Indian audience. By strategically promoting your product and consistently delivering on your promises, you pave the way for success in the dynamic and ever-evolving Indian market.

So, go ahead, put on your creative hat, and let your promotional efforts light up the Indian market, capturing hearts and minds one customer at a time.

## Core Marketing Concepts:

### Needs:

Let's delve into the fascinating realm of needs, one of the core concepts in marketing. Picture yourself as an enthusiastic consumer in India, eagerly searching for the perfect television that meets your desires and expectations. Needs play a crucial role in shaping our purchasing decisions, and understanding the different types of needs can help us make informed choices.

First, we have stated needs, which are the explicit requirements we express when seeking a product or service. For instance, you might say, "I want an inexpensive TV." Here, your stated need revolves around finding a television that fits within your budget. It's a straightforward request, indicating your desire for an affordable option.

However, beneath the surface, lie the real needs, which go beyond the obvious. While you may state the need for an inexpensive TV, your real need could be to find a television that has low or zero maintenance costs. You want a durable and reliable product that won't burden you with frequent repairs or high maintenance expenses. This reflects your underlying concern for long-term affordability and peace of mind.

In addition to stated and real needs, we encounter unstated needs, which are the desires and expectations that we may not explicitly express. As a consumer, you may desire good service from the manufacturer of the TV you purchase. You want to feel valued and supported throughout your ownership journey. Prompt responses to queries, efficient after-sales service, and readily available assistance become important factors that contribute to your overall satisfaction.

Moving on, we come across delight needs, which represent those unexpected and pleasant surprises that go beyond our initial requirements. In your quest for the perfect TV, you might find one that not only meets your stated and real needs but also comes with a home theatre system. This unexpected bonus brings joy and excitement, enhancing your entertainment experience and surpassing your initial expectations. Delight needs aim to create memorable moments and leave a lasting positive impression.

Lastly, we encounter secret needs, which are the desires we may hold privately and may not openly express to others. As a smart buyer, you may have a secret need for your friends to perceive you as someone with impeccable taste and discerning judgment. You want them to admire your choice and view you as a savvy consumer. While this need may not be explicitly stated, it influences your decision-making process and shapes your preferences.

Understanding the different layers of needs allows marketers to craft products, services, and marketing strategies that resonate with customers on a deeper level. By addressing both the stated and real needs, they can fulfil the core requirements and provide value. By recognizing and exceeding the unstated and delight needs, they can create exceptional customer experiences. And by tapping into the secret needs, they can create a sense of identity and self-expression, fostering a strong emotional connection with consumers.

## Wants:

Let's explore the captivating concept of wants, which emanate from our human needs and take on various forms influenced by culture and individual personality. As an Indian reader, you can relate to the diverse wants that arise in our rich and vibrant society.

Needs form the foundation of our desires, representing the essential requirements we seek to fulfil. However, it is when these needs become directed towards specific objects that they transform into wants. Our wants are shaped by our surroundings, influenced by our cultural upbringing, societal norms, and personal preferences.

Imagine you have a need for food, a universal requirement that sustains us all. In an urban Indian setting, your want may manifest as a craving for a delicious pizza. The sight of cheese, flavourful toppings, and a crispy crust evokes a sense of satisfaction and indulgence, fulfilling your desire for a scrumptious meal.

On the other hand, in a rural Indian context, your want might take the form of a hearty plate of rice. The warm aroma, the simplicity of the meal, and its cultural significance create a sense of comfort and contentment, catering to your need for nourishment.

For a child, their want might revolve around a delightful chocolate. The vibrant packaging, the anticipation of unwrapping it, and the delightful sweetness bring joy and happiness, fulfilling their need for a small treat.

In the realm of health and fitness, a fitness-conscious individual may find their want in a protein shake. They seek a convenient and efficient way to replenish their body's nutrients, promote muscle growth, and support their active lifestyle. The nutritional benefits, the smooth texture, and the fitness association fulfil their need for a nourishing and energizing option.

These examples illustrate how wants are intricately connected to our unique backgrounds, experiences, and personalities. They go beyond the basic requirements and reflect our individual desires, tastes, and aspirations.

As marketers, understanding the wants of consumers is crucial in developing products and services that cater to their specific preferences and aspirations. By recognizing the diverse wants that emerge from common needs, they can tailor their offerings to resonate with different segments of the population. From crafting irresistible flavours and packaging to providing convenience and functionality, they aim to fulfil the wants of their target audience, creating a strong bond between the consumer and the brand.

## Demands:

Let's delve into the fascinating concept of demands, which plays a vital role in the world of marketing. As an Indian reader, you'll find this concept relatable as you navigate through a market filled with diverse products and choices.

Demands go beyond mere wants and needs. They represent the desires for specific products that are accompanied by the ability to pay for them. In other words, it's when you have both the desire for a product and the financial means to acquire it that a demand is created.

Imagine you come across a sleek smartphone that catches your eye. You find yourself drawn to its sleek design, advanced features, and the promise of enhanced connectivity. It triggers a desire within you, a want for this specific product.

However, desires alone do not determine demand. It is the combination of desire, the ability to pay for the product, and the willingness to actually make the purchase that gives rise to demand. In this scenario, demand emerges when you possess the financial capability to afford the smartphone and you are genuinely willing to buy it.

To measure demand, companies carefully assess these factors - desire, ability to pay, and willingness to buy. They conduct market research, analyse consumer behaviour, and evaluate economic indicators to gauge the potential demand for their products. By understanding the demands of their target market, companies can align their strategies and offerings to meet the desires of their customers effectively.

The equation "Demand = desire + ability to pay + willingness to buy" encapsulates the essence of this concept. It emphasizes that demand is not solely driven by wants or needs, but by the confluence of multiple factors. Companies rely on this equation to determine the size of their target market, forecast sales, and develop marketing strategies that resonate with the desires and purchasing power of their customers.

By understanding demands, companies can tailor their offerings, pricing, and marketing efforts to attract and satisfy their target audience. They aim to create products and experiences that resonate with the desires of their customers while ensuring they are accessible and affordable.

## Value & Satisfaction:

Let's explore the captivating concepts of value and satisfaction, which lie at the heart of the marketing world. As an Indian reader, you'll find these concepts relatable as you navigate the diverse marketplace in search of products and experiences that meet your expectations.

Value is a powerful notion that encompasses the combination of quality, service, and price. It is the perception we form when we evaluate the overall worth and benefits derived from a product or service. In essence, it's about what we receive in return for what we pay. Value perception is influenced by various factors, such as the quality of the product or service, the level of customer service provided, and the price we are asked to pay.

Think of a time when you purchased a smartphone. You considered its features, performance, and durability. You also took into account the level of service you received from the brand, such as after-sales support and warranty coverage. Additionally, you compared the price of the smartphone with similar offerings in the market. All of these factors contributed to your perception of the value offered by the product. A higher level of quality and service may increase the perceived value, while a higher price may reduce it.

Now, let's turn our attention to customer satisfaction. It is the outcome of the correlation between the performance of a product or service and the expectations of the customer. When a product or service meets or exceeds our expectations, we feel satisfied. It's that feeling of contentment when we receive what we anticipated or even more.

Imagine you book a hotel room for a vacation. You have certain expectations regarding the cleanliness, comfort, and amenities provided. If the hotel meets these expectations, you experience satisfaction. On the other hand, if the hotel falls short of your expectations—for example, if the room is not clean or the staff is unhelpful—you feel dissatisfied.

However, customer satisfaction doesn't stop at simply meeting expectations. It can go beyond that to create a delightful experience. When a product or service exceeds our expectations and provides an exceptional level of performance, we feel delighted. This sense of delight can lead to customer loyalty, as we become more inclined to repurchase from the brand and recommend it to others.

As Indian consumers, we constantly seek value in our purchases and expect products and services to meet our expectations. We evaluate the combination of quality, service, and price to assess the value offered. Similarly, our satisfaction levels are influenced by how well a product or service aligns with our expectations. When our expectations are met or exceeded, we feel satisfied or even delighted, fostering a sense of loyalty towards the brand.

For businesses, understanding the dynamics of value and satisfaction is crucial. By delivering products and services that offer a high perceived value, companies can attract and retain customers. They strive to meet and exceed customer expectations, aiming for satisfaction and delight. Through these efforts, businesses can foster long-term relationships, build customer loyalty, and create a positive brand image.

# Orientations of a Business:

In the world of business, different approaches guide the strategies and actions of organizations. These approaches, known as orientations of business, shape how companies interact with customers, develop products, and pursue their goals. Understanding these orientations provides valuable insights into the mindset and priorities of businesses as they navigate the marketplace. Let's explore the key orientations of business and how they influence decision-making.

## Production Concept:

Imagine you're starting a small business in your town. You have a passion for creating handmade, affordable jewellery. You believe that if you can produce these beautiful pieces on a large scale, you can offer them to customers at a lower price compared to your competitors.

In this scenario, you are following the production concept of business orientation. This concept originated during the post-Industrial Revolution era when mass production became possible. The underlying assumption is that customers will prefer products that are widely available and offered at a lower price.

As you set up your jewellery-making workshop, your focus is on maximizing efficiency and reducing costs. You invest in machinery and tools that help speed up the production process. Your goal is to produce a large quantity of jewellery to meet the anticipated demand.

With the production concept, you may not place a heavy emphasis on marketing research or extensive product development. Instead, your main priority is to manufacture the jewellery at a lower cost, making it affordable for a larger number of customers.

You view marketing as a means to distribute your mass-produced jewellery to those customers who are interested in the product itself, rather than its unique features. Your marketing efforts may involve physical distribution channels, such as setting up a shop in a popular location or participating in local markets.

While the production concept allows you to achieve economies of scale and offer affordable products, it's important to note that it may not prioritize understanding the specific needs and preferences of individual customers. However, for certain products where price and availability are key factors, this orientation can be effective.

## Product Concept:

Imagine you're an entrepreneur with a passion for creating innovative and high-quality mobile phones. You firmly believe that if you focus on designing and manufacturing exceptional products, customers will naturally be drawn to them.

In this scenario, you are following the product concept of business orientation. The product concept revolves around the idea that customers will favour products that offer superior features, performance, or design.

As you embark on your entrepreneurial journey, your main goal is to create a mobile phone that stands out from the competition. You invest time, effort, and resources into extensive research and development. You strive to incorporate cutting-edge technology, sleek designs, and user-friendly interfaces into your product.

Your focus is not only on the physical attributes of the mobile phone but also on its durability, reliability, and overall user experience. You believe that if you can deliver a product that exceeds customer expectations in terms of quality and functionality, it will naturally attract a loyal customer base.

With the product concept, marketing plays a crucial role in highlighting the unique features and benefits of your mobile phone. You emphasize product demonstrations, informative packaging, and engaging advertising campaigns to showcase the exceptional value your product offers.

You pay close attention to customer feedback and use it to refine and enhance your product over time. Continuous improvement and innovation are at the core of your business strategy. By consistently delivering high-quality products, you aim to build a strong brand reputation and foster customer loyalty.

While the product concept places a strong emphasis on creating outstanding products, it's important to balance it with an understanding of customer needs and preferences. While your focus is on the product itself, it's crucial to consider factors such as pricing, distribution, and customer service to ensure a holistic approach to your business.

## Selling Concept:

Imagine you have just started your own business selling fashionable clothing and accessories. You are excited about your unique product range and want to reach as many customers as possible. This is where the selling concept comes into play.

The selling concept of business orientation revolves around the belief that customers will be more inclined to purchase products that are aggressively promoted through various marketing techniques. The assumption is that customers need to be persuaded and convinced to buy a product, rather than naturally seeking it out.

In your clothing business, you understand that simply offering great products may not be enough to attract customers. You realize the importance of promoting your brand through effective advertising, publicity, and sales techniques. You are willing to invest in promotional activities to create awareness and generate interest in your products.

You focus on using multiple channels to reach your target audience. You leverage the power of advertising through print, digital media, and social platforms to showcase your latest collections, highlighting their unique features and benefits. You also collaborate with influencers and fashion bloggers to generate buzz and create a sense of desire among potential customers.

In addition to advertising, you actively engage in salesmanship. You train your sales team to effectively communicate the value and benefits of your products, ensuring they are skilled in addressing customer objections and concerns. Your team is enthusiastic and persuasive, creating a sense of excitement around your brand and encouraging customers to make a purchase.

Sales promotion is another important aspect of the selling concept. You offer special deals, discounts, and incentives to entice customers to buy your products. Limited-time offers and exclusive promotions create a sense of urgency, encouraging impulse buying and attracting customers who may not have initially considered your brand.

While the selling concept places a strong emphasis on promotion and sales, it's important to note that customer satisfaction should not be overlooked. As you interact with customers, you listen to their feedback and address their needs to ensure a positive buying experience. Building strong customer relationships and providing excellent service can lead to repeat purchases and positive word-of-mouth, further boosting your sales.

However, it's important to recognize that the selling concept is not suitable for all types of products or industries. It is commonly used for unsought goods, impulse-buying items, or products that have flooded the market in large quantities. For other types of businesses, adopting a more customer-centric approach, such as the marketing concept, may be more effective in the long run.

## Marketing Concept:

Picture yourself as a passionate entrepreneur who deeply values customer satisfaction and believes in building long-term relationships with your clients. You are determined to make your business successful, not just by selling products, but by truly understanding and meeting the needs of your customers. This is where the marketing concept comes into play.

The marketing concept revolves around the idea that the key to business success lies in identifying and satisfying the needs and wants of your target customers. It places the customer at the center of all business activities and focuses on delivering superior value and satisfaction.

In your journey as an entrepreneur, you recognize that the success of your business depends on understanding the unique needs and desires of your customers. You invest time and resources in conducting market research to gain valuable insights into their preferences, behaviours, and purchasing patterns. This helps you develop a deep understanding of what motivates your customers and how you can serve them better.

With the marketing concept, you go beyond just creating and selling products. You strive to build strong customer relationships by consistently delivering value and exceeding their expectations. You develop a customer-centric approach, where every decision you make is driven by the desire to meet customer needs.

You carefully design your products and services, taking into account the features, quality, and benefits that your customers value the most. You create a product that not only satisfies their basic needs but also provides unique and desirable attributes that differentiate you from your competitors.

To effectively reach your target market, you develop a comprehensive marketing strategy that encompasses various elements such as product positioning, pricing, distribution channels, and promotion. You tailor your marketing efforts to effectively communicate the value and benefits of your offerings to your customers.

Your marketing activities focus on building brand awareness, establishing credibility, and fostering trust with your customers. You leverage different marketing channels, both online and offline, to engage with your target audience and create a positive brand image.

Importantly, you value customer feedback and actively seek it out. You listen to your customers, respond to their concerns, and continuously improve your products and services based on their feedback. By doing so, you build strong customer loyalty and create brand advocates who not only become repeat customers but also recommend your business to others.

The marketing concept recognizes that a satisfied customer is more likely to become a loyal customer, leading to repeat business and positive word-of-mouth recommendations. By consistently delivering superior value and satisfaction, you build a strong foundation for your business growth and long-term success.

Embracing the marketing concept means making a commitment to understanding and serving your customers better than anyone else. It requires a customer-focused mindset, a dedication to continuous improvement, and a genuine passion for meeting customer needs. By adopting this approach, you position your business for sustained success in today's competitive marketplace.

## Societal Concept:

Imagine yourself as a socially conscious entrepreneur who not only cares about the success of your business but also wants to make a positive impact on society. You believe that businesses have a greater responsibility beyond just making profits – they should actively contribute to the well-being of the community and the environment. This is where the societal concept comes into play.

The societal concept revolves around the idea that businesses should not only focus on meeting the needs and wants of their customers but also consider the broader societal implications of their actions. It emphasizes the importance of conducting business in a way that benefits society as a whole.

As an entrepreneur driven by the societal concept, you are committed to operating your business in an ethical and responsible manner. You understand that your business decisions and practices can have a significant impact on the environment, local communities, and various stakeholders.

You take proactive steps to minimize the negative environmental impacts of your operations. This includes adopting sustainable practices such as reducing waste, conserving energy, and using eco-friendly materials. By doing so, you contribute to the preservation of natural resources and help create a cleaner and healthier planet.

Furthermore, you are mindful of the social and cultural aspects of your business. You prioritize fair and ethical treatment of employees, ensuring they receive fair wages, safe working conditions, and opportunities for growth and development. You actively promote diversity, inclusion, and equality within your organization, fostering a positive and inclusive work environment.

In addition to your internal practices, you extend your commitment to societal well-being through various initiatives. You actively engage with local communities, supporting social causes and contributing to their development. Whether it's through charitable donations, volunteering, or partnerships with non-profit organizations, you strive to make a positive difference in the lives of those around you.

You also consider the societal impact of your products or services. You ensure that they meet high standards of quality and safety, and you take into account the potential effects on consumer health and well-being. If possible, you develop offerings that address social issues or provide solutions to pressing problems in society.

By embracing the societal concept, you go beyond the traditional role of a business and become a catalyst for positive change. You understand that businesses have the power to influence and shape society, and you use that power responsibly. Your actions inspire others and set an example for how businesses can operate with integrity and contribute to the greater good.

In a world where societal challenges are ever-present, your commitment to the societal concept sets you apart as a visionary entrepreneur. You understand that true success lies not only in financial prosperity but also in creating a better and more sustainable future for all. By aligning your business goals with the well-being of society, you become a force for positive transformation and leave a lasting impact that goes far beyond your bottom line.

## Factors in Marketing Environment:

The marketing environment consists of various factors that influence a company's marketing activities. These factors can be both internal and external to the organization and have the potential to impact its success in the market. Understanding and adapting to the marketing environment is crucial for businesses to effectively navigate and capitalize on opportunities while mitigating potential threats.

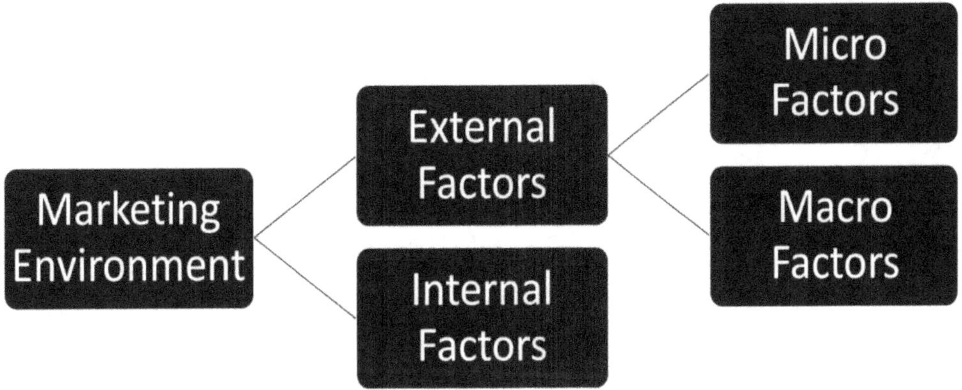


**Internal Factors:**

The internal environment of a company encompasses all the factors that exist within its boundaries and are under the control of its top management team. These factors have a direct impact on the company's marketing efforts and can be altered or modified to align with its strategic objectives. Regular internal audits are conducted to assess the organization's strengths and weaknesses. In the Indian context, the internal environment of a company plays a crucial role in shaping its marketing strategies and overall success. Let's explore some key factors that influence the internal marketing environment:

- **Value System of Founders:** The values and beliefs of the company's founders greatly influence its business choices, mission, objectives, and policies. These values provide a guiding framework for decision-making and shape the company's overall culture.

- **Management Structure:** The way a company's management is structured, whether centralized or decentralized, and the internal power relationships impact how marketing decisions are made and implemented. Efficient communication and coordination among different departments are crucial for successful marketing campaigns.

- **Marketing Channels:** The selection and management of marketing channels, such as distribution networks, wholesalers, and retailers, are important internal factors. These channels play a vital role in reaching customers effectively and delivering products or services to the market.

- **Market of Operation:** The company's target market and the specific segments it serves are internal factors that influence marketing strategies. Understanding the market dynamics, consumer preferences, and competition within the chosen market segment is essential for developing effective marketing plans.

- **Human Resources:** The skills, capabilities, and expertise of various individuals within the organization, including the board of directors, managers, marketing teams, workers, and public relations personnel, significantly impact marketing performance. Building a competent and motivated workforce is crucial for successful marketing initiatives.

- **Company's Image and Brand Equity:** The reputation, image, and brand equity of a company directly influence consumer perceptions and purchase decisions. Developing a strong and positive brand image through effective branding strategies and delivering superior customer experiences are vital internal considerations.

- **Strength of Selling, Product Development, Research Teams, and Customer Service:** The effectiveness and capabilities of these teams directly impact a company's ability to meet customer needs, develop innovative products, conduct market research, and provide excellent customer service. These internal factors contribute to the overall competitiveness and success of the company.

- **Financial Strength:** The financial resources and stability of a company influence its marketing initiatives. Sufficient financial strength enables investments in marketing activities, product development, advertising, and promotional campaigns, helping the company gain a competitive edge.

By focusing on and optimizing these internal factors, companies can enhance their marketing performance, strengthen their brand, and create sustainable competitive advantages in the Indian market. Regular evaluation, improvement, and alignment of these internal elements are crucial for adapting to changing market conditions and achieving marketing success.

## External Factors:

External factors in the marketing environment refer to the elements that exist outside the boundaries of the organization and can influence its marketing activities and overall business performance. These factors are categorized into two types: micro and macro. The micro-environment includes factors that are in close proximity to the company and have a direct impact on its operations, while the macro-environment consists of broader societal forces that affect the entire industry or market.

## Micro Factors:

The micro-environment refers to the specific factors that are in close proximity to a company and directly influence its operations and marketing activities. It's like a circle of influence surrounding the organization, composed of individuals and entities that have a direct impact on its day-to-day functioning. Let's take a closer look at some key elements of the micro-environment.

- **Customers:** Customers are the lifeblood of any business. Understanding their needs, preferences, and purchasing behaviour is crucial for developing effective marketing strategies. In India, with its diverse population and varied cultural backgrounds, businesses must adapt to the unique preferences and demands of different customer segments.

- **Suppliers:** Suppliers provide the necessary resources and inputs for a company's operations. Building strong relationships with reliable suppliers is essential to ensure a steady supply of quality products or services. In India, where the supplier landscape can vary across different regions, it is important for businesses to identify trustworthy suppliers who can meet their requirements efficiently.

- **Competitors:** Competition is a driving force in the market. Understanding and monitoring competitors' strategies, strengths, and weaknesses helps businesses differentiate themselves and stay ahead. In India's dynamic business landscape, where both domestic and international players operate, competition can be intense, requiring companies to constantly innovate and deliver value to their customers.

- **Intermediaries:** Intermediaries, such as distributors, wholesalers, and retailers, play a vital role in the distribution channel. Developing strong partnerships with intermediaries is crucial for reaching customers effectively and ensuring the availability of products or services in the market. In India's vast and diverse market, businesses often rely on intermediaries to navigate the complex distribution networks.

- **Publics:** The micro-environment also includes various publics that can have an impact on a company's reputation and operations. This includes the media, government agencies, local communities, and special interest groups. Maintaining positive relationships with these stakeholders is important for the long-term success and sustainability of businesses in India.

By closely examining the needs and expectations of customers, building strong relationships with suppliers and intermediaries, and monitoring and responding to competitive forces, companies can position themselves strategically and create a favourable business environment. It requires continuous monitoring and adaptation to ensure that the company remains responsive to the ever-changing dynamics of the Indian market.

## Macro Factors:

The macro-environment encompasses the broader external factors that impact an organization's operations and the business environment as a whole. It sets the stage within which companies operate and can significantly influence their strategies and decision-making. Let's delve into some key aspects of the macro-environment and how they relate to the Indian context.

- **Economic Factors:** The economic conditions of a country, such as GDP growth, inflation rates, exchange rates, and consumer spending patterns, shape the business landscape. In India, where economic fluctuations can be common, businesses need to adapt to changing market conditions and consumer purchasing power.

- **Socio-Cultural Factors:** Socio-cultural factors encompass the beliefs, values, customs, and lifestyle of the society. India's rich cultural diversity and traditional values play a significant role in shaping consumer behaviour and preferences. Companies operating in India must consider these factors while developing products, marketing campaigns, and communication strategies that resonate with the local culture and connect with the aspirations of the Indian population.

- **Technological Factors:** Technological advancements have the power to transform industries and disrupt traditional business models. In India, a rapidly evolving technology landscape and increasing digital penetration have opened up new opportunities and challenges for businesses. Embracing technology and innovation is crucial for companies to stay competitive and meet the changing demands of Indian consumers.

- **Political and Legal Factors:** The political and legal environment in India can impact business operations and regulations. Government policies, regulations, and stability play a crucial role in shaping the business environment. Companies need to stay updated with changes in laws, taxation policies, and industry-specific regulations to ensure compliance and mitigate risks.

- **Environmental Factors:** Environmental concerns and sustainability have gained significant importance globally, including in India. Consumers are becoming more conscious of environmental issues, and businesses are expected to adopt sustainable practices. Companies operating in India must consider environmental factors and strive for sustainable operations and responsible business practices.

- **Demographic Factors:** India's large and diverse population with varying age groups, income levels, and geographic locations presents both opportunities and challenges. Understanding demographic trends and segments can help businesses tailor their products and marketing strategies to cater to specific consumer groups effectively.

- **Technological Factors:** Technological advancements have the power to transform industries and disrupt traditional business models. In India, a rapidly evolving technology landscape and increasing digital penetration have opened up new opportunities and challenges for businesses. Embracing technology and innovation is crucial for companies to stay competitive and meet the changing demands of Indian consumers.

By understanding the economic conditions, socio-cultural dynamics, technological advancements, political and legal landscape, environmental concerns, and demographic trends, companies can adapt their strategies, identify emerging opportunities, and mitigate potential risks. A holistic understanding of the macro-environment enables businesses to make informed decisions and develop sustainable business models that align with the needs and expectations of the Indian market.

## MARKETING RESEARCH:

Marketing research is the systematic gathering, recording, and analysis of data about problems relating to the marketing of goods and services. It serves as the "soul" of marketing management, and it is often said that the beginning and end of marketing management are tied to marketing research. It provides valuable insights and knowledge that guide marketers in making informed decisions. Just like generals who ignore enemy signals put themselves at risk, marketers who ignore research are equally vulnerable. Understanding the needs and desires of consumers is crucial, and as Steve Jobs famously said, "People don't know what they want until you show it to them."

## Importance of Marketing Research:

- **Helps in Marketing Mix Decisions:** Marketing research provides valuable information that helps in making effective marketing mix decisions. It helps determine the optimal product features, pricing strategies, promotional activities, and distribution channels to maximize customer satisfaction and business success.

- **Achieves Competitive Advantage:** By conducting thorough market research, companies gain a competitive edge. It helps them understand customer needs, preferences, and expectations better than their competitors, enabling them to develop superior products and services.

- **Leads to Customer Satisfaction:** Marketing research helps companies gain insights into customer preferences, buying behaviour, and satisfaction levels. This information allows businesses to tailor their offerings and provide enhanced customer experiences, leading to higher customer satisfaction and loyalty.

- **Helps in Expanding Markets:** Through market research, companies can identify new market opportunities, evaluate market potential, and understand customer segments that are untapped or underserved. This knowledge enables businesses to expand into new markets and reach a wider customer base.

- **Helps in Forecasting Demand:** Understanding market trends, consumer behaviour, and competitive dynamics enables accurate forecasting of demand. This helps companies plan production, inventory, and resource allocation effectively, minimizing risks associated with overstocking or understocking.

- **Improves Brand Loyalty & Image:** Marketing research helps companies assess brand perception, identify areas of improvement, and develop strategies to enhance brand loyalty and image. By understanding customer sentiments and preferences, businesses can build stronger relationships and foster brand advocacy.

- **Optimum Use of Resources:** Market research enables companies to allocate their resources effectively. By identifying the most promising market segments and focusing on the most profitable opportunities, businesses can optimize their marketing investments and maximize returns.

## Key Areas under Marketing Research:

- **Consumer Research:** Understanding consumers is a fundamental aspect of marketing research. It involves studying consumer profiles, their likes, dislikes, tastes, and preferences. Marketers need to analyse buying patterns and consumer reactions to their products compared to competitors. This research helps in identifying consumer needs and developing strategies to meet those needs effectively.

- **Product Research:** Product research focuses on testing new product launches, reviewing product quality and features, analysing product lines, studying the use of the product, and examining competitors' products. It also includes studying packaging design and materials. By conducting product research, companies can ensure that their products align with consumer expectations, stand out from competitors, and meet the desired quality standards.

- **Pricing Research:** Pricing research involves analysing market price trends, studying competitors' pricing strategies, and evaluating the company's pricing strategy in relation to consumer price perceptions. It also considers changes in the economy that may require adjusting pricing strategies and positioning. Understanding pricing dynamics is essential for setting competitive prices that attract customers while maximizing profitability.

- **Market Research:** Market research provides insights into the size of the market and its potential, the profile of the market in terms of demand, potential market segments, and market characteristics. It helps in analysing market segmentation and conducting market share analysis. Market research enables companies to identify target markets, assess market opportunities, and develop effective marketing strategies tailored to specific customer segments.

- **Sales Research:** Sales research involves forecasting short-term and long-term sales, analysing sales performance, establishing sales quotas and territories, and studying seasonal sales trends. It also considers overall industry trends that may impact sales. By understanding sales patterns and trends, companies can set realistic sales targets, allocate resources effectively, and identify areas for improvement.

- **Promotion Research:** Promotion research focuses on studying the impact of the company's promotional efforts, such as advertising, publicity, salesmanship, and sales promotions. It also involves analysing competitors' promotion tactics and understanding consumer expectations regarding product promotion. This research helps companies develop effective promotional strategies that resonate with their target audience and differentiate them from competitors.

- **Place & Dealer Research:** Place and dealer research involves studying the efficiency of existing distribution channels, assessing the contribution of dealers in sales promotion, and understanding dealer expectations. It also includes studying the incentives provided by competitors to dealers. By understanding the dynamics of distribution channels and dealer relationships, companies can optimize their distribution strategies and build strong partnerships with dealers.

## Consumer Buying Process:

The consumer buying process is a series of steps that individuals go through when making purchasing decisions. Understanding this process is crucial for marketers as it helps them align their marketing efforts with consumer behaviour. Let's explore each stage of the consumer buying process in detail, keeping in mind the Indian context and making it relatable and practical.

- **Need Recognition/Problem Recognition:**

The first stage is recognizing a need or problem. Consumers realize the need for a particular product when they feel it is necessary in their lives. For example, a rural couple may recognize the need for a condom when they want to plan their family. This recognition can be triggered by internal stimuli (such as hunger or thirst) or external stimuli (like exposure to advertisements or attractive product displays).

In India, consumer needs can be classified into different categories. Functional needs arise when consumers require a product to address a specific function or problem. For instance, soap for bathing or a school for education. Social needs arise from the desire for integration, belongingness, or social recognition. Examples include buying a fashionable bag to look good at school or choosing a luxury car to showcase success. Needs for change occur when consumers desire a shift from their regular products or habits, such as switching from Ayurvedic to Allopathic medicines or from traditional 'Datun' to toothpaste.

- **Information Search:**

Once the need is recognized, consumers embark on an information search to gather information about possible solutions to their problem. The extent of information search depends on the complexity of the purchase and the consumer's involvement. Internal information, based on previous experiences and brand opinions, is often sufficient for everyday products. However, for major purchases or when internal information is lacking, consumers turn to external sources such as friends, family, reviews, or the press for additional information.

In India, consumers tend to rely heavily on internal information and recommendations from trusted individuals. They value personal experiences and word-of-mouth opinions when making purchasing decisions. Marketers should focus on building brand credibility and generating positive reviews to influence consumer perceptions and support their decision-making process.

- **Alternative Evaluation:**

At this stage, consumers evaluate the different alternatives available to satisfy their needs. They assess the attributes of each alternative, considering both objective characteristics (product features, functionality) and subjective factors (brand perception, reputation). Consumers use the information gathered during the search stage to classify and prioritize alternatives. This process leads to the formation of the "evoked set," which consists of the brands or products with a higher probability of being purchased. Conversely, the "inept set" includes options that are unlikely to be considered, while the "inert set" represents products for which the consumer has no specific opinion.

In the Indian context, consumers value the perceived value and quality of products. They consider factors such as durability, price, brand reputation, and value for money. Marketers should emphasize the unique selling propositions and benefits of their offerings to differentiate themselves from competitors and attract consumers' attention.

- **Purchase Decision:**

Once the alternatives are evaluated, consumers make their purchase decision. Factors influencing this decision include the information gathered, perceived value, and product features that align with their needs. However, the decision-making process may also be influenced by the quality of the shopping experience, store ambiance (for offline purchases), availability of promotions, return policies, and favourable terms and conditions.

For example, a consumer intending to buy a stereo from a well-known brand may change their decision if they have a negative experience with the salesperson in the store. Similarly, a promotion for a particular yogurt brand in a supermarket could sway a consumer who was considering multiple options within their evoked set.

- **Post-Purchase Behaviour:**

After purchasing and using the product, consumers evaluate its adequacy in meeting their original needs. They assess whether the product lives up to their expectations, leading to feelings of satisfaction or disappointment. This evaluation influences their future buying behaviour and brand loyalty. If the product meets or exceeds expectations, consumers are likely to experience satisfaction and become loyal to the brand. This may result in reduced information search and alternative evaluation for future purchases, as they stick with the familiar and satisfying choice.
On the other hand, if the product fails to meet expectations, consumers may feel disappointed. In such cases, they may repeat the entire consumer buying process for their next purchase, excluding the unsatisfactory brand from their evoked set.

In the Indian market, post-purchase behaviour is particularly important. Consumers value trust and quality, and their opinions can greatly impact brand reputation. Marketers should focus on delivering exceptional customer experiences, addressing any post-purchase concerns promptly, and continuously engaging with consumers to maintain their loyalty.

## Types of Buying Behaviour:

Consumer buying behaviour can be categorized into four types based on the level of consumer involvement and the differences perceived among brands. Understanding these types of buying behaviour helps marketers tailor their strategies and tactics to effectively engage and influence consumers. Let's explore each type in detail:

- ## **Complex Buying Behaviour:**

Complex buying behaviour occurs when consumers are highly involved in a purchase and perceive significant differences among brands. This typically happens when the product is expensive, bought infrequently, risky, and highly self-expressive. In such cases, consumers have limited knowledge about the product category and need to go through a learning process to make an informed decision. They develop beliefs, attitudes, and carefully evaluate various brands before making a thoughtful purchase choice.

For example, when purchasing a new car, consumers may spend a considerable amount of time researching different brands, comparing features, reading reviews, and test driving various models. The marketer of a high-involvement product needs to understand the information-gathering and evaluation behaviour of these consumers. Strategies should focus on providing detailed information about the product's attributes, highlighting the brand's benefits, using print media for communication, and leveraging sales personnel and acquaintances to influence the final brand choice.

- ## **Dissonance-Reducing Buying Behaviour:**

Dissonance-reducing buying behaviour occurs when consumers are highly involved in a purchase but perceive little difference among brands. Similar to complex buying behaviour, this arises when the purchase is expensive, infrequent, and involves risk. Consumers may shop around to gather information but make a relatively quick purchase decision because brand differences are not significant. They may prioritize a good price or purchase convenience.

After the purchase, consumers might experience dissonance or feelings of discomfort if they notice certain undesirable aspects of the product or hear positive things about competing brands. To reduce dissonance, consumers actively seek information that validates their decision. Marketers should focus on supplying beliefs and evaluations that reinforce the consumer's brand choice and alleviate post-purchase dissonance.

For instance, when buying a high-end smartphone, consumers may compare multiple brands and models but ultimately make a decision based on price, availability, or personal preference. Marketers can address dissonance by providing after-sales support, offering warranties, and emphasizing the advantages and unique features of their brand.

- **Habitual Buying Behaviour:**

Habitual buying behaviour occurs when consumers have low involvement in a purchase and perceive minimal brand differences. This typically applies to low-cost, frequently purchased products that consumers buy out of habit rather than strong brand loyalty. Consumers have little interest or involvement in the product category and often reach for the same brand out of familiarity and convenience.

For example, when buying salt, consumers typically choose a brand without much thought or evaluation because the product is perceived as homogeneous. They may not even evaluate the choice after purchase since they have low involvement with the product. Marketers of low-involvement products with few brand differences rely on price and sales promotions to stimulate product trial, as consumers are not strongly committed to any particular brand.

- **Variety-Seeking Buying Behaviour:**

Variety-seeking buying behaviour occurs when consumers have low involvement in a purchase but perceive significant brand differences. In such cases, consumers may engage in frequent brand switching to seek variety rather than due to dissatisfaction. They may have some beliefs about the brands, make choices without extensive evaluation, and evaluate the chosen brand during consumption. However, for the next purchase, they may switch to another brand out of boredom or a desire for a different experience.

For example, when buying cookies, consumers may try different brands to satisfy their cravings for variety or different tastes. Marketers need to adopt different strategies based on their market position. Market leaders focus on encouraging habitual buying behaviour by dominating shelf space, ensuring product availability, and using reminder advertising. Challenger firms, on the other hand, encourage variety-seeking by offering lower prices, deals, coupons, free samples, and advertising that highlights reasons to try something new.

## Pricing Strategies:

Effective pricing strategies are vital for businesses to thrive in today's competitive market. The way products and services are priced can influence customer perception, demand, and ultimately, revenue generation. From adopting innovative approaches to setting competitive prices, businesses employ various strategies to entice customers and gain a competitive edge. Let's explore some of these strategies and their relevance in the Indian market.

- **Skimming the Cream Pricing:**

Skimming the cream pricing is a strategy where a producer sets a high initial price for a new high-end or uniquely differentiated product. This approach is often used for products like luxury perfumes or advanced technical gadgets. The objective is to generate maximum revenue from the market before substitute products appear. Once the market potential is tapped and competition intensifies, the producer can lower the price significantly to capture the lower-end buyers and discourage copycat competitors. For example, when Apple launches a new iPhone model in India, it initially prices it at a premium to attract early adopters before gradually reducing the price to appeal to a wider customer base.

- **Market Penetration Strategy:**

Market penetration strategy focuses on achieving a high volume of sales and deep market penetration for a new product. This approach involves widespread promotion and setting an introductory price that is comparatively low. It is based on the assumption that the product doesn't have a specific price-market segment, exhibits elasticity of demand, and has a market large enough to sustain lower profit margins. The strategy also relies on the expectation that competitors will soon lower their prices. An example of market penetration strategy in India is the launch of a new smartphone with an aggressive pricing strategy to quickly gain market share by offering competitive features at a relatively lower price compared to established brands.

- **Psychological Pricing:**

Psychological pricing is a method based on the belief that certain price points or ranges are more appealing to buyers. This strategy involves setting prices that end in odd numbers, just below round even numbers, such as pricing a product at Rs. 49.95 instead of Rs. 50.00. Although not backed by research findings, proponents of psychological pricing claim that consumers perceive a price of Rs. 49.95 as 'just above Rs. 40' rather than 'just below Rs. 50.' This tactic creates a perception of a lower price, even though the difference may be minimal. Many Indian retailers, especially in the e-commerce sector, adopt psychological pricing techniques to make their products appear more affordable and psychologically appealing to customers.

- **Differential Pricing Strategy:**

Differential pricing involves setting different prices for a product based on various factors such as customer type, quantity ordered, delivery time, or payment terms. This strategy is also known as discriminatory pricing or multiple pricing. In the Indian context, variable pricing is commonly observed, where different prices are charged for the same product in different stores, markets, or zones. Retailers may also offer discounts for bulk purchases or introduce time-specific discounts such as happy hour or closing time discounts for perishable items. For instance, a supermarket in India may offer discounted prices on groceries during specific hours of the day to attract customers during off-peak hours.

- **One Price Strategy:**

The one price strategy entails offering the same price to every customer who purchases the product under the same conditions. This approach eliminates price negotiation and ensures consistency in pricing across the customer base. One price policy promotes transparency and avoids potential disputes arising from price discrimination. For example, travel agencies in India often follow a one price strategy for holiday packages, where the advertised price is inclusive of all costs, including airport taxes and charges. This strategy provides customers with a clear understanding of the total cost of the package without any hidden fees.

- **Premium/Discount Pricing Strategy:**

The premium pricing strategy involves setting a higher price for a product to create an aura of exclusivity, prestige, or snob appeal. This strategy is commonly observed in industries like high-end perfumes, luxury jewellery, clothing, or cars. By positioning the product as exclusive and high-quality, companies can target affluent consumers who are willing to pay a premium for perceived status and luxury. Conversely, discount pricing is a strategy where a product is initially marked up artificially but is then offered at a reduced cost to create a perception of value for the customers. For instance, luxury fashion brands in India may adopt premium pricing strategies for their exclusive designer collections, while retail stores may offer discount pricing on apparel items for a limited time to attract new customers and stimulate sales.

- **Leader Pricing:**

Leader pricing is a common strategy used by Indian retailers to attract customers and generate interest in a business or specific product line. It involves setting lower price points and reducing typical profit margins, often resulting in selling products at a loss. These products are referred to as loss leaders. The purpose of leader pricing is to capture customer attention and drive traffic to the store, with the expectation that customers will also purchase other products with higher profit margins. For example, a supermarket might offer discounted prices on staple food items to entice customers into the store, with the hope that they will also buy other groceries at regular prices.

- **Everyday Low Pricing (EDLP):**

Everyday low pricing (EDLP) is a pricing strategy commonly employed by retail stores in India. Under this strategy, prices are set low and remain consistent every day without the need for special pricing discounts, sales, or price comparisons. The goal of EDLP is to convince consumers that the store offers better and consistently low prices compared to competitors. While competitors may provide periodic promotions with lower prices, EDLP emphasizes the everyday low prices as a long-term advantage. Retail chains like Big Bazaar in India adopt the EDLP strategy to attract and retain price-conscious customers by offering affordable prices on a wide range of products without the need to wait for sales or discounts.

# Segmentation:

Segmentation is a crucial concept in marketing that involves dividing a heterogeneous market into smaller, more homogeneous segments based on certain characteristics or criteria. These segments can then be targeted with tailored marketing strategies to maximize customer satisfaction and business profitability. Market segmentation allows companies to understand their customers better, identify their needs and preferences, and deliver customized offerings. In the Indian context, where diverse consumer groups exist, effective segmentation is particularly important for businesses to effectively cater to the unique needs and preferences of different segments.

There are several bases of market segmentation commonly used in the industry.

- **Geographic Segmentation:**

This involves dividing the market based on geographic factors such as location, climate, population density, or regional characteristics. For example, a beverage company might target different regions in India based on climate conditions. They may promote hot beverages in colder regions like Himachal Pradesh and cold beverages in hotter regions like Rajasthan.

- **Demographic Segmentation:**

Demographic factors such as age, gender, income, occupation, education, and family size are used to segment the market. For instance, a cosmetic brand may target women aged 25-40 with higher income levels who are more likely to be interested in premium beauty products.

- **Sociographic Segmentation:**

Sociographic segmentation considers social and lifestyle factors such as values, beliefs, social class, and lifestyle choices. For example, a luxury car manufacturer may target individuals belonging to high social classes who value prestige and exclusivity.

- ## **Behavioural Segmentation:**

Behavioural segmentation divides the market based on consumer behaviour, including usage patterns, brand loyalty, benefits sought, and occasions of use. An example of this could be a toothpaste brand targeting consumers who seek whitening benefits or cavity protection.

- ## **Psychographic Segmentation:**

Psychographic segmentation focuses on consumers' personality traits, attitudes, motivations, and interests. For instance, a travel agency may target adventure enthusiasts who seek thrilling experiences and outdoor activities.

In addition to the bases of segmentation, there are various types of market segmentation used by businesses:

- ## **Benefits Sought Segmentation:**

This type of segmentation categorizes customers based on the specific benefits they seek from a product or service. For instance, a smartphone manufacturer may target tech-savvy individuals seeking advanced features, while also targeting budget-conscious consumers looking for affordability.

- ## **Gender Segmentation:**

This involves segmenting the market based on gender. Businesses often create products and marketing campaigns tailored specifically for men or women. For example, a clothing brand may offer separate lines of apparel for men and women.

- ## **Income, Lifestyle & Social Class Segmentation:**

This segmentation strategy divides the market based on income levels, lifestyle choices, and social class. For instance, a luxury watch brand may target high-income individuals belonging to the upper class who value luxury and prestige.

- ## **Occasion Segmentation:**

Occasion segmentation involves targeting customers based on specific occasions or events. For example, a confectionery brand may introduce special gift packages during festive seasons like Diwali or Christmas.

- **Interests/Opinions Segmentation:**

This type of segmentation considers consumers' interests, hobbies, and opinions. For instance, a fitness equipment company may target individuals interested in health and wellness or those who prefer eco-friendly products.

- **Usage Segmentation:**

Usage segmentation divides the market based on consumers' usage patterns, such as heavy users, moderate users, or non-users of a product or service. For example, a mobile network provider may offer different plans and packages to cater to different usage levels.

# Targeting:

Targeting is a critical step in the marketing process that involves selecting specific market segments to focus on with tailored marketing strategies. It is the process of identifying and evaluating different segments within a market and then choosing one or more segments that align with the company's objectives and capabilities. Effective targeting allows businesses to allocate their resources efficiently, reach the most relevant audience, and create offerings that meet the specific needs and preferences of the selected target market.
There are five patterns of target market selection that businesses can adopt:

- **Single Segment Concentration:**

This targeting pattern involves selecting a single market segment and directing all marketing efforts towards that segment. The company concentrates its resources, products, and marketing messages on serving the unique needs and preferences of this specific segment. For example, a company may exclusively target luxury car buyers and position its products as high-end and exclusive.

- **Selective Specialization:**

Under selective specialization, a company targets a few distinct segments that share some common characteristics or needs. The company tailors its marketing strategies to meet the requirements of these chosen segments effectively. For instance, a fashion brand might target both young professionals seeking trendy workwear and fashion-forward teenagers looking for casual wear.

- **Market Specialization:**

Market specialization involves focusing on a specific market segment within a particular industry or market. The company aims to become an expert in serving this particular segment and tailors its products, marketing messages, and distribution channels to meet their specific needs. For example, a software company specializing in accounting software exclusively targets small and medium-sized businesses.

- **Product Specialization:**

Product specialization occurs when a company focuses on a specific product or product line to serve multiple market segments. The company develops deep expertise in producing and marketing a specific product category. For instance, a company specializing in fitness equipment might offer a range of exercise machines, targeting various segments such as home users, fitness centers, and rehabilitation centers.

- **Full Coverage (Mass Marketing):**

Full coverage, also known as mass marketing, involves targeting the entire market with a single marketing mix. This strategy assumes that the target market shares similar needs and preferences and can be effectively reached with a standardized marketing approach. Mass marketing is often used for products or services with universal appeal or where customization is not feasible. For example, basic household products like salt or sugar are typically marketed to the mass market without segmenting the audience.

It is essential for businesses to carefully evaluate each targeting pattern and select the most suitable one based on their resources, capabilities, market dynamics, and competitive landscape. The chosen targeting pattern should align with the company's goals and allow them to effectively meet the needs of the selected target market.

# Positioning:

Once the target market is identified, positioning comes into play. Positioning is the process of creating a distinctive image and identity for a product or brand in the minds of the target customers. It involves establishing a unique and favourable perception of the product or brand compared to competitors in the market. There are several positioning approaches or strategies that businesses can adopt:

- **Positioning by Attributes, Features, or Customer Benefits:**
This approach focuses on highlighting the unique attributes, features, or customer benefits of a product or brand. The goal is to position the offering as superior and distinct based on specific characteristics that are important to the target market. For example, a mobile phone company may emphasize the high-quality camera, long battery life, and advanced security features of their product to position it as the best choice for photography enthusiasts.

- **Positioning by Price:**
Positioning by price involves positioning the product or brand based on its price point relative to competitors. This strategy is commonly used when a company wants to position itself as offering the best value for money, either by offering lower prices or by positioning as a premium brand with higher prices. For instance, a budget airline may position itself as a low-cost carrier, appealing to price-sensitive travellers who prioritize affordability.

- **Positioning according to the Users' Category:**
This approach involves positioning the product or brand based on the specific category or group of users it targets. The goal is to create a strong association between the product and the target users. For example, a skincare brand may position its products specifically for sensitive skin or for the aging population, catering to the unique needs of these user categories.

- ## Positioning by Emotional Appeal:

Emotional positioning aims to create an emotional connection with the target market. It focuses on evoking specific emotions, values, or aspirations in consumers to differentiate the product or brand. For example, a soft drink brand may position itself as a symbol of happiness and joy, associating its product with positive emotions and memorable experiences.

- ## Positioning According to Use:

Positioning by use involves associating the product or brand with a specific use or application. It highlights how the product can fulfil a particular need or solve a specific problem for the target market. For instance, a pain relief balm may position itself as a reliable solution for quick pain relief, targeting individuals with muscle aches and joint pains.

- ## Positioning Against Competition:

This strategy involves positioning the product or brand as a superior alternative to competitors in the market. It emphasizes the unique advantages and benefits that set the offering apart from competitors. For example, a detergent brand may position itself as providing better stain removal compared to other brands, targeting consumers who prioritize effective cleaning performance.

- ## Head-to-Head Positioning:

Head-to-head positioning aims to directly compete with a specific competitor by highlighting similar attributes or features. This strategy is effective when the product or brand can offer comparable quality or benefits to the competitor, positioning itself as a viable alternative. For example, a smartphone brand may position its product as a worthy competitor to a well-established brand, offering similar features at a lower price point.

- ## Differentiation Positioning:

Differentiation positioning focuses on highlighting unique and distinctive qualities of the product or brand that make it stand out from competitors. It aims to create a perception of exclusivity and uniqueness in the target market. For instance, a luxury car brand may position itself as the epitome of elegance, luxury, and superior craftsmanship, targeting affluent consumers who value prestige.

- **Positioning by Endorsement:**

Positioning by endorsement involves leveraging the reputation and credibility of influential individuals or organizations to position the product or brand positively. This strategy aims to build trust and credibility among the target market by associating the offering with respected endorsers. For example, a celebrity chef endorsing a cooking appliance can enhance its positioning as a high-quality and reliable product.

- **Positioning by Physical Evidence:**

Positioning by physical evidence focuses on highlighting tangible elements associated with the product or brand to create a favourable perception. It involves emphasizing the quality, design, packaging, or physical appearance of the offering to differentiate it from competitors. For instance, a luxury watch brand may position its products based on their exquisite craftsmanship, intricate detailing, and premium materials.

- **Positioning Process:**

The positioning process involves identifying the target market, conducting market research to understand customer needs and preferences, analysing competitors, and developing a positioning strategy that aligns with the company's objectives. It requires careful market analysis, brand positioning statements, effective communication, and continuous evaluation to ensure the desired positioning is achieved.

- **Leadership Positioning:**

Leadership positioning aims to position the product or brand as the market leader or industry expert. It involves emphasizing market dominance, industry expertise, and innovation to create a perception of superiority in the minds of the target market. For example, an electronics brand may position itself as the leading innovator in the market, offering cutting-edge technology and setting industry trends.

- **Excellence Positioning:**

Excellence positioning focuses on positioning the product or brand as the benchmark for quality, performance, and reliability. It emphasizes consistent delivery of superior products and services to establish a reputation for excellence. For instance, a premium automobile brand may position itself as a symbol of engineering excellence and precision manufacturing, targeting consumers who prioritize exceptional quality.

- **Positioning by Social Values:**

This approach involves aligning the product or brand with specific social values or causes that resonate with the target market. It aims to create an emotional connection based on shared values, such as environmental sustainability, social responsibility, or inclusivity. For example, a skincare brand may position itself as cruelty-free and environmentally friendly, appealing to consumers who prioritize ethical and sustainable choices.

# Chapter 15: Marketing Jargons

Marketing is an essential aspect of any business, and startups are no exception. In fact, marketing plays a crucial role in the success or failure of a startup. It is the process of creating, communicating, and delivering value to customers to fulfil their needs and wants. Without effective marketing, even the best products or services may fail to gain traction in the market.

For entrepreneurs, marketing your startup can be a daunting task, especially with so many jargons and concepts to understand. Let's dwell into some of the common jargons used while marketing your business.

## AB Testing:

AB testing is a way to compare two different things to see which one is better. In the world of business, this can mean testing two different versions of a website or an app to see which one works better. It is useful for businesses because it allows them to make data-driven decisions about what works best for their customers. By testing different things and measuring the results, they can make changes that will help them make more money.

For example, let's say a company has a website where people can buy things. They want to know if changing the colour of the "buy" button from blue to green will make more people buy things. So, they create two versions of the website, one with a blue button and one with a green button, and show each version to different groups of people. Then they can see which version made more people buy things.

## Account-Based Marketing (ABM):

Account-Based Marketing (ABM) is a marketing strategy that focuses on individual accounts or customers, rather than on a larger group. It's a way to personalize marketing efforts and make them more effective. It allows them to focus their marketing efforts on the customers who are most likely to buy their product. By creating personalized marketing materials and using targeted advertising, they can increase the effectiveness of their marketing efforts and make more sales.

For example, let's say a company sells software to other businesses. Instead of trying to market the software to a large group of businesses, they might use ABM to target individual businesses that would be a good fit for their product. They would create marketing materials that are specific to each individual business, and use targeted advertising to reach the people who are most likely to be interested in their product.

## Ad Targeting:

Ad targeting is a way to show advertisements to people who are most likely to be interested in them. Advertisers can use a variety of information to target their ads, including demographics (like age, gender, and location), interests (like hobbies and activities), and online behaviour (like what websites a person visits). It helps them to reach the people who are most likely to be interested in their product. By showing ads to the right people, they can increase the effectiveness of their advertising campaigns and make more sales.

For example, let's say a company sells shoes. They might use ad targeting to show their ads to people who have recently searched for shoes online, or who have shown an interest in fashion. By targeting their ads in this way, they can increase the chances that the people who see their ads will be interested in buying their shoes.

## AdWords:

AdWords is a type of online advertising that allows businesses to create ads that are displayed on search engine results pages. When people search for specific keywords, AdWords ads can appear at the top or bottom of the search results. By appearing at the top of search results, they can increase the chances that people will click on their ad and make a purchase. Additionally, AdWords allows businesses to track the effectiveness of their ads and make changes to improve their performance over time.

For example, let's say a company sells flowers online. They might use AdWords to create an ad that appears at the top of search results when people search for "buy flowers online." By using AdWords, they can increase the visibility of their business and attract more customers.

## Affiliate Marketing:

Have you ever seen a famous YouTuber or an Instagram influencer promoting a product or service in their videos or posts? Well, that's called affiliate marketing! It is a marketing technique where a company partners with an individual or a group of people (usually influencers) to promote their products or services. In this marketing technique, the individual or group promotes the product through their social media platforms, blogs or websites. They share a unique link or code with their audience, which they can use to purchase the product. If someone purchases the product using that link, the company pays the individual or group a commission for each sale made through their unique link.

For example, let's say there's a YouTuber named Rishi who loves to travel and makes videos about his travels. A travel company might approach Rishi to promote their tour packages in his videos. Rishi then shares the company's unique link or code in his videos, and if someone uses that link or code to book a tour package, Rishi gets a commission from the travel company.

## Algorithm:

An algorithm is like a set of instructions that a computer or machine follows to complete a task or solve a problem. You can think of it like a recipe that tells a computer what to do to achieve a certain outcome. Algorithms are used in various industries, including marketing, to improve efficiency and productivity.

In marketing, algorithms are used to analyse data and improve targeting. For example, social media platforms like Facebook and Instagram use algorithms to show users content that is relevant to their interests. These algorithms take into account various factors like the user's age, location, interests, and previous interactions on the platform to show them content that they are most likely to engage with.

## Attribution:

Attribution in marketing refers to giving credit to the marketing channel that contributed the most to a conversion or sale. A conversion can be defined as a desired action taken by a customer, like purchasing a product or filling out a form.

For example, let's say a customer came across a product through a Facebook ad and clicked on the ad to visit the company's website. They didn't make a purchase at that time but returned to the website a week later through a Google search and made a purchase. In this case, attribution gives credit to both the Facebook ad and the Google search for contributing to the sale.

## Audience Segmentation:

Audience segmentation is the process of dividing a target audience into smaller groups based on certain characteristics like age, gender, location, interests, etc. The goal of audience segmentation is to create more personalized and targeted marketing messages for each group.

For example, let's say a company sells both men's and women's clothing. They can use audience segmentation to create separate marketing campaigns for men and women, highlighting the specific products that would appeal to each group. By doing this, they can increase the effectiveness of their marketing campaigns by creating messages that resonate with each audience segment.

## Below the Line (BTL):

In marketing, there are two types of advertising techniques- Above the Line (ATL) and Below the Line (BTL). Above the Line techniques include traditional methods such as television, radio, print, and online advertising. Below the Line techniques are unconventional methods such as events, sponsorships, direct mail, and more.

One example of Below the Line marketing technique in India is the Hindustan Unilever's "Kan Khajura Tesan" campaign. The campaign used mobile phones to reach people in rural India who had no access to traditional media like television or radio. HUL created a missed call number, which when dialled would play entertaining content such as jokes, music, and ads. The campaign was a massive success and reached millions of people in rural areas.

## Billboard:

A billboard is a large outdoor advertising structure used to promote products, services, or brands. They are usually placed in high-traffic areas, such as busy roads, highways, and city centers. Billboards can come in various sizes, from small posters to large digital displays. They can also be static or dynamic, featuring changing messages and images.

An example of a creative billboard advertisement in India is the FeviKwik "Todo Nahi, Jodo" campaign. The billboard featured two broken parts of a pencil and a message that read "Todo nahi, Jodo" which means "Don't break it, fix it." The advertisement was a play on words and the FeviKwik brand's tagline, "FeviKwik jodne wala glue."

## Bot:

A bot is short for "robot," which is a computer program designed to automate tasks. Bots can be programmed to perform a variety of functions, such as customer service, data collection, and social media engagement. Bots can be used to improve efficiency, reduce costs, and provide better customer experiences.

One example of a bot in India is the HDFC Bank's "Eva" bot. Eva is an AI-powered chatbot that can answer customers' queries, provide account information, and help them with various banking services. Eva has been very successful, helping HDFC Bank reduce response times and improve customer satisfaction.

## Brand Awareness:

Brand awareness is the level of familiarity and recognition that customers have with a brand. It is essential for a brand to have high levels of brand awareness to attract new customers and retain existing ones. There are many ways to increase brand awareness, such as advertising, sponsorships, social media, and more.

One example of brand awareness in India is the "KitKat" brand. The brand has created several memorable campaigns, such as "Have a Break, Have a KitKat," which has been around for over 60 years. The brand has also collaborated with popular Bollywood movies, featuring the product in the films and leveraging the stars' popularity. KitKat has created a strong emotional connection with its customers, making it one of the most popular chocolate brands in India.

## Brand Equity:

Brand equity is the value of a brand. It is the added value that a brand name gives to a product or service. In other words, it is the difference between the price that consumers are willing to pay for a product with a particular brand name and the price they are willing to pay for a similar product without that brand name. Brands with high brand equity are valuable assets to a company, and they can help to generate more revenue.

For example, let's take the case of a smartphone brand like Apple. Apple has built a strong brand over the years, and people are willing to pay a premium for Apple products. The brand equity of Apple is high, and it helps the company to charge a premium price for their products.

## Brand Identity:

Brand identity is the visual representation of a brand. It includes the name, logo, colours, design, packaging, and other visual elements that create a distinct image of the brand in the minds of consumers. Brand identity helps to differentiate a brand from its competitors and create a unique image.

For example, the brand identity of Coca-Cola includes its iconic red and white logo, the unique shape of its bottle, and the colour and design of its packaging. These visual elements help consumers to easily recognize Coca-Cola products and differentiate them from other soft drinks.

## Brand Image:

Brand image is the perception of a brand in the minds of consumers. It is the sum of all the impressions and experiences that consumers have with a brand. A positive brand image can help to build trust and loyalty among consumers, while a negative brand image can damage a brand's reputation and sales.

For example, the brand image of Google is associated with innovation, reliability, and simplicity. Consumers trust Google to provide accurate and relevant search results and to protect their privacy. This positive brand image has helped Google to become one of the most valuable brands in the world.

## Brand Loyalty:

Brand loyalty is the degree to which consumers are loyal to a particular brand. It is the willingness of consumers to repeatedly buy products from the same brand, even if there are other options available. Brand loyalty is important for companies because it can help to increase sales and revenue.

For example, Apple has a strong brand loyalty among its customers. Many Apple users are willing to pay a premium for Apple products because they trust the brand and are loyal to it. This loyalty has helped Apple to maintain its position as one of the most valuable brands in the world.

## Brand Management:

Brand management is the process of creating, developing, maintaining, and enhancing a brand's image and reputation. It includes strategies and techniques used to build, manage, and maintain a brand in the market. The ultimate goal of brand management is to create a strong brand that is recognizable, trustworthy, and influential.

For example, when we think of Nike, we immediately associate it with high-quality sports shoes and clothing. This is due to Nike's effective brand management, which includes consistent messaging and branding across all platforms, sponsorships of high-profile athletes and sports events, and a focus on innovation and quality in their products.

## Brand Positioning:

Brand positioning refers to the way a brand is perceived in the minds of consumers. It is the process of creating a unique identity and image for a brand in the marketplace. Brand positioning is a critical component of marketing strategy, as it determines how consumers will perceive and interact with a brand.

For example, if we think of a soft drink brand like Coca-Cola, its brand positioning is all about happiness and sharing good times with family and friends. Coca-Cola's marketing campaigns focus on bringing people together and enjoying moments of happiness, and this positioning has helped to create a strong emotional connection with consumers.

## Branding:

Branding refers to the process of creating a unique name, design, symbol, or other feature that identifies and distinguishes a product or service from others in the market. It is a way of creating an identity for a product or service that sets it apart from its competitors.

For example, when we think of a brand like McDonald's, we immediately recognize its iconic logo, colours, and packaging. McDonald's has invested heavily in branding to create a strong identity and image for its products, which has helped to make it one of the most recognizable and successful brands in the world.

## Bounce Rate:

Bounce rate refers to the percentage of visitors to a website who leave after viewing only one page. It is a metric used to measure the effectiveness of a website in engaging visitors and encouraging them to stay on the site and explore further. A high bounce rate indicates that visitors are not finding what they are looking for or are not engaged with the content on the site.

For example, if a website has a bounce rate of 70%, it means that 70% of visitors left the site after viewing only one page. This could be due to a number of factors, such as slow loading times, poor navigation, irrelevant or uninteresting content, or a lack of clear calls to action. By analysing bounce rates, website owners can identify areas for improvement and make changes to improve engagement and user experience.

## B2B:

Business-to-Business (B2B) is a term used to describe transactions that take place between two businesses. For example, when a company that makes computer chips sells them to a company that manufactures computers, it is a B2B transaction. B2B transactions typically involve larger quantities of goods and services than B2C transactions and often require negotiations between the two parties.

## B2C:

Business-to-Consumer (B2C) is a term used to describe transactions that take place between a business and individual consumers. For example, when you buy a pair of shoes from an online retailer, it is a B2C transaction. B2C transactions typically involve smaller quantities of goods and services and often rely on marketing and advertising to reach individual consumers.

## Business-to-Government (B2G):

Business-to-Government (B2G) is a term used to describe transactions that take place between a business and a government entity. For example, when a company provides software to a government agency, it is a B2G transaction. B2G transactions often involve bidding processes and compliance with government regulations.

## Business-to-Institution (B2I):

Business-to-Institution (B2I) is a term used to describe transactions that take place between a business and institutional customers, such as schools or hospitals. For example, when a company provides office supplies to a hospital, it is a B2I transaction. B2I transactions often require specialized products or services that meet the needs of the institutional customer.

## Business-to-Small Business (B2SB):

Business-to-Small Business (B2SB) is a term used to describe transactions that take place between a larger business and a smaller business. For example, when a supplier sells products to a local retail store, it is a B2SB transaction. B2SB transactions often involve smaller quantities of goods and services and require the smaller business to rely on the larger business for support and resources.

## Buyer Persona:

A buyer persona is a fictional representation of your ideal customer. It is based on data and research on your target audience's behaviour, goals, interests, and demographics. Buyer personas are created to help businesses better understand their customers' needs and preferences so they can create more effective marketing campaigns and tailor their products or services to meet those needs.

For example, let's say you own a toy company in India that sells educational toys for children. Your buyer persona might be a busy parent who values education and wants their child to learn through play. By understanding your buyer persona, you can create marketing materials that appeal to their interests and needs, such as a video ad showcasing the educational benefits of your toys.

## Buyer's Journey:

The buyer's journey refers to the process that a customer goes through before making a purchase. It includes three stages: awareness, consideration, and decision. During the awareness stage, the customer becomes aware of a problem or need they have. In the consideration stage, they research and evaluate different solutions. And in the decision stage, they make a purchase decision.

For example, if someone wants to buy a new phone, their buyer's journey might begin when they realize their current phone is slow and outdated. They then start researching different phone brands and models, comparing features and prices. Finally, they make a decision and purchase the phone that best fits their needs and budget.

## Call-to-Action:

A call-to-action (CTA) is a button, link, or statement that encourages the user to take a specific action, such as making a purchase, subscribing to a newsletter, or filling out a form. CTAs are designed to grab the user's attention and prompt them to take action. They are an essential part of any marketing campaign as they help businesses generate leads and conversions.

For example, if you are running a campaign for a yoga studio in India, your CTA might be "Sign up for a free yoga class today!" This CTA prompts the user to take action and sign up for a class, ultimately leading to more customers for the business.

## Campaign:

A campaign is a coordinated set of activities that are designed to achieve a specific marketing goal. It can be a one-time event or an ongoing effort, and it can be executed through various channels such as email, social media, print ads, or TV commercials.

For example, a food delivery company in India might launch a campaign during the festival season to promote their services. The campaign might include social media posts, email newsletters, and discounts for customers who order during the festival period. The goal of the campaign is to increase sales and attract new customers.

## Chatbot:

A chatbot is a computer program that uses artificial intelligence (AI) to communicate with users via a messaging app or website chat interface. Chatbots are designed to provide automated customer support and assistance, answer questions, and complete simple tasks, such as booking appointments or making purchases.

For example, a food delivery service might use a chatbot on their website to help customers place an order, track their delivery, and provide recommendations based on their previous orders.

## Churn rate:

Churn rate is a measure of customer attrition or the rate at which customers stop doing business with a company over a given period. It is usually expressed as a percentage of the total number of customers.

For example, a mobile service provider may have a churn rate of 2% per month, which means that 2% of their customers stop using their service each month. This can be due to various reasons such as poor customer service, high prices, or better offerings from competitors.

## Click Fraud:

Click fraud is a type of online fraud in which individuals or bots repeatedly click on an online ad with the intention of driving up the advertiser's costs or sabotaging their campaign. This can result in inflated advertising costs for the advertiser, as they are paying for clicks that are not genuine.

For example, a competitor might engage in click fraud to exhaust the advertising budget of a rival company, making it harder for them to reach their target audience. Alternatively, bots might be programmed to click on ads automatically, artificially inflating the number of clicks and impressions. Advertisers use various tools and technologies to detect and prevent click fraud.

## Click-through rate (CTR):

Click-through rate (CTR) is a marketing metric that measures the percentage of people who click on a specific link, usually an ad or a call-to-action (CTA), to visit a website or landing page. CTR is a useful indicator of how successful an advertising campaign is at generating traffic and interest in a product or service. A high CTR means that a larger proportion of people who saw the ad or CTA clicked on it, while a low CTR indicates that the ad may not be resonating with the target audience.

For example, if an ad is displayed to 100 people and 10 of them click on it to visit a website, the CTR is 10%. A higher CTR indicates that the ad is more engaging and relevant to the audience and may lead to more conversions or sales.

## Collateral:

Collateral refers to any marketing material used to promote a product or service, such as brochures, flyers, catalogs, and presentations. The purpose of collateral is to provide information about a product or service to potential customers, and to persuade them to take a desired action, such as making a purchase or requesting more information.

For example, a real estate company may use a brochure to showcase different properties and their features to potential buyers. The brochure may include high-quality images, detailed descriptions, and contact information for the company. By providing this collateral, the real estate company can generate interest in the properties and encourage potential buyers to take the next step in the sales process.

## Commercial:

A commercial is a type of advertisement that is broadcasted on television or radio. The purpose of a commercial is to promote a product or service to a large audience in a short amount of time. Commercials often use a combination of visual and audio cues to capture the attention of viewers and communicate the message of the advertisement.

For example, a soft drink company may create a commercial that features young people having fun and drinking their product on a beach. The commercial may use upbeat music, bright colours, and shots of people laughing and enjoying themselves to convey the message that the drink is fun and refreshing. The goal of the commercial is to create a positive association with the brand and encourage people to buy the product.

## Conversion Funnel:

A conversion funnel refers to the path that a user takes to complete a specific action on a website or online platform, such as making a purchase or filling out a form. The funnel consists of several stages, each representing a step closer to the desired action, and includes different elements such as landing pages, calls to action, and forms.

Imagine that you are planning to buy a toy online. You start by searching for a toy store, then visit their website and browse through different products. Once you find the toy you want, you add it to your cart and proceed to checkout, where you enter your payment and shipping information. This entire process is an example of a conversion funnel.

## Conversion Optimization:

Conversion optimization refers to the process of improving the conversion rate of a website or online platform by optimizing different elements such as content, design, and user experience. The goal of conversion optimization is to increase the percentage of users who take a desired action, such as making a purchase or subscribing to a service.

For example, if an e-commerce website has a high number of visitors but a low conversion rate, conversion optimization techniques can be used to identify the factors that are hindering conversions and to improve them. This can include making changes to the website's layout, simplifying the checkout process, or offering more compelling calls to action.

## Conversion Rate:

The conversion rate refers to the percentage of users who complete a desired action on a website or online platform, such as making a purchase or filling out a form. The conversion rate is calculated by dividing the number of conversions by the number of total visitors, and is a key metric for measuring the effectiveness of a website or online campaign.

For example, if an online store has 1000 visitors and 50 of them make a purchase, the conversion rate would be 5%. A high conversion rate indicates that the website or campaign is successful in engaging and converting users, while a low conversion rate may indicate issues with user experience or messaging.

## Cost Per Action (CPA):

Cost Per Action (CPA) is a marketing metric that measures the cost of acquiring a customer who performs a specific action on a website or online platform, such as making a purchase or filling out a form. CPA is calculated by dividing the total cost of a campaign by the number of conversions, and is commonly used in affiliate marketing and other performance-based advertising models.

For example, if a company spends $1000 on a social media advertising campaign that generates 100 conversions, the CPA would be $10 per conversion. CPA can be used to measure the effectiveness of different advertising campaigns and channels, as well as to optimize marketing budgets and ROI.

## Cost Per Acquisition (CPA):

CPA stands for Cost Per Acquisition, which is the cost an advertiser pays for every conversion or sale that is made. It is a pricing model used in digital advertising, where the advertiser only pays when a desired action is completed. For example, a company running an online shopping website might pay a fixed amount to an advertising platform each time a customer makes a purchase through their ad. The CPA model ensures that the advertiser only pays for the actual conversions made rather than just ad impressions or clicks.

For instance, a company might run a CPA campaign to increase the number of signups for its new service. They can set up an ad campaign on social media and pay for every user who signs up for their service through the ad. This way, the company can track the number of people who signed up through the ad and only pay for those who converted.

## Cost Per Click (CPC):

Cost Per Click (CPC) is a pricing model used in digital advertising, where the advertiser pays a fixed amount every time a user clicks on their ad. CPC is commonly used in search engine advertising, such as Google Ads, where the advertiser bids on specific keywords to appear at the top of search results. The advertiser pays only when someone clicks on their ad.

For example, a company that sells sports shoes might run a CPC campaign on Google Ads by bidding on the keyword "sports shoes". The company will pay every time someone clicks on their ad and is directed to their website. The CPC model is a popular way for companies to drive traffic to their website and increase their online visibility.

## Cost Per Impression (CPM):

Cost Per Impression (CPM) is a pricing model used in digital advertising, where the advertiser pays for every thousand times their ad is displayed on a website. CPM is commonly used in display advertising, where advertisers bid to have their banner ads appear on various websites.

For example, a company that sells travel packages might run a CPM campaign by bidding to have their banner ads displayed on travel-related websites. The company will pay every time their ad is displayed to a user on these websites, regardless of whether the user clicks on the ad or not. The CPM model is a popular way for companies to increase their brand awareness and reach a wider audience.

## Cost Per Lead (CPL):

Cost Per Lead (CPL) is a pricing model used in digital advertising, where the advertiser pays for each lead generated through their ad campaign. A lead is a potential customer who has shown interest in the advertiser's product or service by providing their contact information, such as email or phone number. CPL is commonly used in email marketing and affiliate marketing.

For instance, a company that provides home insurance might run a CPL campaign by partnering with a website that offers home buying advice. The company can offer a free home insurance quote in exchange for the user's contact information. The CPL model allows the company to generate leads that are more likely to convert into paying customers.

## Coupon:

A coupon is a small piece of paper or code that can be redeemed to get a discount or special offer on a product or service. Coupons are often used by businesses to attract new customers or reward loyal ones.

For example, a restaurant might offer a coupon for 10% off the total bill to encourage new customers to try their food. Similarly, an online store might offer a coupon code for free shipping or a discount on the first purchase to incentivize new customers to make a purchase.

## Cross-selling:

Cross-selling is the practice of offering additional products or services to a customer who is already buying something from a business. The goal is to increase the value of the sale by suggesting complementary or related items that the customer might also be interested in.

For example, when you buy a new mobile phone, the salesperson might suggest that you also buy a protective case or screen protector. This is a cross-sell because the additional items are related to the main purchase and can improve the customer's experience.

## Customer Acquisition Cost (CAC):

Customer Acquisition Cost (CAC) is the cost a business incurs to acquire a new customer. It is calculated by dividing the total amount spent on sales and marketing by the number of new customers acquired during a specific time period.

For example, if a business spends Rs. 10,000 on marketing and sales in a month and acquires 50 new customers during that time, the CAC would be Rs. 200 per customer.

## Customer Relationship Management (CRM):

Customer Relationship Management (CRM) is a strategy and technology used by businesses to manage their interactions with customers and potential customers. The goal of CRM is to improve customer satisfaction, retention, and loyalty by understanding their needs and preferences.

For example, a business might use a CRM software to track customer interactions, such as phone calls, emails, and social media messages. This allows the business to provide personalized service and support, as well as track customer preferences and behaviours to improve marketing and sales efforts. In India, many businesses use CRM systems to manage their customer relationships and improve their customer experience.

## Customer Segmentation:

Customer segmentation is the process of dividing customers into groups based on their common characteristics such as age, gender, location, interests, behaviour, and more. This helps businesses create targeted marketing strategies that cater to each group's needs, resulting in better engagement and higher sales.

For example, an e-commerce company might segment its customers based on their purchase history. Customers who buy only during sale periods might be targeted with special offers during the non-sale period to entice them to make purchases. Similarly, customers who buy only premium products can be targeted with premium products and luxury services.

## Customer Lifetime Value (CLV):

Customer Lifetime Value (CLV) is the total amount of money that a customer is expected to spend on a business's products or services over their lifetime. It is a key metric for businesses as it helps them understand the long-term value of each customer and determine the amount of resources they should invest in retaining them.

For example, a company that sells subscription-based software might calculate the CLV of each customer by multiplying the average revenue per user by the length of their subscription. By identifying high CLV customers, the company can invest more in retaining them and providing better customer service.

## Database Marketing:

Database marketing is the practice of using customer data to create targeted marketing campaigns. It involves collecting and analysing customer data to understand their behaviour, preferences, and needs. This data is then used to create personalized marketing messages that are more likely to resonate with each customer.

For example, an e-commerce company might use database marketing to create targeted email campaigns. Customers who have previously purchased sports equipment might receive emails about the latest sports gear, while customers who have previously bought kitchen appliances might receive emails about the latest kitchen gadgets.

## Demographic Segmentation:

Demographic segmentation is the process of dividing customers into groups based on their demographic characteristics such as age, gender, income, occupation, education, and more. It is a widely used segmentation technique as it is easy to collect and analyse demographic data.

For example, a company that sells baby products might segment its customers based on their age and gender. New parents might be targeted with offers on diapers and baby formula, while grandparents might be targeted with gifts for their grandkids. Similarly, a luxury car brand might segment its customers based on their income and occupation. Customers with high incomes and executive positions might be targeted with premium models and luxury features.

## Demographics:

Demographics refer to characteristics that define a particular group of people, such as age, gender, income, education, occupation, and more. These characteristics help businesses understand their target audience and create marketing strategies that appeal to their specific needs and preferences. In India, demographics play a crucial role in marketing as India has a diverse population with people from different regions, religions, cultures, and backgrounds.

For example, a business that sells school supplies might target students aged 6-16, who are attending schools in India. They may further segment their audience based on the age group, gender, and location of the students, to tailor their marketing message and product offerings accordingly.

## Direct mail:

Direct mail refers to a type of marketing where businesses send promotional material, such as postcards, flyers, catalogs, or brochures, directly to their target audience through mail. Direct mail campaigns are usually highly targeted and personalized to maximize their effectiveness.

For example, a business that sells fitness supplements might send a direct mail campaign to people who are interested in fitness and healthy living. They may include a coupon code or a special offer to entice people to make a purchase.

## Display Advertising:

Display advertising is a type of online advertising that involves placing ads on websites, social media platforms, or other digital channels. These ads typically include text, images, or videos and are designed to grab the user's attention and drive them to click on the ad, visit the advertiser's website, or take some other desired action. It is an effective way for businesses to increase their brand awareness and reach their target audience. Advertisers can target their ads based on user demographics, interests, and behaviour, making it easier to reach the right people at the right time.

For example, if you are browsing a website for a new toy, you may see an ad for the same toy on another website you visit later. This is an example of display advertising. In India, popular websites like Times of India, NDTV, and Indian Express display ads from various brands.

## Distribution Channel:

A distribution channel is a set of intermediaries that a product or service passes through before reaching the end customer. In other words, it is the path that a product takes from the manufacturer to the consumer. The distribution channel may include wholesalers, retailers, distributors, and other intermediaries. Choosing the right distribution channel is critical for the success of a business. It determines how quickly and efficiently a product can reach its target market and how much control the business has over the product's price and positioning.

For example, if you want to buy a new smartphone, you can purchase it directly from the manufacturer's website or through a distribution channel, such as a retailer like Amazon or a physical store like Croma. In India, smartphone manufacturers like Xiaomi, Samsung, and Apple use various distribution channels to reach their customers.

## Door-to-Door Sales:

Door-to-door sales is a sales technique where a salesperson goes from door to door, selling products or services directly to consumers. This method of sales was popular in the past when many people didn't have access to the internet, and it was the only way to reach customers. However, it is not commonly used today, as most people prefer to shop online or in physical stores. In India, door-to-door sales are not very common, but it is still used in some industries like water purifiers, home appliances, and insurance.

For example, a salesperson may knock on your door and try to sell you a new vacuum cleaner. They will show you the product, explain its features and benefits, and try to persuade you to buy it.

## E-commerce:

E-commerce, short for electronic commerce, refers to the buying and selling of goods and services over the internet. It is a growing industry in India, with more and more people choosing to shop online for their daily needs. It offers several advantages over traditional shopping, including convenience, a wider selection of products, and competitive pricing. It also allows businesses to reach a larger audience and reduce their overhead costs, making it easier for small businesses to compete with larger companies.

For example, if you want to buy a new dress, you can browse various online stores, select the dress you like, and place an order. The dress will then be delivered to your doorstep. Some popular e-commerce websites in India include Amazon, Flipkart, and Myntra.

## Earned Media:

Earned media refers to the positive publicity and mentions that a business earns through its actions or performance, without paying for it. It can include media coverage, social media shares, influencer mentions, and customer reviews. Earned media is often seen as more trustworthy and credible than paid media because it is not controlled by the business itself.

For example, if a restaurant consistently serves delicious food and provides excellent service, it might receive positive reviews on social media or be mentioned in a food blog. These mentions and reviews are earned media for the restaurant and can help to attract more customers.

## Emotional Appeal:

Emotional appeal is a marketing strategy that aims to evoke an emotional response from consumers to influence their buying behaviour. Advertisements often use emotions such as happiness, sadness, anger, or fear to create a connection with consumers and persuade them to take action.

For example, an advertisement for a chocolate brand might show a happy family enjoying the product together. The advertisement is trying to evoke feelings of warmth, happiness, and togetherness in the viewer, which could then encourage them to buy the chocolate.

## Engagement Rate:

Engagement rate is a metric that measures the level of interaction or engagement that people have with a particular piece of content or a brand on social media. It shows how many people are liking, commenting, sharing, and otherwise engaging with the content. A high engagement rate is desirable because it means that the content is resonating with the audience and generating interest and conversation. This, in turn, can lead to increased brand awareness, more followers, and ultimately, more sales.

For example, let's say a fashion brand in India posts a picture of a new collection on Instagram. The engagement rate would be calculated by looking at how many people liked the post, commented on it, shared it, or saved it. If the post received 100 likes, 20 comments, and 5 shares, the total engagement would be 125. The engagement rate can then be calculated by dividing the total engagement by the number of followers and multiplying it by 100. If the fashion brand has 10,000 followers, the engagement rate would be 1.25%.

## Experiential Marketing:

Experiential marketing is a type of marketing strategy that involves creating an interactive experience for consumers to promote a brand or product. It aims to engage consumers on a deeper level and create a memorable experience that they will associate with the brand.

For example, a company might set up a pop-up shop that allows customers to try out their products or participate in a fun activity related to their brand. By creating an immersive experience, the company can build a stronger connection with its audience and potentially drive sales.

## Frequency:

In marketing, frequency refers to the number of times a person sees an advertisement. The goal of frequency is to create a lasting impression on the consumer's mind by repeatedly showing them the advertisement. The more often a person sees an ad, the more likely they are to remember it.

For example, a television commercial that airs during a popular show will likely have a high frequency, as many people will see it repeatedly. Similarly, a social media ad that appears on a user's feed multiple times a day has a high frequency.

## Frequency Capping:

Frequency capping refers to the practice of limiting the number of times a person sees an ad within a given period. This is done to prevent overexposure and avoid annoying the consumer with the same ad repeatedly.

For example, a marketer may set a frequency cap of three times per day for a particular ad campaign. Once a user has seen the ad three times, they will not see it again for the rest of the day.

## Geo-targeting:

Geo-targeting refers to the practice of delivering ads to specific geographic locations. This is done to ensure that the right message is delivered to the right people in the right place.

For example, a restaurant in Mumbai may use geo-targeting to deliver ads promoting their business to people within a specific radius of their location. This ensures that their marketing efforts are directed towards people who are likely to visit their restaurant.

## Google Analytics:

Google Analytics is a tool used to track and analyse website traffic and visitor behaviour. It helps website owners understand how many people are visiting their website, where they are coming from, what pages they are looking at, and how long they are staying on the website. This information helps website owners improve their website and marketing efforts to better reach their target audience.

For example, if an Indian business owner has a website for selling clothes online, they can use Google Analytics to see how many people are visiting their website from different cities in India. They can also see which pages on their website are most popular and how long people are spending on those pages. This information can help them make decisions about which types of clothes to stock based on what is most popular, and how to improve their website to make it easier for people to buy clothes.

## Gross Impressions:

Gross Impressions refers to the total number of times an advertisement is displayed or shown to a target audience. This includes both the number of people who saw the advertisement once, as well as the number of times it was shown to the same person multiple times.

For example, if an Indian company runs a digital advertisement campaign and the ad is displayed 1000 times on a website, and 500 people see it twice, then the gross impressions of that ad would be 1500. Gross Impressions are a way for companies to measure the overall reach of their advertising campaigns.

## Guerilla marketing:

Guerilla marketing is an advertising strategy that is designed to create buzz and excitement around a product or service through unconventional and unexpected means. It is typically low-cost, high-impact, and relies on creativity and innovation to capture the attention of potential customers. The key to successful guerrilla marketing is to be creative, unexpected, and relevant to the target audience. It is about finding new and innovative ways to promote a product or service, and to engage with potential customers in a way that they will remember and share with others. While guerrilla marketing can be risky, it can also be highly effective and generate a lot of buzz and excitement around a brand.

One famous example of guerrilla marketing in India is the "Jaago Re" campaign by Tata Tea. The campaign aimed to raise awareness about the importance of voting in India and encourage people to vote. They created a series of innovative ads that featured people from different walks of life, holding up signs with messages that urged people to vote. The ads were displayed in unexpected locations, such as on bridges, hoardings, and other public spaces. The campaign was a huge success and helped to increase voter turnout in India.

Another example of guerrilla marketing is the "Red Bull Stratos" campaign. Red Bull sponsored a daredevil named Felix Baumgartner to jump from a helium balloon at the edge of space. The jump was broadcast live on television and the internet, and it generated a huge amount of buzz and excitement around the Red Bull brand. The campaign was a huge success and helped to increase Red Bull's brand awareness and sales.

## Hashtag:

A hashtag is a word or phrase that starts with a hash (#) symbol, used to categorize and index social media posts. Hashtags make it easy for people to find and follow conversations on specific topics, allowing users to connect with others who share similar interests. When a user adds a hashtag to their post, it becomes searchable on that platform.

For example, a user may add the hashtag #travel to their social media post about a recent trip to a popular tourist destination. Anyone searching for the #travel hashtag would be able to find that post, along with others that use the same hashtag.

## High-Involvement Products:

High-involvement products are products that are expensive or involve significant risk, requiring extensive research, evaluation, and comparison before purchase. These products typically require a lot of thought and consideration, as they are often a significant investment for the buyer.

For example, a car or a house is considered a high-involvement product as they are expensive and a buyer needs to consider various factors such as quality, durability, maintenance costs, and resale value before making a purchase decision.

## Inbound Link:

An inbound link, also known as a backlink, is a hyperlink from another website to your website. Inbound links are important for search engine optimization (SEO) as they signal to search engines that other websites view your content as valuable and relevant. Search engines consider the number and quality of inbound links as an indication of the credibility and authority of your website.

For example, if a popular travel website links to a hotel's website, it is considered an inbound link for the hotel's website. This link can help increase the hotel's search engine rankings and drive more traffic to their website.

## Inbound Marketing:

Inbound marketing is a marketing strategy that focuses on creating valuable content and experiences that attract, engage, and delight customers, rather than interrupting them with ads. Inbound marketing is customer-centric and aims to provide helpful and informative content that meets the needs and interests of the target audience.

For example, a company may create blog posts, videos, or podcasts that provide helpful tips and advice on topics related to their product or service. By offering valuable content, the company can attract potential customers to their website and build trust and credibility with their target audience.

## Influencer:

An influencer is someone who has a significant impact on the purchasing decisions of others. This can be due to their expertise, authority, popularity or reach on social media platforms. For example, a popular food blogger or YouTuber may be an influencer in the food industry and have a significant impact on the purchasing decisions of their followers.

Influencer marketing has become a popular way for brands to promote their products or services through influencers. Brands often collaborate with influencers to promote their products or services to their followers, who may trust the influencer's opinion and be more likely to make a purchase.

## Integrated Marketing Communications (IMC):

Integrated Marketing Communications (IMC) refers to the coordination and integration of various marketing communication tools and tactics to deliver a consistent and seamless message to the target audience. This can include advertising, public relations, personal selling, direct marketing, and digital marketing. The goal is to create a unified and consistent message that resonates with the target audience and helps achieve marketing objectives.

For example, a brand may use social media advertising to drive traffic to their website, while also utilizing public relations to get media coverage for their product or service. All of these tactics would be coordinated and aligned with the overall marketing objectives of the brand.

## Key Performance Indicator (KPI):

Key Performance Indicator (KPI) is a measurable metric used to track and evaluate the success of a specific business objective. KPIs are used to monitor progress towards achieving business goals and can vary depending on the industry and business objectives. Examples of KPIs may include revenue, customer acquisition, website traffic, or social media engagement.

For example, a business may set a KPI to increase website traffic by 25% in the next quarter. The KPI would be measured and tracked to determine if the business is on track to meet their goal.

## Keyword:

A keyword is a word or phrase that is used to identify the content of a web page, blog post, or other digital media. Keywords are used in digital marketing to optimize content for search engines and improve search engine rankings. This allows businesses to increase their visibility to potential customers who are searching for specific products or services.

For example, a business selling handmade candles may use the keyword "handmade candles" in their website content to improve their search engine rankings and make it easier for potential customers to find them when searching for handmade candles.

## Landing page:

A landing page is a web page that is created for a specific marketing or advertising campaign with the aim of converting visitors into customers. It's the page a user lands on after clicking on an advertisement or search engine result. Landing pages are designed to provide relevant information and lead visitors to take a specific action, such as making a purchase, filling out a form, or subscribing to a newsletter.

For example, suppose you see an ad for a new online store selling sarees, and you click on it. You will be taken to a landing page for that store where you can see the sarees available and make a purchase. The landing page will be designed to encourage you to make a purchase by displaying the best-selling sarees, offering discounts, and providing clear calls-to-action.

## Lead generation:

Lead generation is the process of attracting and converting potential customers into leads, which are individuals who have expressed interest in your product or service. The purpose of lead generation is to capture the contact information of potential customers so that they can be nurtured into becoming paying customers.

For example, suppose you visit a website that sells fitness equipment. The website offers a free eBook on how to stay fit at home during the pandemic in exchange for your email address. By providing your email, you become a lead for the fitness equipment company, and they can use your email to send you promotional content and information about their products.

## Lead Magnet:

A lead magnet is an incentive offered to potential customers in exchange for their contact information, typically their email address. It's a valuable piece of content that solves a specific problem for the target audience. The lead magnet is designed to attract potential customers, establish trust and authority, and begin the lead nurturing process.

For example, a lead magnet could be an eBook, a free trial, a webinar, a cheat sheet, or a resource list. If you're a fashion brand, your lead magnet could be a style guide for the season. If you're a restaurant, your lead magnet could be a free dessert for new subscribers.

## Low-Involvement Products:

Low-involvement products are products that are purchased frequently, are low in price, and don't require much thought or effort to buy. These products are usually consumed or used quickly and have a short shelf-life.

For example, FMCG products such as toothpaste, shampoo, and soap are low-involvement products. They are affordable, widely available, and require little decision-making. Consumers typically buy these products out of habit or convenience.

## Market Development:

Market Development is a marketing strategy used by companies to increase sales by introducing their existing products to new markets or customer segments. In other words, it is the process of expanding the reach of a company's products or services into new geographic locations or customer groups.

For example, a company that sells organic food products in urban areas may decide to expand into rural areas to increase its customer base. This will involve developing new distribution channels, identifying new customer needs, and adapting the product or service to the specific needs of the new market.

## Market Growth:

Market Growth is a measure of the increase in the size of a particular market over time. It is an important indicator of the health and potential of a market, and helps companies to identify opportunities for growth and expansion.

For example, the Indian mobile phone market has experienced tremendous growth over the past decade, with millions of new customers joining the market each year. This has created opportunities for companies to develop new products and services to meet the needs of this growing market.

## Market Position:

Market Position refers to the place a company occupies in a particular market in relation to its competitors. It is the perception that customers have of the company's products or services, and how they compare to similar offerings from other companies in the same market.

For example, a company that produces premium quality sports shoes may position itself as a high-end brand that offers superior quality and performance compared to other brands in the market. This market position helps the company to attract customers who value quality over price.

## Market Research:

Market Research is the process of gathering and analysing information about a particular market or customer segment. It is a critical component of the marketing process, as it helps companies to understand customer needs, preferences, and behaviour, and to make informed decisions about product development, pricing, promotion, and distribution.

For example, a company that wants to launch a new line of cosmetics in India may conduct market research to gather information about the beauty products market in India, including customer preferences, buying behaviour, and competitive offerings. This information can then be used to develop a marketing strategy that is tailored to the specific needs of the Indian market.

## Market Saturation:

Market saturation is the point where the market for a particular product or service is completely saturated, meaning that the demand for it is completely met, and any further growth is not possible. This usually happens when almost every potential customer already owns the product or service, and there are no new customers left to target.

For example, the market for smartphones in India has become highly saturated over the past few years as almost every adult now owns a smartphone. As a result, smartphone manufacturers are now focusing on offering new features and upgrades to retain their existing customers.

## Market Segmentation:

Market segmentation is the process of dividing a market into smaller groups of consumers with similar needs or characteristics. These groups are known as market segments, and they are based on factors such as demographics, psychographics, behaviour, and geography. By identifying market segments, businesses can develop targeted marketing strategies to better meet the needs of each group.

For example, a company that sells sports shoes may divide its market into different segments such as athletes, fitness enthusiasts, and casual users, and then tailor its marketing messages and product features accordingly.

## Market Share:

Market share refers to the percentage of the total sales revenue of a particular product or service that a company generates within a given market. It is an important metric that helps businesses understand their position in the market relative to their competitors.

For example, if a company sells 1,000 smartphones in a market of 10,000 smartphones, and its competitor sells 3,000 smartphones, the first company's market share would be 10% while the latter's market share would be 30%.

## Marketing Automation:

Marketing automation refers to the use of technology to automate and streamline marketing processes and tasks. This includes activities such as email marketing, social media management, lead generation, and customer relationship management. By automating repetitive and time-consuming tasks, businesses can save time, increase efficiency, and improve the effectiveness of their marketing campaigns.

For example, a company may use marketing automation software to send targeted emails to its subscribers based on their behaviour on the company's website, such as the pages they have visited or the products they have viewed.

This can help the company to nurture leads and increase the chances of converting them into customers.

## Marketing Collateral:

Marketing collateral refers to the collection of materials used to support a company's sales and marketing efforts. This includes any type of media, both physical and digital, such as brochures, flyers, social media posts, email newsletters, videos, and more. The purpose of marketing collateral is to communicate information about a company's products or services to potential customers in a clear and compelling way.

For example, a company may create a brochure that provides an overview of their products or services, showcasing their features and benefits. They may also create social media posts that highlight customer testimonials or behind-the-scenes glimpses of their operations. By using a variety of marketing collateral, companies can reach their target audience through multiple channels and reinforce their brand messaging.

## Marketing Mix:

The marketing mix is a term used to describe the different components of a company's marketing strategy. These components, also known as the "4 Ps," include product, price, promotion, and place. Companies use the marketing mix to create a cohesive and effective plan for selling their products or services.

Product refers to the goods or services that a company offers. Price is the amount of money that customers must pay to purchase the product or service. Promotion includes all of the ways a company advertises and communicates about their product or service to potential customers. Place refers to the channels through which the product is distributed and sold, such as online or in physical stores.

## Marketing Research:

Marketing research is the process of gathering and analysing data about a company's target market, competitors, and industry trends to inform marketing strategy. This data can be collected through various methods, including surveys, focus groups, and market analysis. The goal of marketing research is to provide insights that can help companies make informed decisions about their marketing activities, such as product development, pricing, and promotion.

For example, a company may conduct a survey to understand how their target audience perceives their brand and products compared to competitors. The results of this survey can help the company refine their messaging and adjust their marketing strategy to better meet the needs of their target audience.

## Marketing Strategy:

Marketing strategy is the plan that a company uses to promote and sell their products or services. It includes a variety of tactics, such as advertising, social media marketing, and public relations, and is designed to reach a specific target audience. The goal of marketing strategy is to create a clear and effective plan for promoting a company's products or services to increase sales and revenue.

For example, a company may use a marketing strategy that includes targeted social media advertising, influencer partnerships, and email marketing to reach a specific audience and promote their product. By using a variety of tactics that are tailored to the needs and preferences of their target audience, the company can increase the effectiveness of their marketing efforts and achieve their business goals.

## Media Advertising:

Media advertising refers to the use of different forms of media such as television, radio, newspapers, magazines, billboards, and social media to promote a product or service. The goal of media advertising is to reach a large audience and create brand awareness.

For example, a company may use television commercials to promote a new product. These commercials will air during popular shows or events, such as the Indian Premier League (IPL), to reach a large audience.

## Media Buying:

Media buying is the process of purchasing advertising space or time on various media platforms. This includes negotiating prices, placement, and the specific time and location of the ad.

For example, a company may work with a media buying agency to purchase advertising space during a popular radio program or on a particular website.

## Media Plan:

A media plan is a detailed strategy outlining how a company will use different media platforms to achieve its advertising goals. It includes information such as the target audience, budget, types of media to use, and the specific timing and frequency of ads.

For example, a company may create a media plan to promote a new product launch. The plan may include a mix of television commercials, social media ads, and billboards to reach the target audience.

## Mobile Marketing:

Mobile marketing refers to the use of mobile devices such as smartphones and tablets to promote products or services. This includes a variety of tactics such as SMS (short message service) marketing, mobile apps, and mobile-responsive websites.

For example, a company may create a mobile app to promote a new product or service. The app may include features such as exclusive discounts or special offers to incentivize customers to make a purchase. The company may also use SMS marketing to send targeted messages to customers who have opted in to receive notifications.

## Mobile optimization:

Mobile optimization refers to the process of ensuring that a website or app is optimized for mobile devices like smartphones and tablets. This means that the website or app should be designed to load quickly, be easy to navigate, and be visually appealing on smaller screens. Mobile optimization is important because more and more people are using mobile devices to access the internet, and if a website or app is not optimized for mobile, it can lead to a poor user experience, resulting in low engagement and a high bounce rate.

For example, let's say you have a website that sells clothes. If the website is not mobile optimized, it might take a long time to load on a smartphone, the text might be too small to read, and the images might be too large to fit on the screen. This can lead to a poor user experience, resulting in potential customers leaving the site without making a purchase.

## Native advertising:

Native advertising is a form of paid advertising that blends in with the content on the platform where it is placed. The purpose of native advertising is to make the ads look like they are part of the content, rather than being intrusive or disruptive. Native ads are often seen on social media platforms, where they are designed to match the look and feel of the other posts in a user's feed.

For example, let's say you are scrolling through your Facebook feed, and you come across a post from a company that looks like a regular post from one of your friends. However, if you look closely, you will see that the post is actually a sponsored ad. This is an example of native advertising.

## Non-Traditional Advertising:

Non-traditional advertising is any form of advertising that does not fall under traditional media like television, radio, or print. Non-traditional advertising can take many forms, including social media, influencer marketing, experiential marketing, and guerrilla marketing. The purpose of non-traditional advertising is to reach audiences in new and innovative ways, often by creating memorable and engaging experiences.

For example, let's say you are walking through a mall and see a group of people wearing costumes and handing out samples of a new snack food. This is an example of non-traditional advertising, as it is not a traditional media channel, but rather a way to engage with potential customers in a more interactive way.

## Organic search:

Organic search refers to the process of a user finding a website or content through a search engine like Google, without the use of paid advertising. Organic search results are the listings that appear below the paid advertisements on a search engine results page. The goal of search engine optimization (SEO) is to improve a website's ranking in organic search results, by optimizing the content and structure of the website to make it more appealing to search engines.

For example, let's say you are looking for a new pair of shoes, and you type "shoes for sale" into Google. The first results that appear in the search engine results page will likely be paid advertisements for shoe retailers. However, if you scroll down, you will see organic search results that list websites that offer shoes for sale. These websites have optimized their content and structure to appear higher in organic search results for relevant search terms.

## Out-of-Home Advertising:

Out-of-Home (OOH) Advertising refers to any type of advertisement that targets consumers while they are outside of their homes. These ads can be found on billboards, buses, trains, taxis, and other public places where people gather. OOH advertising is a powerful way to reach consumers and is often used by brands to promote their products or services.

For example, a brand that sells cold drinks may use an OOH advertisement on a billboard at a busy intersection during summer months to target thirsty consumers who are outside In the heat.

## Partnership Marketing:

Partnership Marketing refers to a type of marketing strategy where two or more brands or companies work together to create a marketing campaign that benefits both of them. By pooling their resources, these companies can create a marketing campaign that is more effective and reaches a wider audience than either of them could achieve alone.

For example, a popular sportswear brand and a well-known electronics brand might collaborate on a marketing campaign where they offer a free wearable device with every purchase of a certain shoe model. This will allow both brands to leverage each other's customer bases and increase their reach and visibility.

## Pay-per-click (PPC):

Pay-per-click (PPC) is a type of online advertising where advertisers pay a fee each time a user clicks on one of their ads. These ads can be found on search engines, social media platforms, and other websites. PPC is an effective way to drive traffic to a website or landing page and increase sales or leads.

For example, a business that sells electronic gadgets can use PPC advertising to target users who are searching for electronic gadgets online. The business can create an ad that appears at the top of the search results page when a user types in a relevant keyword. The business will only have to pay when a user clicks on their ad.

## Point of Sale (POS):

Point of Sale (POS) refers to the location where a sale is made. In marketing, POS can refer to both the physical location of a retail store or the digital platform where an online sale is made. POS marketing involves using in-store displays, signs, or other advertising materials to encourage customers to make a purchase at the point of sale.

For example, a brand that sells packaged snacks can use POS marketing by placing eye-catching displays of their products near the cash register or at the end of an aisle to encourage customers to make an impulse purchase. Similarly, an e-commerce website can use pop-up ads or offers on the checkout page to incentivize customers to make a purchase at that moment.

## Point-of-Purchase (POP) Display:

A Point-of-Purchase (POP) display is a marketing tool used to attract customers' attention at the place where they make a purchase decision, such as a store or a restaurant. POP displays are designed to promote a particular product or service by displaying it in an attractive and eye-catching way. These displays can be standalone units or can be integrated into the shelves or counters where products are displayed. They can include elements such as signs, posters, banners, or product samples.

For example, imagine you are shopping for a snack at a convenience store. You see a colourful display of chips, candy, and other snacks at the checkout counter. The display catches your eye, and you decide to buy a bag of chips from the display even though you had not planned on buying any snacks.

## Print Ad:

A print ad is a type of advertising that appears in print media, such as newspapers, magazines, or billboards. Print ads can take many forms, including classified ads, display ads, and advertorials. They are used to promote a product or service to a specific target audience.

For example, a car company might run a print ad in a magazine to promote its latest model to car enthusiasts. The ad might include a picture of the car, a catchy headline, and a description of the car's features and benefits.

## Product Differentiation:

Product differentiation is the process of distinguishing a product or service from its competitors. It is the strategy used by businesses to create a unique identity for their product or service that sets it apart from similar offerings in the market. This can be done through a variety of methods, such as offering a better quality product, providing better customer service, or having a unique design or branding.

For example, a restaurant might differentiate itself from its competitors by offering a unique dining experience, such as live music or a themed atmosphere. This can attract customers who are looking for a different dining experience than they can get at other restaurants.

## Product Life Cycle:

The product life cycle is the pattern of sales and profits over time for a particular product or service. The life cycle typically includes four stages: introduction, growth, maturity, and decline. During the introduction stage, a new product is introduced to the market and sales are low. During the growth stage, sales increase rapidly as more customers become aware of the product. In the maturity stage, sales start to level off as the market becomes saturated with the product. Finally, in the decline stage, sales decrease as the product becomes obsolete or replaced by newer products.

For example, a new smartphone that is introduced to the market goes through the four stages of the product life cycle. When it is first introduced, sales are low as people become aware of the product. As the product gains popularity, sales increase rapidly during the growth stage. In the maturity stage, sales start to level off as the market becomes saturated with the product. Finally, in the decline stage, sales decrease as the product becomes obsolete or replaced by newer smartphones.

## Product Line:

A product line refers to a group of related products that are manufactured or sold by the same company. These products are similar in terms of their function, features, and target audience. Companies often create product lines to appeal to different types of customers or to meet different needs.

For example, a company that sells cosmetics might have a product line for skin care products and another for makeup products. Each product line may have different types of products within it, such as moisturizers, serums, and cleansers in the skin care line, and lipsticks, eyeshadows, and mascaras in the makeup line.

## Product Mix:

A product mix is the combination of all the product lines and individual products that a company sells. It includes everything a company offers to its customers. A company's product mix can vary in terms of product width, depth, length, and consistency.

For example, a grocery store has a product mix that includes food items, household goods, personal care items, and more. Within each category, there are different types of products. In food items, there are canned foods, fresh produce, dairy products, and so on. The product mix of a company is important because it affects the company's revenue and overall performance.

## Product Packaging:

Product packaging is the way a product is presented to the customer. It includes the physical container or wrapper that holds the product, as well as any labelling, instructions, or other materials that come with the product. The packaging of a product is an important part of its marketing strategy because it can influence a customer's perception of the product.

For example, a company that sells snacks might package its products in bright, colourful bags with eye-catching graphics and slogans. This packaging might make the product more appealing to children and teenagers. In contrast, a company that sells health foods might package its products in plain, simple wrappers to appeal to health-conscious adults.

## Product Placement:

Product placement refers to the way a product is positioned or displayed in a retail store or other location where it is sold. This can include the location on a shelf, the way it is arranged with other products, and the signage or advertising that accompanies it. Product placement is an important part of a company's marketing strategy because it can affect the product's visibility and sales.

For example, a company that sells toys might pay for prominent product placement at the front of a toy store or in a display window. This placement can make the product more visible to customers and increase the chances of it being purchased. Similarly, a company that sells snacks might place its products near the cash register or in other high-traffic areas of a grocery store to increase visibility and sales.

## Promotional Mix:

Promotional mix is the combination of various marketing strategies used by companies to promote their products or services to their target audience. These strategies include advertising, personal selling, sales promotion, direct marketing, and public relations. Companies use these strategies in different ways and in different proportions depending on their objectives, target audience, and budget.

For example, a company may use advertising to create brand awareness among a large audience, use personal selling to convince individual customers to buy their products, use sales promotion to encourage customers to make a purchase by offering discounts or freebies, use direct marketing to reach out to specific groups of customers through email or direct mail, and use public relations to create a positive image of the company in the media.

## Public Relations (PR):

Public relations (PR) is the practice of building and maintaining a positive image and reputation for a company or organization among its stakeholders, such as customers, employees, shareholders, and the general public. This involves creating and distributing press releases, organizing events, managing social media, and engaging with the media to promote positive news about the company.

For example, a company may use PR to create awareness about its corporate social responsibility (CSR) activities, such as organizing a charity event, sponsoring a social cause, or promoting sustainability. This helps the company to build a positive image in the eyes of its stakeholders and differentiate itself from its competitors.

## Push Marketing:

Push marketing is a marketing strategy where a company tries to push its products or services onto its customers through various promotional tactics, such as advertising, sales promotions, personal selling, and direct marketing. The objective of push marketing is to create demand for the products or services by promoting them aggressively to the target audience.

For example, a company may use push marketing to promote a new product launch by offering a discount to customers who buy the product within a certain period. This encourages customers to buy the product and create demand for it.

## Qualitative Research:

Qualitative research is a method of research used to gather insights and understanding of people's behaviour, opinions, and attitudes towards a particular product or service. It is typically used to collect data in the form of words, images, and other non-numeric forms.

For example, a company may conduct qualitative research to understand why customers prefer a particular brand over another brand, or to understand how customers use a particular product. This information helps the company to develop better products, improve its marketing strategies, and create a better customer experience. Qualitative research techniques include focus groups, in-depth interviews, and observation.

## Quantitative Research:

Quantitative research is a type of research method that focuses on numerical data and statistical analysis. This type of research aims to collect and measure data in a systematic way in order to come up with objective conclusions. It is commonly used in business, social sciences, and healthcare research. In business, companies use quantitative research to study consumer behaviour, market trends, and other important aspects of their industry.

For example, a company that sells soft drinks may conduct a survey to determine which flavour of soda is the most popular among consumers in a particular region. The company may then use this data to develop new products or marketing campaigns.

## Radio Ad and Radio Advertising:

Radio ads are advertisements that are broadcast on the radio. They are a type of audio advertisement that can be heard by listeners who tune in to the radio station. Radio advertising is a form of marketing that uses radio ads to promote a product, service, or brand.

Radio advertising is a popular form of advertising in India, especially in rural areas where TV and internet penetration is low. Many companies use radio ads to promote their products, such as mobile phones, consumer goods, and automobiles. For example, a company that sells cars may create a radio ad that promotes the features of their new car model, such as fuel efficiency, safety, and comfort.

## Reach:

Reach is a term that is used in marketing to describe the number of people who are exposed to an advertisement or message. It is a measure of the total audience that a particular campaign or advertisement is able to reach. The more people that an advertisement reaches, the higher the reach.

For example, a company that launches a new advertising campaign may measure the reach of the campaign by looking at the number of people who have seen or heard the advertisements. The company may use this information to determine the effectiveness of the campaign and to make changes to future campaigns.

## Relationship Marketing:

Relationship marketing is a marketing strategy that focuses on building long-term relationships with customers, rather than just making one-time sales. The goal of relationship marketing is to create loyal customers who will continue to buy from a company over time. Relationship marketing is especially important in industries such as retail, hospitality, and e-commerce, where repeat business is key to success.

For example, a restaurant may offer a loyalty program to its customers, which rewards them for repeat visits. The loyalty program may include discounts, free meals, or other perks. By offering these incentives, the restaurant is able to build a strong relationship with its customers and encourage them to continue visiting the restaurant.

## Retargeting:

Retargeting is a marketing technique used by businesses to show ads to people who have already interacted with their brand in some way, such as visiting their website or social media page. The idea behind retargeting is that by showing ads to people who have already shown interest in a product or service, businesses can increase the chances of converting them into customers.

For example, if someone visits an online shopping website and browses through a few products, but leaves without making a purchase, retargeting ads can show them those same products again on other websites or social media platforms, reminding them of the products they were interested in.

## Return on Investment (ROI):

Return on investment, or ROI, is a financial metric used to measure the profitability of an investment. In business, ROI is typically used to determine the success of marketing campaigns or other initiatives by comparing the amount of money invested to the amount of money generated as a result.

For example, if a business invests Rs. 10,000 in a marketing campaign and generates Rs. 20,000 in revenue as a result, the ROI would be calculated as (20,000 - 10,000) / 10,000 = 1, or 100%. This means that for every Rs. 1 invested in the campaign, the business earned Rs. 1 in return.

## Sales Funnel:

A sales funnel is a visual representation of the steps involved in converting a potential customer into a paying customer. The idea behind a sales funnel is to guide a customer through each stage of the buying process, from awareness of the product or service to making a purchase.

A typical sales funnel consists of several stages, such as:

1. Awareness: The customer becomes aware of the product or service.
2. Interest: The customer shows interest in the product or service.
3. Consideration: The customer considers the product or service as an option.
4. Purchase: The customer makes a purchase.

Sales funnels can help businesses understand where their customers are in the buying process and which stages may need improvement to increase conversion rates.

## Sales Promotions:

Sales promotions are short-term incentives designed to encourage customers to make a purchase. These promotions can take many forms, such as discounts, coupons, contests, and giveaways. Sales promotions are often used by businesses to boost sales and clear inventory.

For example, let's say a business is running a promotion that offers a 20% discount on all products for a limited time. This promotion is designed to encourage customers to make a purchase while the discount is available.

## Sampling:

Sampling is the process of offering free samples of a product to potential customers. Companies use sampling as a marketing strategy to introduce new products, increase brand awareness, and generate interest in their products. Sampling allows customers to try the product before they make a purchase and helps companies get feedback from customers.

For example, a company that sells a new flavour of chips can offer free samples to customers in a mall or grocery store. The customers can try the chips and provide feedback on the taste, texture, and packaging.

## Search Advertising:

Search advertising is a form of online advertising that displays ads based on the search terms entered by users in a search engine. The ads are displayed on the search engine results page (SERP) and are usually labelled as sponsored or ads. Search advertising allows companies to target customers who are actively searching for a product or service.

For example, when a user searches for "pizza delivery" on Google, the search results will display ads from pizza delivery companies in the area.

## Search Engine Marketing (SEM):

Search Engine Marketing (SEM) is a form of online marketing that promotes a website by increasing its visibility on the search engine results page (SERP). SEM involves paid search advertising, search engine optimization (SEO), and other tactics to drive traffic to a website. SEM is used to increase brand awareness, generate leads, and boost sales.

For example, a company that sells shoes can use SEM to increase its visibility on search engines by using paid search advertising and optimizing its website with relevant keywords.

## Search Engine Optimization (SEO):

Search Engine Optimization (SEO) is the process of optimizing a website to improve its ranking on the search engine results page (SERP). SEO involves making changes to a website's structure, content, and other factors to increase its visibility and relevance to search engines. SEO helps websites rank higher in search engine results, which can drive more traffic to the site.

For example, a company that sells furniture can optimize its website by including relevant keywords in the content, optimizing images, and improving site speed. This can improve its ranking on search engines and attract more customers to the site.

## Social Media Marketing:

Social media marketing is the process of using social media platforms to promote a brand or product to a target audience. Social media platforms like Facebook, Instagram, Twitter, LinkedIn, and YouTube are all used for social media marketing. Social media marketing involves creating and sharing content like posts, stories, videos, and images on these platforms to reach out to potential customers.

For example, a company that sells clothes might create a social media campaign to promote their latest collection. They might create posts and videos that showcase the clothes and their features, and target them towards people who are interested in fashion and clothing.

## Specialty Advertising:

Specialty advertising is a form of advertising that involves promotional products like t-shirts, pens, keychains, or other items with a company's logo or message on them. These items are usually given away for free as part of a marketing campaign, and they are designed to create brand awareness and goodwill.

For example, a company that sells energy drinks might give away free t-shirts or keychains with their logo on them at a sporting event or music festival. This helps to increase brand awareness and create a positive association with the company.

## Sponsored Content:

Sponsored content is a type of advertising that involves paying a content creator to create content that promotes a brand or product. This can take the form of blog posts, videos, or social media posts. The content is designed to be engaging and informative, rather than purely promotional, and is usually created by an influencer or content creator who has a large following.

For example, a company that sells beauty products might sponsor a popular beauty influencer on YouTube to create a video tutorial using their products. The influencer would create the content, but the company would pay them for the promotion.

## Sponsorship:

Sponsorship is a form of advertising that involves sponsoring an event or activity in order to promote a brand or product. This can include sponsoring a sports team, a music festival, or a charity event. In return for the sponsorship, the company's logo or message is usually displayed prominently at the event.

For example, a company that sells cars might sponsor a Formula 1 racing team. The company's logo would be prominently displayed on the race cars and on promotional materials at the events. This helps to create brand awareness and associate the company with high-performance vehicles.

## Strategic Marketing:

Strategic Marketing is a process of planning and implementing marketing activities to achieve business goals. It involves identifying and analysing the target market, evaluating competitors, developing marketing strategies, and executing them effectively. The objective of strategic marketing is to achieve a sustainable competitive advantage by creating a unique position in the market.

For example, if a company wants to launch a new product in India, it needs to analyse the market to identify its target audience, competition, and potential opportunities. Based on this analysis, the company can develop a marketing strategy to promote its product and differentiate it from the competitors.

## Target Audience:

A target audience is a specific group of people who are most likely to be interested in a product or service. It is important to identify the target audience to develop effective marketing strategies that resonate with them. Target audience can be identified based on demographics, psychographics, and behaviour patterns.

For example, a company that sells baby products would target parents and caregivers of young children as their target audience in India.

## Target Marketing:

Target Marketing is a marketing strategy that involves focusing on a specific segment of the market that has a higher likelihood of buying a product or service. The objective of target marketing is to create a more effective and efficient marketing campaign by targeting a specific group of customers.

For example, a company that sells luxury cars in India would target high-income individuals who have a desire for luxury goods.

## Telemarketing:

Telemarketing is a marketing strategy that involves promoting products or services over the phone. It is a direct marketing technique that can be used to generate leads, set up appointments, or sell products directly to customers. However, telemarketing is often considered intrusive and can be annoying to some customers.

For example, a company that provides insurance services in India may use telemarketing to reach potential customers and promote their products.

## Top-of-Mind Awareness (TOMA):

Top-of-mind awareness is the measure of how easily a brand name or a product comes to the consumer's mind when thinking of a particular product or service. It is an important concept in marketing as it helps companies understand how well their brand is recognized and recalled by consumers. TOMA is usually achieved through consistent and effective advertising, and can help companies maintain a competitive edge in the market.

For example, when thinking of a soft drink, the name "Coca-Cola" may immediately come to mind for many people. This is because Coca-Cola has invested in marketing campaigns over the years, and has been successful in creating a strong brand identity that is instantly recognizable.

## Trade Advertising:

Trade advertising is a type of advertising that is aimed at businesses or trade professionals rather than the general public. This type of advertising is used to promote products or services to other businesses, with the aim of increasing sales or building partnerships. Trade advertising is often done through industry publications, trade shows, or targeted online advertising.

For example, a manufacturer of industrial machinery may advertise its products in trade magazines that are read by other manufacturers, or showcase its products at a trade show that is attended by professionals in the industry.

## Trade Show:

A trade show is an event where businesses and organizations come together to showcase their products or services to potential customers, partners, or other businesses. Trade shows are usually held in large exhibition centers or conference halls, and can attract a large number of visitors. They are an important marketing tool for businesses, as they provide an opportunity to reach a large audience, generate leads, and build relationships with other businesses.

For example, the Auto Expo in India is a trade show where automotive manufacturers showcase their latest cars and technology to potential customers, industry experts, and other businesses in the automotive industry.

## Trade Show Marketing:

Trade show marketing is the process of promoting a business, product or service at a trade show. This can include advertising in trade publications, creating a booth or exhibit to showcase products, creating marketing materials such as brochures or flyers, and networking with other businesses and potential customers.

For example, a fashion retailer may create a booth at a trade show to showcase its latest clothing lines to potential customers, and distribute brochures and flyers to attendees to generate interest in its products. The retailer may also network with other businesses in the fashion industry to build relationships and explore new partnership opportunities.

## Unique Selling Proposition (USP):

A unique selling proposition (USP) is a marketing term that describes what sets a product, service, or company apart from its competitors. It is a unique feature or benefit that a product offers, which makes it stand out in the market. A USP is important because it helps a company differentiate its product from the competition and attract customers.

For example, Domino's Pizza in India promotes its 30-minute delivery guarantee as its USP. This promise ensures that the pizza is delivered within 30 minutes, which is faster than its competitors, making it a unique and appealing choice for consumers.

## User-generated content (UGC):

User-generated content (UGC) refers to any content created by users or customers of a brand. This can include photos, videos, social media posts, reviews, and more. UGC is valuable for businesses because it provides authentic and trustworthy content that can help build brand awareness and engagement.

For example, Indian e-commerce website, Myntra, encourages its customers to post photos of themselves wearing the clothes they bought on their website on social media. This UGC helps Myntra to build a community of loyal customers and promote their brand.

## Video Marketing:

Video marketing refers to the use of videos to promote a product or service. It can be used for a variety of purposes, such as building brand awareness, driving website traffic, or increasing sales. Video marketing has become increasingly popular in recent years, with the rise of platforms such as YouTube and TikTok.

For example, Indian mobile phone manufacturer, Xiaomi, uses video marketing to showcase the features of its products and engage with its customers. They create product launch videos, unboxing videos, and product review videos that showcase the features and benefits of their products.

## Viral marketing:

Viral marketing is a marketing technique that uses social media, word-of-mouth, and other channels to promote a product or service. The goal of viral marketing is to create a message or campaign that is so engaging and shareable that it spreads quickly and organically, like a virus.

For example, Indian start-up, Paper Boat, created a viral marketing campaign around its range of traditional Indian drinks. They created a series of videos that showcased the stories and traditions behind the drinks, which went viral on social media and helped to build brand awareness and loyalty.

## Webinar:

A webinar is an online seminar that allows people from different locations to connect and participate in real-time. The word "webinar" is a combination of the words "web" and "seminar." It is an interactive and engaging way to share information, ideas, and knowledge with a large number of people.

For example, a school teacher can conduct a webinar to teach her students remotely during the pandemic. Similarly, a business owner can use a webinar to market their product or service to potential customers located in different parts of the world.

## Website Traffic:

Website traffic refers to the number of people who visit a website. It is an important metric for measuring the popularity and success of a website. The more traffic a website receives, the more likely it is to generate leads, sales, and revenue.

For example, an e-commerce website in India that sells traditional Indian clothes may get a lot of traffic during the festive season of Diwali when people are looking to buy new clothes. On the other hand, a website that provides information on sustainable living may get more traffic during Earth Day.

## White Hat SEO:

Search engine optimization (SEO) is the process of improving the visibility and ranking of a website on search engines like Google. White hat SEO refers to ethical and legitimate SEO techniques that are used to improve a website's ranking. These techniques include creating high-quality content, using relevant keywords, and building high-quality backlinks.

For example, a company that sells organic food products in India may use white hat SEO techniques to optimize their website and improve their visibility on search engines. This may include creating blog posts that provide information on organic food and using relevant keywords in their website content.

## Word of Mouth:

Word of mouth refers to the communication of information about a product or service from one person to another. It is a powerful marketing tool that can influence people's buying decisions. Positive word of mouth can lead to increased sales and revenue, while negative word of mouth can harm a business's reputation.

For example, a restaurant in India that serves delicious food and provides excellent customer service may receive positive word of mouth from its customers. This can lead to more people visiting the restaurant and increased revenue for the business.

# Chapter 16: Customer Relationship Management

## Introduction:

Customer Relationship Management (CRM) is a business strategy that focuses on managing interactions with customers to improve business relationships and ultimately drive sales growth. The goal of CRM is to develop long-term, mutually beneficial relationships with customers by providing personalized service, building trust, and meeting their needs. In today's competitive marketplace, having an effective CRM system is essential for businesses of all sizes to stay ahead of the curve and maintain a loyal customer base.

## What is Customer Relationship Management?

Customer Relationship Management (CRM) is a business strategy that focuses on managing interactions with customers to improve business relationships and ultimately drive sales growth. The concept of CRM has evolved over the years, from simply storing customer data to a more holistic approach that involves analysing customer behaviour, identifying their needs, and developing personalized marketing and communication strategies. Today, CRM is an essential part of any business strategy, allowing businesses to build better relationships with customers and gain a competitive advantage.

## Types of CRM:

There are mainly three types of CRM: Operational CRM, Analytical CRM, and Collaborative CRM.

1. **Operational CRM:** Operational CRM is focused on streamlining business operations and optimizing customer interactions. This type of CRM includes the automation of various business processes such as sales, marketing, and customer service. It enables businesses to improve

efficiency, reduce costs, and provide better service to customers. Operational CRM involves different technologies such as sales automation, marketing automation, and service automation.

2. **Analytical CRM:** Analytical CRM involves the use of data analytics to gain insights into customer behaviour, preferences, and buying patterns. It helps businesses to identify trends and patterns in customer data and develop strategies for improving customer relationships. Analytical CRM enables businesses to make data-driven decisions and personalize marketing and communication strategies for individual customers.

3. **Collaborative CRM:** Collaborative CRM focuses on improving communication and collaboration between different departments within an organization to improve customer service. It involves sharing customer data across departments such as sales, marketing, and customer service to provide a unified customer experience. Collaborative CRM enables businesses to respond to customer inquiries quickly and efficiently and provide personalized service to customers.

## Why is CRM important for businesses?

CRM is important for businesses for several reasons:

1. **Improves customer satisfaction and loyalty:** By better understanding customer needs and preferences, businesses can tailor their marketing and sales efforts to meet those needs, leading to greater customer satisfaction and loyalty.

2. **Increases efficiency:** CRM automates and streamlines sales, marketing, and customer service processes, reducing the time and effort required to manage customer interactions.

3. **Provides insights into customer behaviour:** By analysing customer data, businesses can gain insights into customer behaviour and preferences, enabling them to make more informed decisions about product development and marketing.

4. **Enables personalized marketing:** CRM allows businesses to personalize marketing messages and offers based on customer data, increasing the effectiveness of marketing campaigns.

5. **Facilitates cross-selling and upselling:** By analysing customer data, businesses can identify opportunities for cross-selling and upselling, increasing revenue per customer.

## Implementing CRM best practices

To successfully implement a CRM system, businesses should follow these best practices:

1. **Define clear goals and objectives:** Before implementing a CRM system, businesses should define clear goals and objectives, such as improving customer satisfaction, increasing revenue, or reducing customer churn.
2. **Choose the right CRM system:** Businesses should choose a CRM system that is aligned with their goals and objectives and meets their specific needs.
3. **Ensure data quality:** Accurate and complete data is essential for a successful CRM program. Businesses should ensure that data is entered consistently and is regularly updated.
4. **Train employees:** Employees should be trained on how to use the CRM system effectively and how it can benefit their work.
5. **Continuously measure and improve:** Businesses should regularly measure the success of their CRM program and make adjustments as needed to ensure that it is meeting its goals and objectives.

## Measuring the success of CRM

Measuring the success of a CRM program is essential to ensure that it is meeting its goals and objectives. Some key metrics to track include:

1. **Customer satisfaction:** Customer satisfaction surveys can be used to track how well the CRM program is meeting customer needs and expectations.
2. **Customer retention:** Tracking customer retention rates can provide insight into the effectiveness of the CRM program in building customer loyalty.

3. **Revenue per customer:** Tracking revenue per customer can help identify opportunities for cross-selling and upselling.
4. **Customer acquisition cost:** Tracking customer acquisition cost can help identify areas where the CRM program can be improved to reduce costs.

There are several CRM solutions available in India, catering to the needs of different types and sizes of businesses. Some of the top CRM solutions in India are:

1. **Zoho CRM:** Zoho CRM is a cloud-based CRM software that offers a comprehensive range of features, including lead management, sales automation, marketing automation, and customer service. It is a popular choice among small and medium-sized businesses in India.

2. **Salesforce CRM:** Salesforce is a leading cloud-based CRM provider that offers a wide range of solutions for sales, marketing, and customer service. It is a popular choice among large enterprises and mid-sized businesses in India.

3. **Freshsales CRM:** Freshsales is a cloud-based CRM solution that offers features such as lead scoring, lead tracking, and sales automation. It is a popular choice among small and mid-sized businesses in India.

4. **HubSpot CRM:** HubSpot CRM is a free cloud-based CRM software that offers features such as contact management, deal management, and email tracking. It is a popular choice among startups and small businesses in India.

5. **Microsoft Dynamics CRM:** Microsoft Dynamics CRM is a cloud-based CRM solution that offers features such as sales automation, customer service, and marketing automation. It is a popular choice among large enterprises in India.

6. **Pipedrive CRM:** Pipedrive is a cloud-based CRM solution that offers features such as pipeline management, deal tracking, and sales forecasting. It is a popular choice among small and mid-sized businesses in India.

7. **SugarCRM:** SugarCRM is an open-source CRM solution that offers features such as lead management, sales automation, and customer service. It is a popular choice among small and mid-sized businesses in India.

8. **Insightly CRM:** Insightly is a cloud-based CRM solution that offers features such as lead management, project management, and email tracking. It is a popular choice among small businesses and startups in India.

9. **Agile CRM:** Agile CRM is a cloud-based CRM solution that offers features such as contact management, deal tracking, and email marketing. It is a popular choice among small and mid-sized businesses in India.

10. **Bitrix24 CRM:** Bitrix24 is a cloud-based CRM solution that offers features such as contact management, lead management, and sales automation. It is a popular choice among small businesses in India.

## Conclusion:

Customer Relationship Management (CRM) is an essential part of any business strategy. It helps businesses to improve customer satisfaction, increase sales, streamline business operations, and provide data-driven insights. By implementing an effective CRM system, businesses can build better relationships with customers and gain a competitive advantage in today's marketplace.

# Chapter 17: Managing Your Finances

Financial management is an essential part of running any successful business. Proper financial management ensures that a company is using its resources effectively to achieve its goals. It involves planning, organizing, directing, and controlling financial resources to achieve the organization's objectives. This section will discuss why financial management is important and how it can help a business succeed.

The role of financial management in ensuring business success cannot be overemphasized. Financial management provides a framework for planning and controlling financial resources to achieve the objectives of the organization. It enables businesses to allocate resources effectively and make informed decisions.

Poor financial management can have a devastating effect on a business. It can lead to financial instability, increased debt, and bankruptcy. When a company does not have a proper financial management system in place, it can result in financial mismanagement, which can cause operational difficulties, and ultimately affect the company's bottom line.

On the other hand, good financial management can lead to increased profitability, better decision-making, and improved cash flow management. With proper financial management, a company can determine its financial position, identify areas that need improvement, and take necessary actions to improve its financial performance.

Setting financial goals and objectives that align with overall business goals is an important aspect of financial management. Financial goals and objectives provide a framework for a company's financial planning and decision-making process.

When setting financial goals and objectives, it is important to ensure they are realistic and achievable. Unrealistic goals can lead to disappointment, frustration, and a lack of motivation. Realistic goals, on the other hand, provide a sense of direction and motivation to achieve them.

Financial goals and objectives can be used to measure performance and progress. They provide a benchmark for a company to measure its financial performance against the desired outcomes. This allows businesses to identify areas that need improvement and take necessary actions to improve their financial performance.

# Budgeting:

A budget is a financial plan that outlines a company's expected revenues and expenses over a specific period, typically a year. Creating a budget is an essential component of financial management for any business. A budget helps a business to plan for the future, manage its resources effectively, and allocate funds to priority areas.

A budget helps a business to set realistic financial goals and objectives, measure performance and progress, and identify areas for improvement. A budget can help to control spending, reduce waste, and improve cash flow management.

There are several different types of budgets that a business can create, including an operating budget, capital budget, and cash budget. An operating budget outlines a company's expected revenues and expenses for its day-to-day operations, while a capital budget outlines its investment in long-term assets. A cash budget is a detailed plan of a company's expected cash inflows and outflows for a specific period.

## Creating a Budget:

Creating a budget involves several steps. The first step is to gather the necessary financial data, including historical financial statements and sales projections. A business should also consider its business growth plans and any changes in market conditions that may impact its revenue and expenses.

Once the necessary financial data is collected, the next step is to identify and categorize expenses. Expenses can be classified as fixed, variable, or semi-variable. Fixed expenses, such as rent and salaries, remain constant regardless of changes in sales volume, while variable expenses, such as raw materials and shipping costs, vary depending on sales volume. Semi-variable expenses, such as utilities and maintenance costs, have both fixed and variable components.

After identifying and categorizing expenses, the next step is to create a revenue forecast based on historical sales data, market trends, and any other relevant factors. The revenue forecast should be realistic and based on reliable data.

Once the revenue forecast and expense categories are established, the next step is to create a budget template. The budget template should include a summary of revenue and expenses, as well as a detailed breakdown of each expense category.

Finally, the business should review and adjust the budget as necessary. It is important to consider different scenarios and make adjustments based on changes in market conditions or unexpected events.

## Monitoring and Adjusting the Budget:

A business should regularly review its budget performance to ensure that it is on track to achieve its financial goals and objectives. There are several strategies that a business can use to monitor its budget performance. One effective strategy is to compare actual revenue and expenses to the budgeted amounts. This helps to identify any areas where the business is overspending or underspending. Another strategy is to use financial ratios to analyse the business's financial performance.

If the business identifies any budget variances, it should take steps to adjust the budget as necessary. This may involve cutting expenses, increasing revenue, or revising financial projections. It is important to consider the impact of any changes on the overall business goals and objectives before making adjustments.

# Financial Reporting

Financial reporting involves the preparation and presentation of financial information, which is used to provide insight into the financial health of a business. This section covers the basics of financial reporting, including financial statements, financial ratios, and other financial reports that can be used to make informed decisions.

## Financial Statements:

Financial statements are essential reports that provide an overview of a company's financial health. There are three primary financial statements that every business owner should be familiar with: the income statement, balance sheet, and cash flow statement.

The income statement, also known as the profit and loss statement, summarizes a company's revenues, expenses, and net income or loss for a specific period. The purpose of the income statement is to show the profitability of a company's operations over a given period. Revenue includes all money earned by the company from sales, while expenses include all costs incurred in generating those revenues, such as salaries, rent, and supplies. The difference between revenues and expenses is the net income or loss.

The balance sheet is a snapshot of a company's financial position at a specific point in time. It presents the company's assets, liabilities, and equity. Assets are things that a company owns, such as cash, inventory, and property. Liabilities are amounts owed to others, such as loans or accounts payable. Equity represents the amount of money that the company's owners have invested in the business. The balance sheet equation is Assets = Liabilities + Equity, which means that the total assets of a company must be equal to the sum of its liabilities and equity.

The cash flow statement provides information about the cash inflows and outflows of a company for a specific period. It shows how much cash is generated from operating activities, such as sales, how much is invested in capital expenditures, and how much is used to pay off debt or distribute to shareholders. The purpose of the cash flow statement is to provide insight into a company's liquidity, or its ability to meet its financial obligations.

## Financial Ratios:

Financial ratios are quantitative tools used to analyse a company's financial performance. These ratios are derived from the financial statements and can provide insight into the company's liquidity, profitability, solvency, efficiency, and overall financial health. Financial ratios can be used by investors, creditors, and managers to make informed decisions about the company.

Financial ratios can be classified into several categories based on the type of analysis they provide. Some of the common financial ratios are:

**1. Liquidity Ratios:** Liquidity ratios measure a company's ability to meet its short-term obligations. The most commonly used liquidity ratios are:

- **Current Ratio:** Current ratio is calculated by dividing current assets by current liabilities. It indicates whether the company has enough current assets to pay off its current liabilities. A current ratio of 1 or higher is considered good.

- **Quick Ratio:** Quick ratio is calculated by dividing quick assets (current assets minus inventory) by current liabilities. It is a more conservative measure of liquidity as it excludes inventory, which may not be easily convertible to cash. A quick ratio of 1 or higher is considered good.

**2. Profitability Ratios:** Profitability ratios measure a company's ability to generate profits. The most commonly used profitability ratios are:

- **Gross Profit Margin:** Gross profit margin is calculated by dividing gross profit by revenue. It indicates the amount of profit the company makes on its sales after deducting the cost of goods sold. A higher gross profit margin indicates a more profitable company.

- **Net Profit Margin:** Net profit margin is calculated by dividing net income by revenue. It indicates the percentage of revenue that is left after all expenses, including taxes, have been deducted. A higher net profit margin indicates a more profitable company.

**3. Solvency Ratios:** Solvency ratios measure a company's ability to meet its long-term obligations. The most commonly used solvency ratios are:

- **Debt-to-Equity Ratio:** Debt-to-equity ratio is calculated by dividing total debt by total equity. It indicates the proportion of the company's funding that comes from debt. A lower debt-to-equity ratio indicates a less leveraged company.

- **Interest Coverage Ratio:** Interest coverage ratio is calculated by dividing earnings before interest and taxes (EBIT) by interest expense. It indicates the company's ability to meet its interest payments. A higher interest coverage ratio indicates a more solvent company.

**4. Efficiency Ratios:** Efficiency ratios measure how efficiently a company uses its resources. The most commonly used efficiency ratios are:

- **Inventory Turnover Ratio:** Inventory turnover ratio is calculated by dividing cost of goods sold by average inventory. It indicates how many times the company's inventory is sold and replaced during a period. A higher inventory turnover ratio indicates a more efficient company.

- **Accounts Receivable Turnover Ratio:** Accounts receivable turnover ratio is calculated by dividing revenue by average accounts receivable. It indicates how many times the company collects its accounts receivable during a period. A higher accounts receivable turnover ratio indicates a more efficient company.

However, it is important to note that financial ratios should be used in conjunction with other financial information and should not be the only factor considered when making investment or lending decisions.

## Other Financial Reports:

In addition to financial statements and ratios, businesses can also benefit from other financial reports that provide useful insights into their financial health. Two examples of such reports are budget vs. actual reports and variance reports.

**Budget vs. Actual Reports:** These reports compare the actual financial performance of a business against the budgeted or planned performance. This comparison helps to identify where the business is performing better or worse than expected and can highlight areas where adjustments need to be made. For example, if a business has budgeted for $10,000 in revenue in a given month but only generates $8,000 in actual revenue, a budget vs. actual report will reveal the $2,000 variance. By analysing the variance, the business can identify the reasons for the difference and take corrective action if necessary.

**Variance Reports:** Variance reports provide more detailed information about the differences between actual performance and budgeted performance. They break down the variances into smaller categories and provide explanations for the differences. For example, a variance report might show that the variance in revenue was due to a lower volume of sales or a decrease in the selling price of products.

To use these reports to make informed decisions, it is important to analyse the data and identify the root causes of variances. If there are positive variances, the business may want to identify what actions led to the better-than-expected performance and consider replicating those actions. On the other hand, if there are negative variances, the business may want to investigate the reasons behind them and take corrective action if necessary.

# Financial Forecasting:

Financial forecasting is an essential tool for businesses to plan and prepare for their financial future. It involves estimating the future financial performance of a business by analysing historical financial data and taking into account various external factors that may impact its operations. In this section, we will discuss the importance of financial forecasting for businesses, common forecasting methods, and how to use financial forecasts to make informed decisions.

## What is Financial Forecasting?

Financial forecasting refers to the process of predicting a company's financial performance in the future based on historical data, current market trends, and other factors. Financial forecasting is an important tool for businesses to help them plan their future financial activities, set goals, and make informed decisions. The process of financial forecasting involves analysing historical financial data, identifying trends, and making assumptions about future business activities.

Financial forecasting is crucial for businesses for several reasons. Firstly, it helps businesses plan and budget for future expenses and revenue. This, in turn, helps businesses make informed decisions about investments and other financial activities. Secondly, financial forecasting helps businesses identify potential financial risks and opportunities. By analysing historical financial data and current market trends, businesses can anticipate potential challenges and make proactive decisions to mitigate risks. Finally, financial forecasting helps businesses evaluate their performance over time. By comparing actual financial data to projected financial data, businesses can determine if they are meeting their financial goals and make necessary adjustments.

## Common Financial Forecasting Methods:

There are several methods that businesses can use for financial forecasting. Some of the most common methods include:

- **Trend Analysis:** This involves analysing historical financial data to identify trends and patterns that can be used to predict future financial performance.
- **Regression Analysis:** This involves analysing the relationship between various financial variables to predict future financial performance.
- **Market Research:** This involves analysing market trends and consumer behaviour to predict future financial performance.
- **Expert Opinion:** This involves using the opinions and insights of industry experts to predict future financial performance.

## Creating a Financial Forecast

Creating a financial forecast involves several steps. These include:

- **Collecting and analysing historical financial data.**
- **Identifying trends and patterns in the data.**
- **Identifying and analysing external factors that may impact future financial performance, such as changes in the market, consumer behaviour, or industry trends.**
- **Making assumptions about future business activities, such as sales growth, expenses, and investments.**
- **Creating a projected income statement, balance sheet, and cash flow statement based on the above factors.**

It is important to note that creating an accurate financial forecast can be challenging, and there is no guarantee that the forecast will be completely accurate. However, by using a combination of financial forecasting methods and careful analysis of historical data and external factors, businesses can create a realistic financial forecast that can be used to guide decision-making.

When creating a financial forecast, businesses should consider several factors that can impact future financial performance. Some of these factors include:

- **Market trends and consumer behaviour**
- **Changes in the industry**
- **Business growth plans**
- **Sales growth**
- **Expenses**
- **Investments**
- **Interest rates**
- **Inflation**

By taking these factors into account, businesses can create a financial forecast that is realistic and accurate.

**Common Forecasting Mistakes to Avoid:**

When creating a financial forecast, there are several common mistakes that businesses should avoid. These include:

- **Overestimating revenue:** This can lead to unrealistic financial projections and inaccurate decision-making.
- **Underestimating expenses:** This can lead to financial shortfalls and missed opportunities.
- **Ignoring external factors:** External factors, such as changes in the market or industry, can have a significant impact on financial performance and should be taken into account when creating a financial forecast.
- **Not revising the forecast:** Business environments can change rapidly, and a financial forecast should be regularly revisited and revised to reflect these changes.
- **Not seeking expert advice:** Financial forecasting can be complex, and seeking the advice of financial experts can help businesses create more accurate forecasts.

## Using Financial Forecasts:

Once a financial forecast has been created, it can be used to make informed business decisions. Financial forecasts can help businesses identify potential financial risks and opportunities, set financial goals, and plan for future investments and expenses. By regularly revising financial forecasts, businesses can adjust their financial plans and strategies based on changing market conditions and business performance.

Financial forecasts should be regularly revised to reflect changes in the business environment and to ensure that they remain accurate and relevant. By regularly revising financial forecasts, businesses can ensure that they are making informed decisions based on the most current information available.

Financial forecasts can help businesses identify potential financial risks and develop strategies to manage them. For example, if a financial forecast predicts a potential cash flow shortfall, a business may decide to delay investments or reduce expenses to conserve cash. Alternatively, if a financial forecast predicts strong sales growth, a business may decide to increase marketing and advertising spending to take advantage of the opportunity.

In conclusion, managing your finances is an essential skill that can help you achieve your financial goals and secure your financial future. By creating a budget, tracking your expenses, and monitoring your investments, you can gain control over your finances and make informed financial decisions. It is important to keep in mind that financial management requires ongoing effort and attention, and that it is never too late to start managing your finances more effectively. With the help of technology and financial management tools, you can simplify and streamline your financial management process, making it easier to achieve your financial goals. By implementing the strategies and techniques discussed in this chapter, you can take control of your finances and build a strong financial foundation for your business.

# Chapter 18: Raising Capital for your Finances

One of the most significant challenges faced by entrepreneurs and startups is raising capital to finance their businesses. Raising capital is a complex process that requires a lot of research and planning. In this chapter, we will discuss various ways to raise capital and how to choose the right financing option.

## Debt, Equity, and Hybrid Financing:

When raising capital for a business, there are three main types of financing to consider: debt, equity, and hybrid financing.

Debt financing involves borrowing money from a lender that must be paid back with interest. Debt financing can come from a variety of sources, such as banks, credit unions, or private lenders. The advantage of debt financing is that the lender has no ownership in the business, and the borrower retains full control. Debt financing can also be less expensive in the long run than equity financing, as interest payments are tax-deductible. However, debt financing can also come with high interest rates, strict repayment terms, and the risk of default if the business is unable to make payments.

Equity financing involves selling ownership shares in the business to investors in exchange for capital. The advantage of equity financing is that there is no obligation to repay the investment, and the investor takes on the risk of the business's success or failure. Equity financing can also bring in valuable expertise and connections from investors. However, equity financing can be more expensive in the long run than debt financing, as investors typically expect a higher return on investment. Additionally, giving up ownership can mean giving up control over important decisions.

Hybrid financing involves a combination of debt and equity financing. This can be beneficial for businesses that want to maintain some control over decision-making while also minimizing the risk of high interest payments. Hybrid financing can take many forms, such as convertible debt or preferred equity. The advantage of hybrid financing is that it allows businesses to customize their financing to their specific needs. However, hybrid financing can also be complex and difficult to negotiate.

When deciding which type of financing to pursue, businesses should consider factors such as their current financial situation, their goals for growth and expansion, and the amount of control they are willing to give up. For example, a business with a solid revenue stream and a strong credit history may be better suited for debt financing, while a startup with high growth potential may benefit more from equity financing. Ultimately, the best financing option will depend on the unique circumstances of each business.

## Bootstrapping and Self-financing:

Bootstrapping and self-financing refer to a method of financing a business using personal savings and profits generated from the business rather than seeking external funding. This approach is particularly useful for entrepreneurs who may not have access to significant external funding or who want to maintain full control over their business.

Bootstrapping involves using personal savings, credit cards, or loans from family and friends to start and run the business. This method requires careful management of finances and a focus on minimizing costs to maintain profitability.

Self-financing refers to using profits generated by the business to fund growth and expansion rather than seeking external funding. This approach requires the business to be profitable and generate sufficient cash flow to fund growth and expansion.

The advantage of bootstrapping and self-financing is that the entrepreneur retains full ownership and control over the business. Additionally, since there is no external funding, there are no repayment terms, no interest rates, and no equity dilution.

However, there are also some drawbacks to bootstrapping and self-financing. Since the business relies solely on personal savings and profits generated, the funds may be limited, which could limit growth opportunities. Additionally, there may be a higher risk involved since the entrepreneur is not receiving outside expertise or validation.

## Angel Investors:

Angel investing refers to the process of raising capital for a business venture from high net worth individuals or groups who are interested in investing in startups. These individuals are known as angel investors and typically invest in early-stage companies. Angel investors provide more than just funding; they also offer their expertise, industry knowledge, and networks to help the business grow.

Finding angel investors can be done through various channels, including personal networks, angel investor groups, online platforms, and referrals from professionals. It is important to carefully research potential investors and ensure that they are a good fit for the business. When pitching to angel investors, it is essential to have a clear and concise business plan that outlines the business's mission, target market, growth potential, and financial projections. It is also crucial to demonstrate the team's competence and expertise, as well as the uniqueness of the product or service being offered.

Angel investing has several advantages for startups, including access to funding, industry knowledge, and networks. However, there are also some potential drawbacks to consider. Angel investors may require a significant equity stake in the business or have expectations for a quick return on their investment. It is essential to carefully consider the terms of any investment and ensure that they align with the business's long-term goals. It is also important to have a solid plan in place for managing investor relationships and expectations.


## Venture Capital:

Venture capital is a type of financing that is typically provided to early-stage, high-growth companies that have the potential to disrupt their industries and generate significant returns for investors. Venture capitalists (VCs) invest in these companies in exchange for an ownership stake, with the expectation of eventually realizing a return on their investment through an initial public offering (IPO), acquisition, or other exit event.

VCs typically raise money from institutional investors such as pension funds, endowments, and family offices. They then use this capital to invest in a portfolio of startups that they believe have the potential to generate significant returns. VCs typically invest in startups that have already demonstrated some traction and have a strong team, unique technology or business model, and a clear path to growth and profitability.

Finding venture capitalists can be challenging, as they typically invest in a very small percentage of the companies that approach them. One approach is to leverage personal networks and connections to get introductions to VCs. Entrepreneurs can also attend startup events, pitch competitions, and conferences to network with VCs and other investors.

When pitching to venture capitalists, it's important to have a clear and compelling business plan that highlights the potential of the startup and how it plans to disrupt its industry. VCs are looking for startups that have a clear path to growth and profitability, as well as a strong team that can execute on the plan. It's also important to be prepared to answer tough questions about the business model, market size, and competition.

In addition to funding, VCs can provide valuable support and guidance to startups, including strategic advice, introductions to potential customers and partners, and access to talent and resources. However, it's important to carefully evaluate potential VC partners to ensure that they share your vision and are aligned with your goals and values.

## Crowdfunding:

Crowdfunding is a method of raising funds for a business or project by soliciting contributions from a large number of people, typically via the internet.

Crowdfunding can be broadly categorized into four types: donation-based, reward-based, equity-based, and debt-based.

Donation-based crowdfunding involves people contributing to a cause or project without expecting any return. This is usually done for charitable or social causes.

Reward-based crowdfunding involves people contributing to a project or business in exchange for a reward or incentive, such as a pre-order of the product or service being offered.

Equity-based crowdfunding involves people investing in a company in exchange for equity, or ownership, in the business. This is typically used by early-stage startups that are looking for funding but may not be able to secure traditional venture capital.

Debt-based crowdfunding involves people lending money to a business or project with the expectation of repayment with interest over time.

To run a successful crowdfunding campaign, it is important to have a clear and compelling idea that resonates with potential supporters. The campaign should also have a clear target and timeline, as well as a marketing strategy to attract and engage potential supporters.

## Government schemes:

In India, there are various government financing schemes and grants available for startups. Some of the major schemes include the Startup India scheme, which provides funding and support to startups in various sectors, and the Stand-Up India scheme, which provides loans to women and marginalized entrepreneurs. Additionally, there are various state-level schemes and programs that provide funding and support to startups in their respective regions. To qualify for these schemes, startups typically need to meet certain criteria related to their size, sector, and stage of development.

# Chapter 19: Business Plan

As an aspiring entrepreneur or a business owner looking to grow and scale your venture, creating a well-crafted business plan is a crucial step towards success. A business plan serves as a roadmap that outlines your vision, strategies, and goals, and provides a comprehensive understanding of your business to potential investors, lenders, and stakeholders.

In this chapter, we will delve into the fundamental aspects of developing a robust business plan that will guide you through the various stages of your entrepreneurial journey. Whether you are just starting out or seeking to expand an existing business, a well-structured business plan will serve as a blueprint for success.

A business plan is not just a document to secure financing; it is a strategic tool that helps you clarify your business idea, assess the market, define your target audience, identify your competition, and articulate your value proposition. It provides a framework for making informed decisions, setting realistic goals, and monitoring your progress along the way.

Throughout this chapter, we will explore the key components of a business plan in detail, explaining their importance and providing practical guidance on how to develop each section effectively. We will also discuss various tips, techniques, and best practices to ensure that your business plan stands out and captures the attention of potential investors or lenders.

Remember, a well-crafted business plan not only helps you attract funding but also serves as a valuable resource for managing your business, aligning your team, and adapting to changes in the market. It is a living document that should be regularly reviewed and updated to reflect the evolving nature of your business and its environment.

So, let's dive into the world of business planning and discover how to develop a compelling and effective business plan that sets the foundation for your entrepreneurial success.

# Executive Summary:

The executive summary is a critical component of a business plan as it serves as an introduction and overview of your entire document. It is typically the first section that potential investors, lenders, or stakeholders will read, so it needs to be concise, engaging, and compelling. The purpose of the executive summary is to grab the reader's attention, provide a summary of your business idea, and entice them to continue reading the rest of your business plan.

The executive summary should capture the essence of your business and convey the key points that make your venture unique and promising. It should include the following elements:

1. **Company Overview:** Begin by introducing your company and providing a brief overview of its history, mission, and vision. Explain the nature of your business, the products or services you offer, and the market you operate in.

2. **Problem and Solution:** Clearly define the problem or need that your business aims to address. Explain how your product or service offers a unique solution to this problem and how it provides value to your target customers. Highlight any competitive advantages or innovative features that set your solution apart.

3. **Target Market:** Identify your target market and describe the demographics, characteristics, and behaviours of your ideal customers. Explain the size and growth potential of your target market and outline how your business is positioned to capture a significant share of it.

4. **Business Model:** Provide a high-level overview of your business model, including your revenue streams, pricing strategy, and distribution channels. Explain how you plan to generate revenue and achieve profitability.

5. **Competitive Advantage:** Highlight the key factors that differentiate your business from competitors. This may include unique features, proprietary technology, strategic partnerships, or intellectual property. Emphasize why customers will choose your product or service over alternatives.

6. **Financial Summary:** Provide a snapshot of your financial projections, including revenue forecasts, profitability, and expected return on investment. Summarize key financial metrics and highlight the potential for growth and profitability.

7. **Funding Requirements:** If you are seeking funding, clearly state the amount of funding you require and how it will be utilized. Explain the purpose of the funds and the expected outcomes or milestones that will be achieved with the investment.

Remember, the executive summary should be concise and to the point. Aim to keep it within one to two pages, providing enough information to give a clear understanding of your business idea without overwhelming the reader with excessive details. It should serve as a compelling teaser that leaves the reader intrigued and eager to learn more about your business.

## Company Description:

The Company Description section of a business plan provides an overview of your company, giving readers a clear understanding of what your business is all about. It serves as an introduction to your venture, highlighting key aspects that set your company apart and providing insight into its purpose, mission, and values.

In this section, you need to provide a detailed and concise description of your company's background, history, and current status. It should paint a clear picture of who you are, what you do, and why your business is unique and promising.

Here are some key components to include in your Company Description:

1. **Business Name and Legal Structure:** Begin by stating the official name of your company and its legal structure (e.g., sole proprietorship, partnership, corporation). This information helps establish your business's identity and legal standing.

2. **Mission Statement:** Express your company's mission statement, which defines its purpose, values, and long-term aspirations. A mission

statement should be concise, inspiring, and reflect the core values and goals of your business.

3. **Vision Statement:** Articulate your company's vision, which describes the future direction and desired outcomes of your business. It should outline your aspirations and what you aim to achieve in the long run. A compelling vision statement helps create a sense of purpose and guides decision-making.

4. **Business History and Milestones:** Provide a brief overview of your company's history, highlighting key milestones and achievements. This could include significant events, product launches, awards, or major partnerships. Showcase the progress and growth your company has experienced to instil confidence in potential investors or lenders.

5. **Legal and Ownership Structure:** Describe the legal structure of your company, such as whether it is a sole proprietorship, partnership, limited liability company (LLC), or corporation. Outline the ownership structure, including the names and roles of key stakeholders, partners, or shareholders.

6. **Industry and Market Analysis:** Discuss the industry in which your business operates, providing an overview of its size, growth potential, and key trends. Include relevant market research to demonstrate your understanding of the market landscape and the opportunities and challenges it presents.

7. **Unique Selling Proposition (USP):** Highlight your company's unique selling proposition, which sets you apart from competitors and establishes your value proposition to customers. Clearly communicate the advantages and benefits that your products or services offer.

8. **Target Market:** Define your target market by describing the specific customer segments you aim to serve. Include demographic information, psychographic characteristics, and their needs or pain points that your business addresses. This demonstrates your market understanding and helps investors or lenders see the potential market demand for your offerings.

9. **Competitive Advantage:** Identify and explain the competitive advantages that give your company an edge over competitors. This could include factors such as proprietary technology, intellectual property, unique expertise, strategic partnerships, or cost advantages. Showcase how these advantages contribute to your market positioning and growth potential.

10. **Future Growth Opportunities:** Briefly discuss future growth opportunities and expansion plans for your company. This could include potential new markets, product diversification, strategic partnerships, or scalability plans. Show that you have a clear vision for the future and a roadmap for continued success.

Remember, the Company Description section sets the foundation for the rest of your business plan. It should be concise, engaging, and provide a compelling overview of your company's identity, purpose, market positioning, and growth potential. Tailor the description to your target audience, whether it be investors, lenders, or potential business partners, and ensure that it aligns with the overall tone and goals of your business plan.

## Market Analysis:

The Market Analysis section of a business plan is a critical component that provides a comprehensive evaluation of the industry, market, and target customers. It helps entrepreneurs gain a deep understanding of the market they operate in and identify opportunities and challenges that can impact their business's success.

In this section, you need to conduct thorough research and present relevant data and insights to support your analysis. By demonstrating a solid grasp of the market dynamics, trends, and customer needs, you can effectively position your business and develop strategies to capitalize on market opportunities.

Here are the key elements to include in your Market Analysis:

1. **Industry Overview:** Begin by providing an overview of the industry in which your business operates. Describe the size, growth rate, and key trends that shape the industry landscape. Highlight any significant

factors such as technological advancements, regulatory changes, or market disruptions that could impact the industry's future.

2. **Target Market Segmentation:** Define and segment your target market based on specific characteristics such as demographics, psychographics, behaviours, or geographic locations. Identify the key customer segments you plan to serve and explain why these segments are attractive and relevant to your business. Show a deep understanding of your target customers' needs, preferences, and pain points.

3. **Market Size and Growth Potential:** Estimate the total addressable market (TAM) for your product or service. Analyse the market size in terms of revenue, volume, or units sold. Support your analysis with data from credible sources or industry reports. Additionally, provide insights into the market's growth potential, highlighting any projected growth rates or emerging trends that can create opportunities for your business.

4. **Competitive Analysis:** Identify and analyse your direct and indirect competitors. Assess their strengths, weaknesses, market share, pricing strategies, distribution channels, and overall market positioning. Identify what sets your business apart from competitors and articulate your unique value proposition. Understand your competitive landscape to determine how you can differentiate and gain a competitive edge.

5. **Customer Buying Behaviour:** Explore how customers make purchasing decisions in your industry. Understand the factors that influence their buying behaviour, such as price sensitivity, brand loyalty, product quality, convenience, or customer service. Analyse any existing market research or customer surveys to gain insights into customer preferences, motivations, and purchasing patterns.

6. **Market Entry Barriers:** Identify any barriers or challenges that may impede new entrants into the market. These could include high capital requirements, regulatory restrictions, strong incumbent players, or technological complexities. Assess how these barriers may impact your business and develop strategies to mitigate or overcome them.

7. **Market Trends and Future Outlook:** Analyse the current market trends and anticipate future developments. Identify emerging technologies, changing consumer preferences, or shifts in market

demand that could impact your business. Stay updated with industry publications, market research reports, and expert insights to ensure your analysis reflects the most current trends and projections.

8. **SWOT Analysis:** Conduct a SWOT analysis, evaluating the strengths, weaknesses, opportunities, and threats facing your business in the market. Highlight your business's unique strengths and how they align with market opportunities. Identify potential weaknesses or threats and outline strategies to address them.

By conducting a comprehensive Market Analysis, you can gain valuable insights into your industry and target market, enabling you to make informed decisions and develop effective marketing and growth strategies. It helps you understand your customers, competitors, and market dynamics, ensuring that your business is well-positioned to capitalize on opportunities and navigate challenges. Remember to use credible sources and data to support your analysis and continually update your Market Analysis as the market evolves.

## Organization and Management:

The Organization and Management section of a business plan provides an overview of the structure, key personnel, and roles within the company. This section highlights the management team's expertise, demonstrates their ability to execute the business plan, and instils confidence in potential investors or lenders.

In this section, you will introduce your company's organizational structure, key management team members, and their roles and responsibilities. Additionally, you should outline any advisory board or external consultants who contribute to the company's strategic decision-making. The goal is to convey that your team has the necessary skills, experience, and knowledge to drive the success of the business.

Here are the key elements to include in the Organization and Management section:

1. **Organizational Structure:** Describe the legal structure of your company, whether it is a sole proprietorship, partnership, limited

liability company (LLC), or corporation. Explain the reasoning behind your chosen structure and how it aligns with your business goals. Provide an organizational chart that illustrates the hierarchy and relationships among different roles and departments within the company.

2. **Management Team:** Introduce the key members of your management team and highlight their qualifications, expertise, and relevant experiences. Include their names, positions, and a brief background that highlights their skills and accomplishments. Demonstrate how their skills and experiences complement each other and contribute to the success of the business. If you have any notable advisors or consultants, mention their names and their specific roles in guiding the company.

3. **Roles and Responsibilities:** Clearly outline the roles and responsibilities of each member of the management team. Explain how their individual contributions align with the overall objectives of the business. Emphasize any unique or specialized skills that are critical to the success of your business. This will give investors or lenders confidence in the team's ability to execute the business plan effectively.

4. **Staffing Plan:** Outline the staffing requirements and any additional key personnel needed to support the growth of the business. Describe the qualifications and skills required for each position. Include a timeline for hiring and the associated costs. Demonstrating that you have considered the staffing needs of your business shows that you have thought through the operational requirements and are prepared for growth.

5. **Board of Directors or Advisory Board:** If applicable, mention any board of directors or advisory board members. Highlight their expertise and how their guidance will benefit the company. This adds credibility to your business by demonstrating that you have sought external perspectives and have access to valuable industry insights.

6. **Management Compensation and Ownership:** Provide an overview of how management is compensated, including salaries, bonuses, equity ownership, and any other incentives. Explain how these compensation structures align with the company's performance and

long-term goals. Investors will be interested in understanding how the management team's interests are aligned with the success of the business.

7. **Key Relationships:** Identify any strategic partnerships or key relationships that are essential to your business operations. This could include suppliers, distributors, or other businesses that contribute to your value chain. Explain the importance of these relationships and how they support your business's growth and competitive advantage.

By including a comprehensive Organization and Management section in your business plan, you demonstrate that your team has the necessary skills and expertise to execute the business strategy effectively. It conveys a sense of stability, competence, and credibility to potential investors or lenders. Remember to highlight the strengths and qualifications of your team, and emphasize how their collective experience and skills will contribute to the success of your business.

## Products or Services:

The Products or Services section of a business plan provides an in-depth description of the products or services your company offers. This section is crucial as it showcases the value proposition of your business and demonstrates how your offerings meet the needs of your target market. It helps investors and stakeholders understand the unique features, benefits, and competitive advantages of your products or services.

When describing your products or services, consider the following key elements:

1. **Product or Service Description:** Start by providing a clear and concise description of your products or services. Explain what they are, how they work, and the specific problems they solve for customers. Highlight any unique features or innovations that set your offerings apart from competitors. Include relevant technical specifications or details that are important for customers to know.

2. **Benefits and Value Proposition:** Clearly articulate the benefits customers can expect from using your products or services. Explain how your offerings add value and address customers' pain points or needs. Describe the advantages and positive outcomes customers can achieve by using your products or services. This helps investors and stakeholders understand the potential demand and market opportunity for your offerings.

3. **Competitive Advantage:** Identify and communicate your competitive advantage. This could be factors such as superior quality, lower cost, unique features, proprietary technology, or a differentiated approach to delivering value. Highlight why customers would choose your products or services over those offered by competitors. This demonstrates your understanding of the competitive landscape and how your offerings stand out in the market.

4. **Intellectual Property:** If applicable, discuss any intellectual property (IP) associated with your products or services. This could include patents, trademarks, copyrights, or trade secrets. Explain how your IP protects your competitive advantage and adds value to your business. Investors and stakeholders are often interested in understanding the level of protection and potential barriers to entry that your IP provides.

5. **Development Stage and Roadmap:** Describe the current stage of development for your products or services. If they are already in the market, provide information on their sales performance, customer feedback, and any planned updates or enhancements. If they are still in development, outline your roadmap for bringing them to market, including key milestones, timelines, and resource requirements. This demonstrates your ability to execute your product or service strategy effectively.

6. **Pricing Strategy:** Discuss your pricing strategy and how it aligns with your target market and overall business objectives. Explain the rationale behind your pricing structure, taking into account factors such as production costs, market demand, competitor pricing, and perceived value. Consider any pricing models, discounts, or promotional strategies that may be relevant to your products or services.

7.  **Future Opportunities:** Briefly mention any potential future opportunities for expanding or diversifying your product or service offerings. This could include new features, product extensions, additional market segments, or complementary offerings. Investors and stakeholders are interested in understanding your vision for the future and the potential for growth beyond your initial offerings.

By providing a comprehensive and compelling description of your products or services, you showcase the value they provide to customers and the market opportunity they represent. It is important to convey a clear understanding of your offerings, their unique features and benefits, and how they differentiate you from competitors. Remember to focus on the customer perspective and explain why customers would choose your products or services over alternatives. This section is critical for investors and stakeholders to assess the viability and potential success of your business.

## Marketing and Sales Strategy:

The Marketing and Sales Strategy section of a business plan outlines how you plan to attract and retain customers, promote your products or services, and ultimately generate revenue. This section is crucial as it demonstrates your understanding of the target market, competition, and the steps you will take to effectively reach and engage potential customers.

When developing your marketing and sales strategy, consider the following key elements:

1.  **Target Market:** Clearly define your target market or customer segments. Identify the specific characteristics, needs, and preferences of your ideal customers. This includes demographics (age, gender, location, etc.), psychographics (lifestyle, interests, values, etc.), and any other relevant factors. Understanding your target market helps you tailor your marketing efforts and messages to resonate with your intended audience.

2.  **Market Analysis:** Conduct a thorough analysis of your industry, market trends, and competition. Identify your competitors and analyse

their strengths, weaknesses, and market positioning. Understand the market size, growth potential, and any emerging opportunities or challenges. This information helps you identify gaps in the market that you can leverage and develop effective marketing strategies.

3. **Unique Selling Proposition (USP):** Define your unique selling proposition or competitive advantage. Determine what sets your products or services apart from the competition and why customers would choose you over alternatives. Your USP could be based on factors such as superior quality, innovative features, exceptional customer service, competitive pricing, or a differentiated approach to meeting customer needs. Communicate your USP clearly to differentiate yourself in the market.

4. **Marketing Channels:** Outline the channels and methods you will use to reach your target market. This includes both online and offline channels such as websites, social media platforms, email marketing, content marketing, advertising, public relations, direct sales, partnerships, and more. Consider the most effective channels for reaching your target audience and allocate resources accordingly. Additionally, discuss any strategic alliances or partnerships that can help you extend your reach.

5. **Marketing Tactics:** Detail the specific marketing tactics and campaigns you will implement to promote your products or services. This may include online advertising campaigns, search engine optimization (SEO), social media marketing, content creation, events, trade shows, public relations efforts, and more. Provide a timeline and budget for each tactic to ensure effective execution. Clearly define the key performance indicators (KPIs) you will use to measure the success of your marketing efforts.

6. **Sales Approach:** Explain your sales approach and the strategies you will use to convert leads into paying customers. Describe your sales process, including lead generation, qualification, nurturing, and closing techniques. Discuss the sales team structure, if applicable, and the training and support you will provide to ensure their success. Provide

sales forecasts and projections based on your market analysis and anticipated conversion rates.

7. **Customer Retention:** Outline your strategies for customer retention and fostering long-term customer relationships. Discuss how you will provide exceptional customer service, address customer feedback, and encourage repeat purchases. Consider loyalty programs, customer referral programs, and other initiatives to maximize customer lifetime value.

8. **Budget and ROI:** Include a budget for your marketing and sales activities. Break down the costs associated with each marketing tactic and estimate the return on investment (ROI) you expect to achieve. This demonstrates your financial planning and helps investors understand how you will allocate resources to drive revenue growth.

By developing a comprehensive marketing and sales strategy, you demonstrate your ability to effectively reach your target market, generate demand for your products or services, and convert prospects into customers. Your strategy should align with your overall business objectives, target market insights, and competitive landscape. Regularly review and adjust your marketing and sales strategies based on customer feedback, market trends, and performance metrics to ensure their ongoing effectiveness.

## Financial Projections:

The Financial Projections section of a business plan provides an overview of the financial performance and viability of your business over a specific period, usually three to five years. It includes forecasts of revenue, expenses, and profitability, as well as key financial metrics and assumptions. This section is crucial for investors, lenders, and stakeholders as it demonstrates the financial feasibility and potential return on investment of your business.

When creating your financial projections, consider the following key components:

1. **Sales Forecast:** Start by estimating your sales revenue for each product or service category. This can be based on market research,

historical data, industry benchmarks, and anticipated market demand. Project your sales volume and price per unit, taking into account factors such as seasonality, market trends, and competitive landscape. Break down your sales forecast by month or quarter for the first year and then annually for the following years.

2. **Cost of Goods Sold (COGS):** Calculate the direct costs associated with producing or delivering your products or services. This includes raw materials, manufacturing costs, direct labour, packaging, and any other variable costs directly related to your sales. By subtracting the COGS from your sales revenue, you can determine your gross profit margin.

3. **Operating Expenses:** Estimate your fixed and variable operating expenses, including rent, utilities, salaries, marketing expenses, insurance, office supplies, and any other costs required to run your business. Categorize your expenses into different cost categories and specify any major assumptions or changes in costs over time. Be realistic and provide detailed justifications for your expense projections.

4. **Profit and Loss Statement:** Prepare a projected Profit and Loss (P&L) statement, also known as an income statement. This statement summarizes your revenues, COGS, operating expenses, and ultimately calculates your net income or loss. It provides a snapshot of your business's financial performance and profitability. Include the P&L statement for each year of the forecasted period.

5. **Cash Flow Projections:** Cash flow projections are essential for understanding the inflows and outflows of cash in your business. Prepare a cash flow statement that outlines your projected cash inflows (such as sales revenue, loans, or investments) and outflows (such as expenses, loan repayments, and taxes) over the forecasted period. This statement helps you identify potential cash flow gaps, plan for working capital needs, and assess your business's ability to meet financial obligations.

6. **Balance Sheet:** Include a projected balance sheet, which provides a snapshot of your business's financial position at a specific point in time. It includes your assets (such as cash, inventory, equipment), liabilities

(such as loans, accounts payable), and owner's equity. The balance sheet helps assess the solvency and financial stability of your business.

7. **Break-Even Analysis:** Conduct a break-even analysis to determine the point at which your revenue equals your expenses, resulting in neither profit nor loss. This analysis helps you understand the level of sales volume or revenue required to cover your costs. It is particularly useful for assessing the viability of a new product or service, pricing strategies, and overall financial risk.

8. **Financial Ratios and Metrics:** Calculate and include key financial ratios and metrics that provide insights into your business's financial health and performance. Examples include gross profit margin, net profit margin, return on investment (ROI), current ratio, and debt-to-equity ratio. These ratios help evaluate profitability, liquidity, efficiency, and leverage.

9. **Assumptions:** Clearly state the assumptions underlying your financial projections. This includes factors such as market growth rates, pricing assumptions, cost trends, inflation rates, and any other variables that significantly impact your financial performance. Justify your assumptions with relevant market research, industry data, and historical trends.

Remember, financial projections are not set in stone and will evolve as your business progresses. Regularly review and update your projections as you gather more information and data. It's essential to be realistic, transparent, and accurate in your financial projections to gain the trust and confidence of potential investors, lenders, and stakeholders.

By presenting comprehensive and well-structured financial projections, you can demonstrate your understanding of your business's financial dynamics, showcase its growth potential, and attract the necessary funding to support your entrepreneurial journey.

## Funding Request:

The Funding Request section of a business plan outlines the specific amount of funding you are seeking from investors or lenders to support your business's growth and operations. This section is crucial as it demonstrates your financial needs and how the requested funds will be utilized to achieve your business objectives.

When preparing your Funding Request, consider the following key components:

1. **Funding Amount:** Clearly state the specific amount of funding you are requesting. This should be based on a thorough analysis of your financial projections, taking into account your startup costs, working capital needs, expansion plans, and any other funding requirements. Be specific and provide a breakdown of how the funds will be allocated.

2. **Use of Funds:** Describe in detail how the requested funds will be used to support your business's growth and operations. Specify the key areas where the funds will be invested, such as product development, marketing and sales initiatives, hiring additional staff, purchasing equipment or inventory, expanding to new markets, or improving infrastructure. Provide a clear and logical justification for each expense to demonstrate the potential impact on your business's success.

3. **Milestones and Timelines:** Outline the milestones you plan to achieve with the requested funding and establish a timeline for accomplishing these milestones. Milestones may include product launches, market penetration goals, revenue targets, customer acquisition targets, or expansion plans. By setting measurable and realistic milestones, you can demonstrate a clear path to growth and success.

4. **Funding Structure:** Specify the desired funding structure, such as equity financing, debt financing, or a combination of both. Explain the reasoning behind your chosen funding structure and how it aligns with your long-term business goals and financial projections. If seeking equity financing, indicate the percentage of ownership you are willing to offer in exchange for the funding.

5. **Exit Strategy:** Discuss your proposed exit strategy for investors or lenders. Explain how they can expect to realize a return on their investment, whether it's through a planned acquisition, an IPO, or other strategic opportunities. Demonstrating a clear and viable exit strategy

can provide investors with confidence that their investment will yield a favourable return.

6. **Risk Assessment:** Address the potential risks and challenges associated with your funding request. Acknowledge any market risks, competitive pressures, regulatory concerns, or other factors that may impact your business's ability to achieve its goals. Provide a thorough risk assessment and explain the strategies you have in place to mitigate these risks and maximize the likelihood of a successful outcome.

7. **Financial Projections:** Include a summary of your financial projections, highlighting the anticipated revenue growth, profitability, and return on investment. This will help investors or lenders understand the financial potential of your business and assess the viability of your funding request. Refer to the detailed financial projections in the Financial Projections section of your business plan for more comprehensive information.

8. **Requested Terms and Conditions:** Clearly state the specific terms and conditions you are seeking from potential investors or lenders. This may include the desired interest rate, repayment schedule, collateral requirements, equity ownership percentage, or any other relevant terms. Be realistic and consider industry standards and market conditions when formulating your requested terms and conditions.

9. **Contact Information:** Provide your contact information, including your name, position, email address, phone number, and any other relevant details. Encourage potential investors or lenders to reach out to you for further discussions or to request additional information.

Remember, the Funding Request section is your opportunity to make a compelling case for why investors or lenders should provide the requested funds. It should be concise, persuasive, and supported by data and financial projections. Clearly articulate the funding needs of your business, the potential for growth and profitability, and the strategies in place to mitigate risks and ensure a successful outcome.

## Implementation Plan:

The Implementation Plan section of a business plan outlines the specific actions and strategies you will undertake to bring your business concept to life and achieve your stated objectives. It provides a roadmap for executing your business plan and guides your team in implementing the necessary steps to launch and operate your business successfully.

When developing your Implementation Plan, consider the following key components:

1. **Goals and Objectives:** Clearly define the goals and objectives you aim to achieve during the implementation phase. These should align with the overall vision and mission of your business. Goals can be broad, such as increasing market share or launching new product lines, while objectives should be specific, measurable, attainable, relevant, and time-bound (SMART).

2. **Action Steps:** Break down the implementation process into actionable steps or tasks. Each step should be specific, with a clear description of what needs to be done, who will be responsible, and the timeline for completion. Assigning responsibilities ensures accountability and ensures that each task is completed in a timely manner.

3. **Timeline:** Develop a timeline or project schedule that outlines the sequence of activities and their respective deadlines. This timeline should cover the entire implementation phase, from initial preparations to full operation. Consider dependencies between tasks and factor in any external factors that may impact the timeline, such as regulatory approvals or supplier lead times.

4. **Resource Allocation:** Identify the resources required to execute your implementation plan effectively. This includes financial resources, human resources, technology, equipment, and any other assets necessary to support your operations. Determine how these resources will be acquired, allocated, and managed throughout the implementation process.

5. **Team and Responsibilities:** Specify the roles and responsibilities of key team members involved in the implementation. This includes members of your management team, project managers, department

heads, and any external consultants or contractors. Clearly define each person's responsibilities, reporting structure, and communication channels to ensure smooth coordination and collaboration.

6. **Budget and Financial Considerations:** Outline the budgetary requirements for implementing your business plan. Identify the estimated costs associated with each activity or task and allocate funds accordingly. Consider one-time costs, ongoing expenses, and any contingency plans for unforeseen circumstances. Regularly monitor and review your budget to ensure financial discipline and alignment with your business objectives.

7. **Key Milestones:** Establish key milestones or checkpoints throughout the implementation phase. These milestones mark significant achievements or progress points and allow you to assess the effectiveness of your strategies and make any necessary adjustments. Each milestone should have specific deliverables or outcomes that contribute to the overall success of your business.

8. **Monitoring and Evaluation:** Develop a system for monitoring and evaluating the progress of your implementation plan. This includes defining key performance indicators (KPIs) that measure the effectiveness of your strategies and track the achievement of your goals and objectives. Regularly review and analyse the data to identify areas for improvement and make informed decisions.

9. **Risk Management:** Identify potential risks and challenges that may arise during the implementation process and develop strategies to mitigate them. This includes assessing market risks, operational risks, financial risks, and any other factors that may impact the successful execution of your plan. Develop contingency plans and alternative courses of action to address potential setbacks.

10. **Continuous Improvement:** Emphasize the importance of continuous improvement and adaptability throughout the implementation phase. Monitor market trends, customer feedback, and industry developments to identify opportunities for innovation and growth. Regularly review and update your implementation plan to ensure it remains relevant and aligned with the evolving needs of your business.

The Implementation Plan serves as a guide for executing your business plan effectively. It provides a structured approach to turning your vision into reality by outlining the specific steps, responsibilities, timelines, and resource requirements. By carefully planning and managing the implementation process, you increase the likelihood of achieving your business objectives and positioning your company for long-term success.

## Appendix:

The Appendix section of a business plan is an optional but valuable component where you can include supplementary information and supporting documents that provide further depth and credibility to your plan. It is a space to include any additional information that is relevant to understanding your business, but may not be necessary to include in the main body of the plan.

Here are some elements you may consider including in the Appendix section:

1. **Market Research Data:** If you have conducted extensive market research and gathered a significant amount of data, charts, or graphs, you can include them in the Appendix. This can include market analysis reports, industry trends, customer surveys, competitor analysis, or any other research findings that support your business plan.

2. **Product or Service Documentation:** Include any technical specifications, product catalogs, patents, or prototypes related to your products or services. This can provide a more comprehensive understanding of your offerings and demonstrate their unique features or competitive advantages.

3. **Legal Documents:** Include copies of any relevant legal documents, such as licenses, permits, trademarks, copyrights, or contracts that are important for your business operations. This helps provide credibility and transparency to potential investors or lenders.

4. **Resumes and Biographies:** Include resumes or biographies of key members of your management team, highlighting their relevant experience, expertise, and accomplishments. This allows readers to assess the qualifications and capabilities of the individuals driving the business forward.

5. **Financial Statements:** Include detailed financial statements, such as balance sheets, income statements, and cash flow statements, for the past few years, if available. This provides a historical perspective on your business's financial performance and demonstrates your ability to manage finances effectively.

6. **Letters of Support or Recommendation:** If you have received letters of support or recommendation from industry experts, advisors, customers, or other stakeholders, you can include them in the Appendix. These letters can attest to the viability and potential of your business, adding credibility to your plan.

7. **Marketing Collateral:** Include samples of your marketing materials, such as brochures, flyers, advertisements, or website screenshots. This gives readers a visual representation of your branding, messaging, and promotional efforts.

8. **Legal and Regulatory Compliance:** Include documentation related to compliance with relevant laws, regulations, and standards in your industry. This can include certifications, permits, environmental impact assessments, or any other compliance-related documents.

9. **Additional Financial Information:** If there is any additional financial information that supports or supplements the financial projections presented in the main body of the plan, include it in the Appendix. This can include detailed revenue breakdowns, cost analyses, or other financial data that stakeholders may find useful.

10. **Any Other Supporting Documentation:** Include any other relevant documents, such as market studies, product testing results, customer testimonials, or letters of intent from potential clients or suppliers. These documents can enhance the credibility and persuasiveness of your business plan.

The Appendix section allows you to provide readers with comprehensive and detailed information that supports the content presented in the main body of your business plan. It is important to organize the information in a logical and easily accessible manner, ensuring that it complements and enhances the understanding of your business and its potential for success.

Remember, a business plan is not a static document but rather a dynamic tool that evolves with your business. It should be regularly reviewed, updated, and adjusted as you gather new information, encounter challenges, and seize opportunities. Embrace the feedback and insights you receive from investors, mentors, and industry experts to continuously improve and refine your plan.

A well-prepared business plan sets the foundation for success and provides you with a roadmap to navigate the complexities of the business world. It guides your decision-making, helps you stay focused on your goals, and enables you to seize opportunities with confidence. Whether you are starting a new business, seeking funding, or looking to scale your existing venture, a well-crafted business plan is an invaluable asset that can propel you towards your entrepreneurial aspirations.

As you embark on your entrepreneurial journey, take the time to develop a comprehensive and well-thought-out business plan. Invest the effort to articulate your vision, outline your strategies, and demonstrate the financial viability of your venture. By doing so, you increase your chances of attracting the right investors, securing funding, and turning your entrepreneurial dreams into a successful reality.

# Chapter 20: Creating a Pitch Deck

In the world of entrepreneurship and startup funding, the pitch deck has become an essential tool for effectively communicating your business idea and capturing the attention of potential investors. A pitch deck is a concise and visually compelling presentation that highlights the key aspects of your business, such as the problem you're solving, your solution, target market, competitive advantage, and financial projections. This chapter will guide you through the process of creating a compelling pitch deck that effectively showcases your business and increases your chances of securing funding.

## Understanding the Purpose of a Pitch Deck:

The primary purpose of a pitch deck is to capture the interest of investors and convince them of the potential of your business. It serves as a condensed version of your business plan, presenting the most critical information in a concise and engaging manner. A well-crafted pitch deck can help you make a memorable impression, generate investor interest, and ultimately lead to further discussions and potential funding opportunities.

## Key Components of a Pitch Deck:

- **Problem Statement:** Clearly define the problem or pain point your target audience is facing and highlight its significance. Explain why existing solutions are inadequate or inefficient.

- **Solution:** Present your unique solution or product that addresses the identified problem. Clearly articulate the value proposition and how it solves the problem better than existing alternatives.

- **Market Opportunity:** Demonstrate the size and growth potential of your target market. Provide market research, data, and insights to support your claims. Highlight any market trends, customer segments, or untapped opportunities.

- **Business Model:** Describe your business model and revenue generation strategy. Explain how you plan to monetize your product or service and achieve profitability. Include details on pricing, distribution channels, and potential partnerships.

- **Competitive Advantage:** Differentiate your business from competitors and highlight your unique selling points. Showcase your competitive advantages, such as proprietary technology, intellectual property, strategic partnerships, or a strong team.

- **Marketing and Sales Strategy:** Outline your marketing and sales approach to reach your target customers and generate revenue. Describe your customer acquisition strategy, distribution channels, and marketing tactics. Include any early traction or customer testimonials.

- **Team:** Introduce the key members of your team and their relevant expertise. Highlight their accomplishments, industry experience, and how their skills contribute to the success of the business. Investors often invest in teams rather than just ideas.

- **Financial Projections:** Provide a summary of your financial projections, including revenue forecasts, profitability, and key financial metrics. Highlight any notable milestones achieved or future funding needs.

- **Funding Request:** Clearly state the amount of funding you are seeking and how you plan to utilize the funds. Provide a breakdown of the funding allocation and the expected impact on the business.

- **Appendix:** Include any additional supporting materials, such as product demonstrations, market research data, customer testimonials, or press coverage. This section can be customized based on the specific needs of your pitch.

## Crafting a Compelling Pitch Deck:

- **Keep it concise:** Aim for a pitch deck that is no longer than 10-15 slides. Be concise and focus on the most critical information. Use bullet points, visuals, and charts to convey your message effectively.

- **Tell a compelling story:** Structure your pitch deck as a narrative that captivates and engages the audience. Start with a strong opening that grabs attention, outline the problem, present your solution, and build momentum towards your business's potential.

- **Visuals and design:** Use visually appealing graphics, charts, and images to enhance the presentation and make it visually engaging. Ensure consistency in fonts, colours, and overall design to maintain a professional and polished look.

- **Keep the language simple:** Avoid jargon or technical terms that may confuse or alienate your audience. Use clear and concise language that is easy to understand for individuals with varying levels of business knowledge.

- **Focus on the problem and solution:** Clearly articulate the problem your target market is facing and emphasize how your solution addresses that problem effectively. Highlight the unique features, benefits, and competitive advantages of your product or service.

- **Showcase market opportunity:** Use market research and data to demonstrate the size, growth potential, and attractiveness of your target market. Provide insights into market trends, customer demographics, and any untapped opportunities that make your business viable and scalable.

- **Present a compelling business model:** Clearly explain how your business generates revenue and achieves profitability. Outline your pricing strategy, sales channels, customer acquisition plan, and any strategic partnerships or collaborations that contribute to your business model's success.

- **Highlight the team:** Introduce the key members of your team, emphasizing their relevant experience, expertise, and accomplishments. Investors often invest in people, so showcase the strengths of your team and how their collective skills contribute to the success of the business.

- **Present financial projections:** Provide a summary of your financial projections, including revenue forecasts, cost structure, and key financial metrics such as gross margin, net profit, and break-even point. Use visuals, charts, and graphs to make the financial information easily understandable and compelling.

- **Include a clear funding request:** Clearly state the amount of funding you are seeking from investors and explain how the funds will be utilized to drive business growth and achieve key milestones. Provide a breakdown of the funding allocation, indicating how it will impact various aspects of your business.
- **Practice and refine your pitch:** Rehearse your pitch deck presentation multiple times to ensure smooth delivery and confidence. Seek feedback from trusted advisors or mentors to refine your pitch, making it more compelling and effective.

## Conclusion:

A well-crafted pitch deck is a powerful tool in your entrepreneurial journey. It enables you to present your business idea, showcase its potential, and secure funding from investors. By understanding the key components and crafting a compelling narrative, visuals, and financial projections, you can create a pitch deck that effectively communicates the value and viability of your business. Remember to practice your presentation and seek feedback to continuously improve and refine your pitch deck. With a compelling pitch deck in hand, you'll be well-prepared to captivate investors and take your business to new heights.

# Chapter 21: Scaling and Growing Your Startup

Scaling and growing a startup is an exciting yet challenging phase in the entrepreneurial journey. It involves expanding your business operations, increasing market reach, and achieving sustainable growth. This chapter will guide you through the essential strategies, considerations, and best practices for effectively scaling and growing your startup.

## 1. Develop a Growth Strategy:

- **Define Your Vision:** Clearly articulate your long-term vision and goals for the business. Identify the key milestones you aim to achieve during the scaling process.

- **Market Expansion:** Analyse your target market and identify opportunities for expansion. Consider entering new geographic markets, targeting different customer segments, or diversifying your product/service offerings.

- **Customer Acquisition and Retention:** Develop strategies to acquire new customers and retain existing ones. Focus on enhancing customer experience, implementing effective marketing campaigns, and leveraging customer feedback for product/service improvement.

- **Strategic Partnerships:** Explore partnerships with complementary businesses or industry leaders to leverage their resources, expertise, and customer base. Strategic alliances can help accelerate growth and provide access to new markets.

- **Technology Adoption:** Embrace technology solutions and innovations that can streamline operations, improve efficiency, and enhance customer engagement. Evaluate emerging technologies that align with your business objectives and can give you a competitive edge.

## 2. Build a High-Performing Team:

- **Talent Acquisition:** Recruit skilled professionals who align with your business culture, values, and growth objectives. Look for individuals with relevant experience, a passion for your industry, and a track record of success.
- **Leadership Development:** Invest in developing leadership skills within your team. Empower managers to lead effectively, delegate responsibilities, and foster a positive and growth-oriented work environment.
- **Employee Engagement:** Create a work environment that promotes employee engagement, satisfaction, and growth. Offer competitive compensation packages, provide opportunities for professional development, and foster a culture of open communication and collaboration.
- **Scalable Organizational Structure:** Ensure that your organizational structure is adaptable and scalable to accommodate future growth. Regularly assess and realign roles and responsibilities to optimize efficiency and support the evolving needs of your business.

## 3. Strengthen Operational Efficiency:

- **Streamline Processes:** Continuously evaluate and optimize your business processes to enhance efficiency and productivity. Identify bottlenecks, automate repetitive tasks, and implement scalable systems and tools.
- **Supply Chain Management:** Evaluate your supply chain to ensure timely and cost-effective delivery of products/services. Establish strong relationships with suppliers, optimize inventory management, and consider outsourcing non-core functions, if necessary.
- **Financial Management:** Maintain robust financial controls and systems to monitor cash flow, profitability, and key financial metrics. Implement financial forecasting and budgeting practices to ensure sound financial management during the scaling phase.
- **Scalable Infrastructure:** Assess your infrastructure needs to accommodate growth. This includes physical infrastructure, such as

office space and equipment, as well as digital infrastructure, such as IT systems and software.

## 4. Customer-Centric Approach:

- **Customer Feedback and Insights:** Continuously gather customer feedback to understand their evolving needs, preferences, and pain points. Leverage customer insights to drive product/service enhancements and differentiate your offerings in the market.
- **Personalization and Customization:** Tailor your products/services to meet the specific needs of your target customers. Implement personalized marketing strategies, customize solutions, and offer flexible pricing or packaging options.
- **Customer Success and Support:** Prioritize customer success by providing exceptional support and service. Build strong relationships with customers, proactively address their concerns, and strive for long-term customer satisfaction and loyalty.

## 5. Funding and Capital:

- **Funding Options:** Evaluate various funding options to fuel your growth. These may include venture capital, angel investors, crowdfunding, bank loans, or government grants. Assess the pros and cons of each option and align them with your business goals and growth strategy.
- **Financial Planning:** Develop a comprehensive financial plan that outlines your funding requirements, projected revenue, expenses, and profitability. Determine the amount of capital needed to support your growth initiatives and create realistic financial projections.
- **Investor Relations:** Build strong relationships with investors and communicate your growth plans effectively. Provide regular updates on key milestones, financial performance, and strategic initiatives. Maintain transparency and accountability to gain trust and support from investors.

- **Bootstrapping:** Consider bootstrapping as a viable option for funding your startup's growth. Bootstrapping involves using your own resources, generating revenue, and reinvesting profits back into the business. This approach allows you to maintain control and ownership while minimizing external dependencies.

## 6. Continuous Innovation:

- **Research and Development:** Allocate resources for research and development activities to drive innovation and stay ahead of the competition. Foster a culture of experimentation and encourage employees to generate new ideas and solutions.
- **Product and Service Expansion:** Continuously enhance your product or service offerings to meet evolving customer needs and market demands. Conduct market research, gather customer feedback, and invest in product/service development to remain competitive.
- **Agile Decision-Making:** Adopt an agile decision-making process that allows you to quickly respond to market changes and adapt your strategies accordingly. Stay informed about industry trends, monitor competitors, and make data-driven decisions to seize growth opportunities.

## 7. Scalable Marketing and Sales:

- **Digital Marketing:** Leverage digital channels, such as social media, search engine optimization (SEO), content marketing, and online advertising, to reach a wider audience, generate leads, and increase brand visibility.
- **Sales Strategy:** Develop a scalable sales strategy that aligns with your growth objectives. Hire and train a sales team, implement effective sales processes, and leverage customer relationship management (CRM) tools to manage and track sales activities.
- **Customer Acquisition Cost:** Monitor and optimize your customer acquisition cost (CAC) to ensure that your marketing and sales efforts

are cost-effective. Identify the most effective channels and strategies that yield a high return on investment.

- **Customer Retention:** Focus on customer retention strategies to maximize customer lifetime value (CLV). Implement customer loyalty programs, provide excellent customer support, and foster strong relationships with your existing customer base.

## 8. Monitor Key Performance Indicators (KPIs):

- **Metrics and Analytics:** Define and track key performance indicators (KPIs) that align with your growth objectives. Measure metrics such as revenue growth, customer acquisition rate, customer churn rate, gross margin, and customer satisfaction.

- **Data-Driven Decision Making:** Analyse data and derive actionable insights to make informed decisions. Utilize analytics tools and software to monitor and analyse business performance, identify trends, and optimize your growth strategies.

- **Regular Evaluation and Course Correction:** Regularly evaluate your progress against your growth goals. Identify areas of improvement, adjust strategies as needed, and iterate on your approach to ensure continued growth and success.

Scaling and growing your startup requires a strategic and proactive approach. By developing a clear growth strategy, building a high-performing team, strengthening operational efficiency, adopting a customer-centric approach, securing appropriate funding, fostering innovation, implementing scalable marketing and sales strategies, and monitoring key performance indicators, you can navigate the challenges and seize opportunities for sustainable growth. Remember, scaling is a continuous process, and it requires adaptability, perseverance, and a commitment to delivering value to your customers.

# Chapter 22: Overcoming Challenges and Staying Motivated

Entrepreneurship is a journey filled with challenges, obstacles, and uncertainties. It requires resilience, perseverance, and a strong sense of motivation to overcome these hurdles and keep moving forward. This chapter explores the common challenges faced by entrepreneurs and provides strategies to overcome them while maintaining motivation and focus on your goals.

## 1. Embracing the Entrepreneurial Mindset:

- **Embrace Failure as a Learning Opportunity:** Understand that failure is an inherent part of the entrepreneurial journey. Instead of being discouraged by setbacks, view them as valuable learning experiences that can propel you forward.
- **Develop a Growth Mindset:** Cultivate a mindset that thrives on challenges and embraces continuous learning and improvement. Believe in your ability to adapt, learn new skills, and overcome obstacles along the way.
- **Practice Resilience:** Build resilience to bounce back from setbacks and rejections. Develop coping mechanisms, seek support from mentors or peers, and maintain a positive outlook even during challenging times.

## 2. Identifying and Addressing Common Challenges:

- **Financial Constraints:** Lack of capital or cash flow can be a significant challenge for startups. Seek funding options, explore cost-saving measures, and focus on generating revenue early on to alleviate financial constraints.
- **Market Competition:** Competing in a crowded market requires differentiation and a deep understanding of your target audience.

Develop a unique value proposition, identify your competitive advantage, and continuously innovate to stay ahead.

- **Team Building and Management:** Hiring and managing a competent team can be challenging. Define clear roles and responsibilities, foster a positive work culture, provide professional development opportunities, and communicate openly to build a cohesive and motivated team.
- **Time Management and Prioritization:** As an entrepreneur, you have numerous tasks competing for your attention. Prioritize effectively, delegate tasks where possible, and adopt time management techniques to optimize productivity and focus on high-impact activities.
- **Balancing Work and Personal Life:** Entrepreneurship can be demanding, often blurring the lines between work and personal life. Establish boundaries, practice self-care, and create a support system to maintain a healthy work-life balance.

## 3. Seeking Support and Building Networks:

- **Mentorship:** Seek guidance from experienced mentors who can provide valuable insights, advice, and support. They can help you navigate challenges, make informed decisions, and offer a fresh perspective on your business.
- **Entrepreneurial Communities:** Engage with entrepreneurial communities and networks to connect with like-minded individuals facing similar challenges. Attend industry events, join professional organizations, and participate in networking activities to build a support system and gain valuable connections.
- **Peer Groups and Mastermind Sessions:** Join peer groups or participate in mastermind sessions where entrepreneurs come together to share experiences, challenges, and solutions. These platforms provide support, accountability, and opportunities for collaborative problem-solving.

## 4. Staying Motivated and Focused:

- **Set Clear Goals:** Define specific, measurable, achievable, relevant, and time-bound (SMART) goals for your business. Break them down into actionable steps, and regularly review and revise them as needed.
- **Celebrate Milestones and Small Wins:** Acknowledge and celebrate the milestones and small wins along your entrepreneurial journey. Recognize your progress and use these moments as motivation to keep pushing forward.
- **Find Inspiration:** Surround yourself with positive influences and sources of inspiration. Read books, listen to podcasts, attend conferences, or follow successful entrepreneurs who motivate and inspire you.
- **Practice Self-Care:** Take care of your physical, mental, and emotional well-being. Prioritize exercise, healthy eating, quality sleep, and activities that recharge and rejuvenate you. This will help maintain your energy, focus, and motivation.
- **Review Your Why:** Reflect on your purpose and the reasons why you embarked on the entrepreneurial journey in the first place. Reconnect with your passion and vision for your business, as they can serve as powerful motivators during challenging times.
- **Break Tasks into Manageable Chunks:** Overwhelm can often lead to a lack of motivation. Break down complex tasks into smaller, more manageable steps. This will not only make them feel less daunting but also provide a sense of progress and accomplishment as you complete each step.
- **Seek Feedback and Accountability:** Share your goals and progress with trusted individuals who can provide constructive feedback and hold you accountable. This can be a mentor, a business coach, or a fellow entrepreneur. Regular check-ins and discussions will help you stay focused and motivated.
- **Continuously Learn and Grow:** Invest in your personal and professional development. Attend workshops, conferences, and webinars related to your industry. Engage in continuous learning through reading books, taking online courses, or joining relevant

communities. Embrace new knowledge and skills to stay ahead in your entrepreneurial journey.

- **Visualize Success:** Create a vision board or a visualization practice that helps you envision your success. Picture yourself overcoming challenges, achieving your goals, and enjoying the rewards of your hard work. Visualization can reinforce your motivation and serve as a powerful tool to manifest your desired outcomes.
- **Stay Persistent:** Understand that success rarely happens overnight. Entrepreneurship is a long-term endeavour that requires persistence and resilience. When faced with obstacles, remind yourself of the purpose behind your business and stay committed to your goals. Embrace the mindset that setbacks are temporary roadblocks, and with determination, you will find a way to overcome them.

Overcoming challenges and staying motivated is essential for the success of any entrepreneur. By adopting an entrepreneurial mindset, addressing common challenges proactively, seeking support, and maintaining focus and motivation, you can navigate the ups and downs of entrepreneurship with confidence. Remember, challenges are opportunities for growth and learning. Stay committed, believe in your abilities, and keep pushing forward, and you will find yourself on the path to entrepreneurial success.

# Chapter 23: Legal and Regulatory Compliance

The chapter on "Legal and Regulatory Compliance" explores the crucial aspects of ensuring legal adherence and regulatory compliance in the realm of business. In today's dynamic and ever-evolving business landscape, understanding the legal obligations and regulatory frameworks is essential for entrepreneurs and startups. This chapter aims to provide you with valuable insights into the legal and regulatory landscape, enabling you to navigate through the complexities and ensure compliance.

## Business Entity Formation:

In the journey of starting a business, one of the crucial decisions is determining the appropriate business entity. The choice of business entity can have far-reaching implications, impacting the structure, liability, taxation, and legal obligations of the business. In this chapter, we will delve into the concept of business entity formation, focusing on the different types of business entities in India, namely, sole proprietorship, partnership, limited liability company (LLC), and private limited company. We will explore the advantages, disadvantages, and legal obligations associated with each type, empowering you to make an informed decision that aligns with your startup's goals and circumstances.

## 1. Sole Proprietorship:

### Definition:

A sole proprietorship is the simplest form of business entity, owned and operated by a single individual. It is not considered a separate legal entity from its owner, and the owner has complete control and unlimited personal liability for the business's obligations.

### Advantages:

- **Ease of Formation:** Establishing a sole proprietorship is relatively simple and cost-effective, requiring minimal formalities or legal documentation.
- **Direct Decision-making:** The owner has full control over business decisions without the need for consultations or consensus.
- **Tax Benefits:** Profits and losses of the business are treated as the owner's personal income, enabling them to avail certain tax benefits and deductions.
- **Flexibility:** Sole proprietors can easily adapt to changing business needs, making quick decisions and implementing changes.

## Disadvantages:

- **Unlimited Liability:** The owner bears personal liability for the business's debts and obligations, which could potentially put personal assets at risk.
- **Limited Resources:** Sole proprietors may face challenges in raising capital as they solely rely on personal funds or loans.
- **Limited Growth Potential:** The business's growth and expansion may be limited due to the inherent limitations of being a one-person operation.
- **Lack of Continuity:** The business's continuity is dependent on the owner's presence, and it ceases to exist upon the owner's demise or inability to continue.

## Legal Obligations:

- **Registration:** Though not mandatory, it is advisable to obtain the necessary licenses and registrations specific to the nature of the business.
- **Taxation:** Sole proprietors are required to comply with income tax regulations and file returns accordingly.

- **Compliance:** Adhering to applicable laws, regulations, and business-related compliances, such as maintaining proper books of accounts.

## 2. Partnership:

### Definition:

A partnership is a business structure formed by two or more individuals who agree to share profits and losses. It can be classified as a general partnership or a limited liability partnership (LLP).

### Advantages:

- **Shared Responsibility:** Partners contribute their expertise, resources, and skills, allowing for shared decision-making and workload distribution.
- **Combined Resources:** Partners can pool financial resources, making it easier to secure capital and investments.
- **Flexibility:** Partnerships offer greater flexibility in terms of managing the business, allocating profits, and modifying the partnership agreement.
- **Taxation:** Like sole proprietorships, partnerships enjoy pass-through taxation, where profits and losses are passed on to partners' personal income tax returns.

### Disadvantages:

- **Unlimited Liability:** In a general partnership, each partner has unlimited personal liability for the partnership's debts and obligations.
- **Shared Decision-making:** Differences in opinions or conflicts among partners can lead to disputes and hinder decision-making processes.
- **Dissolution Challenges:** The partnership dissolves upon the exit or death of a partner, necessitating partnership agreements and succession plans.

### Legal Obligations:

- **Partnership Deed:** A written agreement outlining the terms, rights, and responsibilities of each partner is essential to establish clarity and avoid future disputes.
- **Registration:** Partnerships can be registered under the Indian Partnership Act, 1932, though it is not mandatory.
- **Compliance:** Partnerships must comply with applicable tax laws, maintain proper accounts, and file tax returns accordingly.

## 3. Limited Liability Company (LLC):

### Definition:

A limited liability company (LLC) combines elements of a partnership and a corporation, providing limited liability to its members (owners). It is a separate legal entity distinct from its members.

### Advantages:

- **Limited Liability:** Members' personal assets are protected from the company's debts and liabilities.
- **Flexible Management:** LLCs offer flexibility in structuring management, allowing for member-managed or manager-managed arrangements.
- **Taxation Flexibility:** LLCs have the option to be taxed as a partnership or a corporation, providing flexibility in tax planning.
- **Credibility and Perpetuity:** The separate legal entity status enhances credibility, and the business continues even if a member exits or passes away.

### Disadvantages:

- **Compliance Requirements:** LLCs have certain compliance obligations, including maintaining proper records, holding annual meetings, and filing annual returns.
- **Complexity:** Compared to sole proprietorships and partnerships, LLCs involve more formalities in terms of formation and ongoing compliance.

- **Limited Funding Options:** Raising capital through external sources may be challenging due to the lack of established frameworks like equity shares.
- **Formation:** LLCs must be registered with the Registrar of Companies (RoC) under the provisions of the Companies Act, 2013.
- **Compliance:** Annual filings, maintenance of statutory registers, and adherence to company law provisions are essential for LLCs.

## Private Limited Company:

## Definition:

A private limited company is a business entity that offers limited liability protection to its shareholders and has a separate legal existence from its owners. It is characterized by its restricted ownership, limited number of shareholders, and prohibition on public trading of shares.

## Advantages:

- **Limited Liability:** Shareholders' personal assets are safeguarded from the company's debts and obligations.
- **Separate Legal Entity:** The company is distinct from its shareholders, providing credibility and potential for long-term existence.
- **Fundraising Potential:** Private limited companies can attract investment through the issuance of shares to private investors.
- **Transferability of Ownership:** Shares can be transferred among shareholders, facilitating changes in ownership and potential exit strategies.

## Disadvantages:

- **Restrictions on Ownership:** The number of shareholders is limited, and the transfer of shares is restricted, reducing flexibility in ownership.

- **Complex Compliance:** Private limited companies have more stringent compliance requirements, including annual filings, audits, and regulatory obligations.
- **Costs and Formalities:** Establishing and maintaining a private limited company involves costs related to registration, compliance, and legal formalities.
- **Confidentiality Challenges:** Certain company information, such as financial statements, may be accessible to the public, impacting privacy.

## Legal Obligations:

- **Formation:** Private limited companies must be registered with the Registrar of Companies (RoC) under the provisions of the Companies Act, 2013.
- **Compliance:** Annual filings, maintenance of statutory registers, conducting regular board meetings, and adhering to company law provisions are essential for private limited companies.

Each of these business entities has its own unique characteristics, advantages, disadvantages, and legal obligations. When considering the appropriate business entity for your startup, it is crucial to carefully assess your business objectives, risk tolerance, funding requirements, and long-term vision.

Please note that the information provided here is a general overview and not exhaustive. It is highly recommended to seek professional advice from legal and financial experts specializing in Indian business laws to ensure compliance with the latest regulations and to make well-informed decisions.

# Intellectual Property Protection:

Intellectual property (IP) protection is a critical aspect of business strategy in today's knowledge-driven economy. It encompasses various forms of creative and innovative assets, such as trademarks, copyrights, patents, and trade secrets. This part of chapter provides a comprehensive overview of the importance of IP protection, delves into the different types of IP assets, explains the detailed process of registration in India, highlights enforcement mechanisms, and outlines the potential consequences of IP infringement.

## Importance of Intellectual Property Protection:

Effective IP protection is vital for businesses to capitalize on their innovations, creativity, and investments. The following reasons highlight the significance of safeguarding intellectual property:

- **Preserving Market Differentiation:** Trademarks enable businesses to establish unique brand identities, distinguishing their products or services from competitors and fostering consumer recognition and loyalty.
- **Securing Competitive Advantage:** Copyrights protect original artistic, literary, musical, and dramatic works, granting creators exclusive rights to reproduce, distribute, and publicly display their works. This helps businesses maintain a competitive edge by preventing unauthorized use and reproduction.
- **Encouraging Innovation:** Patents encourage inventors to disclose their inventions by granting them exclusive rights. This stimulates innovation by providing inventors with the assurance of legal protection and the ability to reap the benefits of their inventions.
- **Safeguarding Trade Secrets:** Trade secrets, such as proprietary formulas, customer lists, and business strategies, give businesses a competitive advantage by keeping valuable information confidential. Protecting trade secrets ensures that competitors cannot unfairly benefit from proprietary knowledge.
- **Investor Confidence and Funding Opportunities:** A strong IP portfolio enhances the attractiveness of a business to potential investors, increasing the chances of securing funding for growth and expansion.

## Intellectual Property Assets:

- **Trademarks:** Trademarks protect brand names, logos, symbols, or any distinctive sign that identifies and distinguishes goods or services in the marketplace. They establish brand recognition, consumer trust, and brand loyalty.

- **Copyrights:** Copyright protection extends to original artistic, literary, musical, and dramatic works. It grants creators exclusive rights to reproduce, distribute, publicly display, or perform their works. Copyrights safeguard creative expressions and ensure fair use of copyrighted materials.

- **Patents:** Patents protect inventions, granting inventors exclusive rights to prevent others from making, using, selling, or importing their patented inventions without permission. Patents encourage innovation by providing inventors with a limited monopoly on their inventions.

- **Trade Secrets:** Trade secrets refer to confidential business information that provides a competitive advantage. They include formulas, processes, methods, customer lists, and marketing strategies. Protecting trade secrets ensures the continued advantage and profitability of a business.

## Process of Registration in India:

In India, the registration process for various intellectual property assets involves the following steps:

- **Trademark Registration:** The registration process includes conducting a comprehensive trademark search to ensure the uniqueness of the proposed mark. Applicants must file an application with the Trademarks Registry, provide relevant information, and pay the prescribed fees. The application undergoes examination, publication, and registration stages, leading to the issuance of a trademark registration certificate.

- **Copyright Registration:** While copyright protection is automatic upon the creation of an original work, registering copyrights with the Copyright Office provides additional benefits. The process involves filing an application, depositing copies of the work, and paying the required fees. Upon examination, the Copyright Office issues a registration certificate.

- **Patent Registration:** Patent registration involves a detailed and rigorous process governed by the Patent Act. It includes drafting a patent application, conducting a prior art search, and filing the application with the Indian Patent Office. The application undergoes examination, publication, and grant stages before a patent is granted.
- **Trade Secret Protection:** Trade secrets are not subject to registration. Instead, businesses must implement robust internal practices to maintain confidentiality, such as implementing access controls, non-disclosure agreements, and employee training programs.

## Enforcement of Intellectual Property Rights:

Enforcing intellectual property rights is crucial to protect against infringement. The following mechanisms can be utilized:

- **Cease and Desist Notices:** Issuing cease and desist notices to infringing parties is an initial step to stop unauthorized use and inform them of the violation.
- **Civil Litigation:** Filing a lawsuit in civil court can be pursued to seek legal remedies, including injunctions, damages, and account of profits. Legal representation by an experienced intellectual property attorney is essential for navigating the complex legal process.
- **Alternative Dispute Resolution:** Mediation or arbitration can provide alternative means to resolve IP disputes outside of the courtroom, offering more cost-effective and expedient solutions.

## Potential Consequences of IP Infringement:

IP infringement can lead to severe consequences for infringers, including:

- **Legal Liabilities:** Infringers may face legal action, resulting in monetary damages, injunctions, and court-ordered injunctions to cease infringing activities.
- **Reputational Damage:** Infringement can tarnish a business's reputation and diminish consumer trust, impacting its market position and long-term viability.

- **Loss of Market Share:** Infringement can lead to the loss of market share as consumers may switch to genuine products or services offered by IP rights holders.
- **Criminal Penalties:** In severe cases of deliberate infringement, criminal charges can be pursued, resulting in fines and imprisonment.

## Contracts and Agreements:

Contracts and agreements form the foundation of business relationships and transactions, providing clarity, protection, and enforceability. For startups, understanding and effectively drafting these legal documents is essential to mitigate risks, establish favourable terms, and ensure smooth operations. There are several types of contracts and agreements, few of them are mentioned below:

### Client/Customer Contracts:

Client/customer contracts are fundamental in establishing the terms and conditions of providing goods or services to clients or customers. Key aspects to consider include:
- **Scope of Work:** Clearly define the scope, deliverables, timelines, and responsibilities of both parties involved in the transaction.
- **Payment Terms:** Specify payment schedules, modes of payment, and any additional charges, ensuring a mutual understanding of financial obligations.
- **Intellectual Property Rights:** Address ownership and usage rights of any intellectual property created or utilized during the engagement.
- **Termination and Dispute Resolution:** Outline conditions for termination, including notice periods, and establish mechanisms for resolving disputes.

### Vendor Agreements:

Vendor agreements govern the terms and conditions of purchasing goods or services from suppliers or vendors. Key considerations include:

- **Product/Service Specifications:** Clearly define the quality standards, specifications, and requirements of the products or services being procured.
- **Pricing and Payment Terms:** Address pricing structures, payment terms, discounts, and any applicable penalties for non-compliance.
- **Delivery and Performance:** Outline expectations regarding delivery timelines, performance benchmarks, and remedies for non-compliance.
- **Confidentiality and Intellectual Property:** Establish obligations of confidentiality and address intellectual property rights related to the vendor's products or services.

## Partnership Agreements:

Partnership agreements are crucial when entering into business ventures with other individuals or entities. Key provisions to include are:

- **Roles and Responsibilities:** Clearly define the roles, responsibilities, and decision-making authority of each partner, fostering transparency and avoiding conflicts.
- **Profit and Loss Distribution:** Specify the distribution of profits and losses among partners, considering factors like capital contributions and involvement in the business.
- **Governance and Decision Making:** Establish procedures for decision-making, voting rights, and dispute resolution mechanisms to ensure effective management.
- **Exit Strategies and Dissolution:** Address mechanisms for partner exits, buyouts, and dissolution of the partnership, safeguarding the interests of all parties involved.

## Non-Disclosure Agreements (NDAs):

Non-disclosure agreements are essential when sharing confidential information with external parties. Key considerations include:

- **Definition of Confidential Information:** Clearly define what constitutes confidential information, ensuring comprehensive protection.

- **Purpose and Scope:** Specify the purpose of sharing confidential information and limit its use to the intended scope.
- **Non-Disclosure and Non-Use Obligations:** Establish obligations of non-disclosure and non-use, including restrictions on sharing information with third parties.
- **Duration and Remedies:** Determine the duration of the agreement's validity and outline remedies for breach, such as injunctive relief or monetary damages.

## Employment Contracts:

Employment contracts govern the relationship between employers and employees. Key provisions to address are:

- **Job Description and Responsibilities:** Clearly define the employee's role, duties, and responsibilities, providing clarity and avoiding ambiguity.
- **Compensation and Benefits:** Specify the employee's salary, incentives, benefits, leave policies, and any other entitlements.
- **Non-Compete and Non-Solicitation:** Include clauses restricting employees from engaging in competing activities or soliciting clients or employees upon termination.
- **Termination and Confidentiality:** Outline grounds for termination, notice periods, and provisions for protecting confidential information after the employment ends.

As a startup founder, it is crucial to be aware of various other legalities that govern your business. While the following topics provide a brief overview, it is recommended to delve deeper into these concepts to ensure compliance and mitigate legal risks.

- **Regulatory Compliance:** Every industry has specific regulations that startups must adhere to. These may include data protection and privacy laws like GDPR and CCPA, as well as industry-specific regulations such as healthcare or finance. Familiarize yourself with these regulations to safeguard your business and customer data.

- **Startup India Registration:** The Startup India initiative aims to support and nurture startups in India. Understand the benefits, eligibility criteria, and documentation required for registering your startup under this program. It can provide access to resources, networking opportunities, and financial incentives to boost your growth.

- **Tax Obligations:** Startups have tax obligations, including GST registration for selling goods and services, income tax, and other applicable taxes. It's essential to understand the registration process, compliance requirements, and potential tax incentives or exemptions available for startups to optimize your tax planning.

- **Employment Laws:** Hiring practices, employment contracts, employee benefits, termination procedures, and compliance with labour laws are crucial for creating a productive and legally compliant work environment. Familiarize yourself with these laws to ensure fair and lawful employment practices.

- **Fundraising and Securities Laws:** When raising funds for your startup, you need to navigate the legal framework and comply with securities laws. Understand the regulations governing fundraising activities, such as crowdfunding regulations and investor disclosures, to ensure compliance and build trust with investors.

- **Corporate Governance:** Maintaining proper corporate governance practices is essential for startups. This includes conducting board meetings, establishing shareholder agreements, and complying with company laws. Upholding good corporate governance enhances transparency, accountability, and investor confidence.

- **Ongoing Compliance:** Legal and regulatory compliance is an ongoing process. Stay informed about periodic filings, renewals, annual reports, and other obligations relevant to your business. Ensure you meet these requirements to maintain good standing and avoid penalties.

Remember, this overview provides a starting point only, and further exploration of these topics will empower you with the knowledge needed to navigate the legal landscape. Consult with legal professionals or experts in each area to gain a comprehensive understanding tailored to your specific startup's needs.

# Chapter 24: Few Jargons in Startup

- **Bootstrap:** To start and grow a business using personal savings or minimal external funding.
- **Idea Stage:** The initial phase of a startup where the idea is conceptualized and validated.
- **Proof of Concept:** Demonstrating the feasibility and potential of a product or service to attract investors or customers.
- **Angel Investor:** An individual who provides capital for startups in exchange for equity ownership or convertible debt.
- **Seed Funding:** The initial capital raised by a startup to support product development, market research, and early-stage activities.
- **Incubator:** An organization that provides startups with resources, mentorship, and support to help them grow and succeed.
- **Accelerator:** A program or organization that offers mentorship, funding, and resources to startups to accelerate their growth and scale.
- **Exit Strategy:** A plan outlining how a startup's founders, investors, or shareholders intend to monetize their investment and ultimately sell or exit the company.
- **Founder-Market Fit:** The alignment of a startup founder's skills, experience, and passion with the target market and industry.
- **Runway:** The amount of time, typically measured in months, that a startup can continue operating with its existing cash reserves.
- **Burn Rate:** The rate at which a startup spends its cash reserves or incurs losses over a specific period.
- **Pivot:** A strategic change in a startup's business model, product, or target market in response to market feedback or changing circumstances.
- **Series A, B, C Funding:** Different stages of funding rounds in which startups secure financing as they grow.

- **Valuation:** The estimated worth of a startup, often determined by factors such as revenue, growth potential, market size, and comparable company analysis.
- **Due Diligence:** The process of conducting a comprehensive investigation and analysis of a startup's financial, legal, and operational aspects before entering into an investment or partnership.
- **Equity:** Ownership interest in a startup, represented by shares or stock. Equity holders have a claim on the company's assets and earnings.
- **Cap Table:** A table that outlines the ownership structure of a startup, including details of shareholders, equity ownership percentages, and types of equity held.
- **Vesting:** The process by which employees earn the right to exercise their stock options or receive their allocated equity over time.
- **Exit Strategy:** A plan outlining how a startup's founders, investors, or shareholders intend to monetize their investment and ultimately sell or exit the company.
- **IPO (Initial Public Offering):** The first sale of a company's shares to the public, allowing it to raise capital and become publicly traded.
- **Unicorn:** A startup valued at over $1 billion.
- **Mezzanine Financing:** Intermediate-stage financing between the initial rounds of funding and an IPO or acquisition.
- **Bridge Financing:** Short-term financing provided to startups to bridge the gap between two funding rounds or to sustain operations.
- **Dilution:** The reduction in existing shareholders' ownership percentage when new shares are issued.
- **Run Rate:** Extrapolating current financial performance over a specific period to estimate future performance, often on an annual basis.
- **Churn Rate:** The rate at which customers or subscribers discontinue their relationship with a company, often expressed as a percentage.
- **Cash Flow:** The movement of money into and out of a company.

- **Gross Margin:** The difference between sales revenue and the cost of goods sold (COGS), indicating the profitability of a company's core operations.
- **Net Profit:** Net profit is the total revenue a company generates after deducting all expenses, taxes, and interest.
- **Pro Forma Financial Statements:** Projected financial statements that provide estimates of a startup's future performance, including income statements, balance sheets, and cash flow statements.
- **EBITDA (Earnings Before Interest, Taxes, Depreciation, and Amortization):** A measure of a company's operating performance and profitability, excluding certain non-cash expenses and financing costs.
- **Unit Economics:** The financial analysis of individual products or services to determine their profitability and contribution to overall company performance.
- **Term Sheet:** A non-binding agreement that outlines the basic terms and conditions of an investment, including valuation, investment amount, and investor rights.
- **Exit Event:** A liquidity event that allows investors and shareholders to sell their ownership stake in a company, such as an IPO, acquisition, or merger.
- **Product-Market Fit:** The stage at which a product or service satisfies the market demand and achieves significant traction with its target audience.
- **Growth Hacking:** A marketing strategy focused on rapid experimentation, data analysis, and creative techniques to achieve scalable growth.
- **Monetization:** The process of generating revenue from a product, service, or user base.
- **Scalability:** The ability of a startup to handle increased workload, expand its operations, and grow its customer base without significant resource constraints.

- **Intellectual Property (IP):** Legal rights protecting intangible assets, such as patents, trademarks, copyrights, and trade secrets.
- **Agile:** An iterative and flexible approach to project management and product development, emphasizing collaboration and adaptability.
- **Runway:** The amount of time, typically measured in months, that a startup can continue operating with its existing cash reserves.
- **Gamification:** Incorporating game elements, such as points, rewards, and leaderboards, into non-game contexts to engage and motivate users.
- **Freemium:** A business model that offers basic services or products for free while charging for premium features or additional functionality.
- **User Acquisition:** The process of attracting and onboarding new users or customers to a product or service.
- **Customer Lifetime Value (CLTV):** The estimated revenue a business expects to generate from a single customer throughout their entire relationship with the company.
- **SaaS (Software as a Service):** A software licensing and delivery model in which software is hosted centrally and accessed by users over the internet.
- **Burnout:** Physical and mental exhaustion caused by prolonged stress and overwork, commonly experienced by startup founders and employees.
- **Boot Camp:** An intensive training or educational program designed to accelerate learning or skills development in a short period.
- **Pivot:** A strategic change in a startup's business model, product, or target market in response to market feedback or changing circumstances.
- **Disruption:** The process by which a new technology, product, or business model fundamentally changes the existing market landscape.

# Conclusion

Congratulations! You have reached the end of "Startup from Scratch," a comprehensive guide that has provided you with a solid foundation for starting your own venture. Throughout this journey, you have acquired valuable knowledge and practical insights to navigate the dynamic landscape of entrepreneurship in India. As you reflect on your accomplishments, remember that the entrepreneurial path is not without its challenges. However, even in the darkest of times when you feel like giving up, there is always a glimmer of hope and support to guide you forward.

Entrepreneurship is a rollercoaster ride, and there will be moments when you question your decisions and face obstacles that seem insurmountable. During these trying times, it is important to stay motivated and find inspiration to fuel your determination. Surround yourself with a supportive network of mentors, advisors, and fellow entrepreneurs who can lend their expertise, provide guidance, and offer a fresh perspective. Seek out communities, both online and offline, where you can connect with like-minded individuals, share your experiences, and learn from their journeys.

Remember that success rarely comes without setbacks. Embrace the lessons learned from your failures and use them as stepping stones to further refine your business strategy. Stay curious, continuously educate yourself, and adapt to the ever-evolving market dynamics. The entrepreneurial landscape in India is dynamic and presents immense opportunities for growth and innovation. Keep a watchful eye on industry regulations, tax implications, and emerging trends specific to your business domain. By staying informed and proactive, you can ensure that your startup remains resilient and adaptable in the face of challenges.

As you embark on this exciting journey, maintain a growth mindset and never stop learning. Seek out niche knowledge, explore new markets, and consider international expansion opportunities. The possibilities for your startup are limitless, and with the passion, resilience, and determination you possess, you are well-equipped to make a meaningful impact in your industry.

Always remember that success is not just measured by financial gains but also by the positive impact you create. Stay true to your vision and the values that drive your entrepreneurial endeavour. Let your startup be a force for good, addressing societal needs and making a difference in the lives of your customers and communities.

In the world of entrepreneurship, it is crucial to remember that success is not solely defined by external validation or financial metrics. It is also about personal growth, resilience, and the pursuit of a purpose-driven life. Embrace the challenges as opportunities for self-discovery and development. Remember that even the most renowned entrepreneurs faced moments of doubt and uncertainty. It is during these moments that you have the chance to dig deep within yourself and discover the true extent of your capabilities. Believe in your vision, trust your instincts, and never underestimate the power of your dreams. With unwavering determination and an unwavering belief in yourself, you have the potential to surpass your own expectations and build a remarkable legacy through your startup journey.

Finally, I want to extend my heartfelt best wishes to you on your new venture. The journey ahead may be challenging, but armed with the knowledge, insights, and resources gained from this book, you are well-prepared to navigate the path of entrepreneurship. Embrace the adventure, seize opportunities, and forge your own path to success.

May your startup journey be filled with resilience, perseverance, and the fulfilment of your wildest dreams. Remember, you have the power to shape the future, make a difference, and leave a lasting legacy. Believe in yourself, stay focused, and let your entrepreneurial spirit soar. The world is waiting for the impact you will create.

Wishing you boundless success, fulfilment, and a remarkable entrepreneurial journey!

www.ingramcontent.com/pod-product-compliance
Lightning Source LLC
Chambersburg PA
CBHW080925260726
48661CB00010B/3801